OP 1st 12⁵²

THE FRANCES PARKINSON KEYES COOKBOOK

THE FRANCES PARKINSON KEYES COOKBOOK

BOOKS BY FRANCES PARKINSON KEYES

Fiction

THE ROYAL BOX	FIELDING'S FOLLY
STEAMBOAT GOTHIC	THE GREAT TRADITION
JOY STREET	PARTS UNKNOWN
DINNER AT ANTOINE'S	HONOR BRIGHT
CAME A CAVALIER	THE SAFE BRIDGE
THE RIVER ROAD	SENATOR MARLOWE'S DAUGHTER
ALSO THE HILLS	LADY BLANCHE FARM
CRESCENT CARNIVAL	QUEEN ANNE'S LACE
ALL THAT GLITTERS	THE CAREER OF DAVID NOBLE

THE OLD GRAY HOMESTEAD

Non-fiction

THE COST OF A BEST SELLER
THERESE: SAINT OF A LITTLE WAY
ALL THAT IS LOUISIANA
THE GRACE OF GUADALUPE
BERNADETTE OF LOURDES
ALONG A LITTLE WAY
CAPITAL KALEIDOSCOPE
SILVER SEAS AND GOLDEN CITIES
LETTERS FROM A SENATOR'S WIFE

Juvenile

ONCE ON ESPLANADE

THE

Frances Parkinson Keyes

COOKBOOK

1955

DOUBLEDAY & COMPANY, INC., GARDEN CITY, N. Y.

*With gratitude and affection
to all the friends
whose cooperation and contributions
have made this book possible*

Contents

Part One

THE NEW ENGLAND BRIDE

MY MOTHER'S HOUSE

My mother's house has stood foursquare
A hundred years and more—
A walk of ancient cobblestones
Leads to its deep-set door.

This cobbled walk is flanked with trees
And lilacs in a row,
And bright against the clapboarding
The tiger lilies glow.

The clapboarding is yellow chrome,
The sturdy shutters green,
The window glass is many-paned,
With iridescent sheen.

The parlor paneling is white,
The parlor mirror tall,
And little candles, side by side,
Stand primly in the hall.

We take the candles in our hands,
And mount the stairs, and find
The quiet chambers, where the soft
Warm firelight is kind.

It flickers gently on the wall,
And on the patchwork quilt.
(It flickered so, long years ago,
When first the house was built.)

And year by year those pleasant flames
Are kindled for our friends,
And when they find our lighted hearths
Their restless roving ends.

So come with me, at any time,
And seek that deep-set door—
My mother's house still stands foursquare
As in the days of yore!

Pine Grove Farm, North Haverhill, New Hampshire

*I*T IS customary to describe brides who know nothing about the culinary arts as unable to make a piece of toast. I did not belong to that category, though my mother did, not only on the several occasions when she was a bride, but all her life, and she lived to be ninety-one. (She could, however, make a very passable French omelet and she could dress and mix a green salad better than anyone I have ever known.) I could, at the time of my marriage, boil coffee, prepare tea, brew raspberry shrub, pop corn, toast marshmallows, pull molasses candy, scramble eggs, and make not only toast but baking powder biscuit and chocolate fudge.

None of this prowess was due to my mother, whose presence in the kitchen was customarily confined to a leisurely, late morning visit, during the course of which she sat in a large rocker, placed where it would not be in the cook's way; from this vantage point, she either made suggestions or gave orders, according to her mood and the exigencies of the situation. I must say that the results thus achieved were astonishingly good; while she could not herself cook, she was nearly always successful in teaching some other inexperienced person how to do so. She used to say that if a dish were unsatisfactory after the third attempt at amendment and improvement, it was pointless to waste any more breath on a beginner; but she was usually able to save breath in this respect as in most others. The first attempt at a new *pièce de résistance* might be a flat failure; but the second usually had passable and the third excellent results. In those days she did not change cooks very often, and she was highly regarded both as a housekeeper and as a hostess. However, her success was not founded on intensive supervision, much less on grueling personal toil; a good housekeeper, in her opinion, was not someone who worked hard herself, but who knew how to make others work hard; and an accomplished hostess was not someone who confronted her guests with flushed cheeks, a worried expression and disordered dress—it was someone who smiled engagingly while extending a jeweled hand, and whose beautiful clothes were worn with an air of accustomed ease.

Since this was her attitude, it is not surprising that she should seek to have it emulated by her only daughter. She did not object to corn popping which, in our circles, was done by the members of the younger generation over the open fire in the library and consumed on the premises, after the golden kernels had become white and fluffy and had been removed from a wire cage attached to the end of a long pole and well salted and buttered; popcorn had not then become universally regarded as an almost indispensable accessory to moving pictures, purchased ready-made, in a paper bag, before the picture began and crunched with increasing force as the plot unfolded. (Of course, there were no moving pictures, either, in the sense that we use the term today, though the "Biograph" was a favorite feature at Keith's Vaudeville Theater in Boston and doubtless elsewhere.) When marshmallows, pricked by the prongs of a long-handled fork, and carefully toasted, supplemented the corn popping, she did not object to those, either—after all, they were also prepared for consumption in the library; and when the first craze for fudge making obsessed the teen-agers of the day, she accepted the theory that it was less upsetting to have this delicacy made on the kitchen stove than in a chafing dish on the dining room table, though the chafing dish craze had begun at about the same time. Gradually, she also accepted the fact that the kitchen, where the fudge would be made, was quite likely to be her own, whereas the candy pulling had always taken place in someone else's, and she had been able to ignore it; and as most of the time

I especially remember chicken fricassees, shepherd's pies, stews with dumplings, escalloped oysters, brown Betties and pan dowdies for regular family meals; for company, broilers in summer, venison as a matter of course in the autumn, trout as a matter of course in the late spring, but turkey only for Thanksgiving and Christmas. In the cool and refreshing category was our favorite late summer supper: a salad which my mother mixed in a bowl shaped like a large lettuce leaf and which we ate with two kinds of homemade bread—white and whole wheat—and homemade cottage cheese; after this, peaches with sugar and cream, also mixed in a bowl on the table, and two kinds of homemade cake, usually one dark and one light. (Most people had three kinds of cake for supper, but my mother limited us to only two at a time.)

Speaking of food that was cool and refreshing, I should not fail to say that the back piazza was also the home of the ice cream freezer, which, when not in use, was turned on its side at the edge of the granite steps to drain and dry, but which seldom had a chance to dry out very thoroughly, as it was in fairly constant use. "Boughten" ice cream, like boughten bread, was unheard of; the grinding noise, associated with its freezing, was as familiar a sound on Sunday morning as the ringing church bells; and it was also understood that the dasher, when removed from the can still dripping, was the lawful prerequisite of the young, as were the saucepans in which frosting had been made. But Sundays were not the only days when we had a frozen dessert. We always had it for a party, and two extra persons could be designated as constituting a party, if one of them were grown-up. We always had it when anyone in our household or a neighboring household was ill, or threatened with illness, or convalescent. We always had it when berries or fruit were so abundant that it was impossible for a small family to can them all or to eat them all in their natural state. Oh, the raspberry sherbet that came off that back piazza! Oh, the peach ice cream! My mouth waters yet at the memory of them! How glad I am that, in those days, no one—at least, no one in Newbury, Vermont—had ever heard of calories or vitamins, as I said before, but simply believed that normal amounts of any appetizing and nourishing food were necessary to health. What is more, everyone lived to a ripe old age, and I cannot remember a single person who was either over or under weight.

Twice a week, Mr. Greenleaf, who was our butcher, pulled up beside the back piazza with his horse-drawn meat cart, opened it from the rear and invited examination of its contents and selection therefrom. The first purchase was almost invariably a shin of beef and a knuckle of veal, which went into an iron pot, filled with cold water and placed on the stove beside the omnipresent teakettle, and eventually became transformed into excellent soup. After the soup meat, a leg of lamb, lamb chops, a rib roast of beef, a pot roast, beefsteak, beef or lamb for stew, a loin roast of pork, pork chops and homemade sausage were carefully chosen—not all at the same time, of course, but in pretty rapid rotation. Sometimes there would be a roast of veal as well and when this was the case, Mr. Greenleaf gave us the sweetbreads and the liver—he would not dream of charging for "innards," he said. I think he gave us the cat's meat, too, but as to that I am not sure—it may have cost five cents. My mother loved to carve, and did it beautifully; so Mr. Greenleaf's roasts always appeared in due time, still intact, on the dining room table. But the cart was an adjunct of the back piazza, and the icebox which stood there permanently the first repository for the meats. We had our own chickens which, rather inconsistently, in the light of her general lack of interest in such matters, my mother enjoyed feeding—the only utilitarian service she ever performed. She carried a large bowl and wore a large apron and a large straw hat, completely out of harmony with the rest of her wardrobe. But though Mr. Greenleaf did not supply our chickens, he secured our turkeys for Thanksgiving and Christmas from some friend of his who lived "out back,"* which was where our maple sugar also came from.

* I.e., any one of the villages slightly to the west of Newbury, among the hills, which was not on the railroad, by which those of us who lived

Mr. Hale, who kept the general store, also made back piazza purchases easy for his customers. He did not come himself, like Mr. Greenleaf, and the horse-drawn vehicle driven by his clerk, Mr. Slack, was not called a meat cart, but a delivery wagon. Mr. Slack would take orders for anything from a yeast cake to a barrel of flour and later the same day, he would come back and bring it to us—even if it were only the yeast cake and though we were a mile and a half from the general store; bills were rendered once a year. All in all, it was a pleasant and helpful service, which I have appreciated all the more since I have spent a good deal of time in a town where no foodstuffs can be charged or delivered except milk, and where endless hours are spent in cash and carry grocery stores; but in the days when I lived at the Oxbow, it never had quite the same intimate association with immediate household needs as Mr. Greenleaf's meat cart. After all, I rode horseback every day; I could go to the village and get the yeast cake myself and bring it back in my pocket; and we did not need a barrel of flour very often. Meat was different; I could not bring that back in my pocket and we did need it every day.

But to return to the back piazza and its various associations with the kitchen where I learned so little. My Cousin Mary, who lived across the street, and my Cousin Ellen, who lived just a quarter of a mile away, had similar kitchens, and in those I was made most welcome, for Cousin Mary and Cousin Ellen did their own cooking and turned out meals which, to this day, I have never seen surpassed. Cousin Mary knew how to make more different kinds of pie than any woman in that part of Vermont; and Cousin Ellen's motto that the only way to be a good cook was to have a free hand and no conscience produced marvelous results. But neither one suggested that she might teach me something of her lore, perhaps because neither guessed how eager a pupil I would have been; and it was not until a few weeks before my marriage, when my fiancé and I decided to

in the Valley so proudly benefited—the Connecticut and Passumpsic, built by my future father-in-law.

spend our honeymoon at a small camp he had built on a nearby lake, that I suddenly woke up to the fact there would be no cook there. I flew for help to the mother of one of my bridesmaids and asked her what she could do for me. She said I could come to supper and that, besides the preserves and the cake which were already made, we would have baking powder biscuit, scrambled eggs and coffee. She did her best to show me how to prepare them and we ate the results—such as they were—that night.

Fortunately, my bridegroom knew more about cooking than I did. He was used to camping, and he had been brought up in a household where, despite abundant household help, most of his female relatives took an active part in the preparation of meals, until they were well on in years, instead of making suggestions from a rocking chair. He praised my biscuits, said he never drank coffee, and that he preferred eggs fried in bacon fat, along with the bacon itself and potatoes, rather than scrambled eggs. I had never even heard of eating potatoes for breakfast, and though I had heard of bacon and eggs for this meal, I had never seen them served on that occasion, either. He took the most tactful possible way of preventing early morning arguments by rising before I did, building a wood fire in the rather primitive stove, and luring me kitchenward by fragrant scents. I watched him with increasing wonder and admiration, drank my coffee and ate my toast while he stowed away a hearty meal, and humbly dried the dishes which he washed with expert swiftness. When it came to keeping the camp in order, I could do better, and he commended my expert bed making, dusting, sweeping and scrubbing as beyond his capacities. But by dinnertime, I was humbled again. Steaks were broiled and potatoes baked with no help from me; I could only do the dishes. Our families— especially his family—sent us hampers covered with white cloths and containing frosted cakes, roasted meats, salad materials and other hearty items for our bill of fare, and these helped very greatly; but by mutual consent, we decided to skip supper, which we could do by eating our dinner around midafternoon and having crackers and cheese with whiskey and soda before bedtime. This, incidentally, was my introduction to highballs and nightcaps.

Though nothing was said on the subject to hurt my feelings, I left the camp determined that never again would I be so hampered by ignorance. However, on our return to Pine Grove Farm, my mother-in-law's capable Swedish staff was in charge and I was no more welcome in the kitchen there than I had been at the Oxbow. Shortly afterward, I lost all interest in food and by the time I regained it, I was enjoined to "save my strength." My first baby was only six weeks old when I was so badly burned that I was incapacitated for months; and the burns were hardly healed when another long siege with nausea began. It was not until I was on my feet after the birth of my second baby that I was able to make the announcement which, for nearly three years, had been unwillingly withheld: for the next three years, unless I was actually flat on my back again, I was going to make all the bread, cake and pastry eaten in that house, and I was going to learn as much as possible about other edibles and experiment with them myself.

This probably would not seem like much of a proclamation today, especially when I add that I had two capable, kind and willing helpers: Mary Phillips, a Nova Scotian cook, and Ina Danforth, whose role was then described as that of second maid, though she had never done that sort of work before, and was a very fine cook herself, as I well knew, as she had lived with my mother during part of my early girlhood. But the house at Pine Grove Farm had twenty-five rooms, which were kept in a state of scrubbed and shining cleanliness which I have never since achieved and which—if I may be pardoned for saying so—I have never seen achieved elsewhere. On the ground floor, the every-day cleaning was always done before breakfast; and when I say "cleaning," I do not refer to the casual process known as "passing the mop" with which I have since become familiar in the South. I mean that all the flat surfaces of furniture were carefully dusted and all rugs carpet-swept; that faded flowers and over-flowing ashtrays were removed and scrap baskets emptied; that fresh towels replaced the soiled ones in the well-tended lavatory. By eight o'clock, this and the living room, library, front hall—which measures twenty by forty feet—den and dining room were all in complete order. By ten o'clock, the bedrooms, bathrooms and corridors on the second floor had received similar treatment. But this was only the beginning. Once a week, one room on each story was *really* cleaned. That is to say, all small pieces of furniture were taken out of it and all large ones moved to permit thorough treatment of the floor. Everything was washed or polished or both. The baseboards, the backs of pictures, the lintels of doors—none of these was overlooked. The rugs, of course, were taken out doors to be beaten and, in wintertime, they were left spread on the snow, so that if any dirt still remained in them, it would show on the glistening white surface. The hired man helped with the rugs and with the outsides of those windows which could be reached only by a ladder. All others were the responsibility of the female contingent and there are over fifty windows in the house. Even the cellar stairs were scrubbed once a week, the brass door handles and andirons polished twice a week. And just to make assurance doubly sure, in addition to all this, came spring house cleaning and fall house cleaning as regularly as the seasons rolled around. This meant that the two attics, the cellar and the china closet were due for complete overhauling, that every book in the house was taken from its place and "clapped" as well as dusted, that registers were unscrewed and lifted up, so that lurking dirt could be removed from underneath them, and that every inch of white paint was washed with soap and water.

Cleaning on this scale has now, I believe, more or less vanished from the earth. At all events, it has been greatly mitigated by vacuum cleaners and other mechanical aids. The same is true of laundry. But in those days every bit of washing and ironing was also done by hand, in the house, and this at a period when a clean tablecloth every day was taken as a matter of course, when babies and small children, whether boys or girls, wore frilly white clothes, and young ladies four starched petticoats at a time, not to mention ruffled drawers, chemises and dresses. The clothes-horses in our house were really a sight to see, on ironing day; and then there were the diapers, which did not get ironed and which were hung apart. . . .

So, after all, the work in the house could hardly be called light, apart from the cooking. Moreover, as I have said before, no loaf of boughten bread, no store ice cream ever darkened the door; and no canned baked beans, fruits, berries or pickles, no tenderized ham, was so much as thought of. Everything was prepared at home, whether this was just for the "family" or for "dress-up company," and "dress-up company" could mean any-where from three to three hundred. When I announced that I intended to make all our bread, cake and pastry, this meant that in addition to doing the chamber work and sewing; caring, with Ina's help, for a two-year-old child and a six-months'-old baby; entertaining my own and my husband's friends; and lending a hand here, there and everywhere, I was undertaking to make an average of from six to sixteen loaves of bread a week, from six dozen to sixteen dozen rolls, from one to four cakes a day, and the same number of pies. It meant that, despite this visible amount of work, I must go cautiously, rather than impetuously, about my labors; when there was a cake in the oven, there was the omnipresent danger that it might fall if anyone walked heavily or hastily across the kitchen floor; and this danger was increased if the oven door were opened, so real technique was necessarily developed, as far as the latter action was concerned for, in the absence of present-day oven control and indicators, there was no sure way of finding out whether any dish were done, except by looking at it and feeling of it. Once it had become visible, a straw, plucked from the nearest broom and carefully thrust into the thickest part of a cake or a loaf of bread, was the usual gauge by which it was tested, though the degree to which it had "shrunk away from the pan" was also a fairly reliable indication of its progress.

Most important of all, however, my new and earnest resolu-tion meant that I must be ingenious, as well as industrious and

cautious, since, in spite of—or rather, because of—the spaciousness and comparative luxury of my ready-made home, there was
crying need for rigid economy in the present to make up for
casual extravagance in the past; and because my husband's
family and political guests expected him to set a good table—
which meant a lavish one.

I was very eager not only to do all this reasonably well, but to
excel in doing it. New standards had been set for me, and I
wanted first to meet these and then to surpass them. For instance,
all the married women with whom I was acquainted in Newbury, except my mother—and then, she was only intermittently
married!—made currant jelly and crab apple jelly and wild grape
jelly and a few of them made currant-raspberry jelly; not a single
one made raspberry jelly without the addition of currants to
insure extra firmness; and a surreptitious glance at the latest
edition of Fanny Farmer's Cookbook, which soon occupied a
place second only to the Bible in my personal library, informed
me that this was the most critically difficult of all jellies to make,
and should never be attempted, if berries were inferior or overripe. However, my mother-in-law not only attempted raspberry
jelly every year, she made it in large quantities, from berries
picked in our own pasture, and never once did it fail to jell.
When I eventually gathered the reins of management at Pine
Grove Farm into my own hands, I also made raspberry jelly every
year—twice as much as she had; and after the jelly bags had
dripped, I put the squeezed berries back on the stove a second
time, added sugar and water, and achieved an excellent syrup
for use in beverages and sauces. . . . All the married women with
whom I was acquainted in Newbury—except my mother—made
excellent pies; but none of them made puff paste. My mother-
in-law's Swedish cook, Alma, made it to perfection; her lobster
vol-au-vent was a masterpiece and, indeed, there was nothing in
the realm of pastry which she could not achieve. After her departure from Pine Grove Farm, I dismantled one of the ancient
washstands that had been stowed away in the attic, had the
marble top moved to the kitchen pantry, and used this as the

slab recommended by Fanny Farmer for the preparation of puff paste. But though the marble slab itself cost nothing, the *cannelons*—delicate cornucopias of puff paste filled with sweetened whipped cream—the sweetbread and mushroom patties, the dainty tartlets of all sorts, which came into being thereon, ran into tall money. I soon realized that vaulting ambition had o'erleapt itself and was in danger of falling on the other.

Ina helped most with economy. (I must, however, qualify that statement by saying it was Mary who had the perspicacity to realize that, on a dairy farm, the most economical way to make bread was with whole milk and no shortening; and I have never eaten better bread—except, perhaps, my Cousin Mary's—than resulted from this method. It was also Mary who pointed out that the baked beans, left over from Saturday night supper and Sunday breakfast, when they were of course served hot, would make the basis for a good salad Sunday night and then, hot again, the basis for soup on Monday; and it was Mary who taught me to make Brewis, of which I had never heard before, out of leftover brown bread, and which I have never seen served except in my own house—I cannot imagine why, as it is an excellent substitute for a breakfast cereal and equally good for the main dish of small children's supper.) Ina did not subscribe to Cousin Ellen's school of thought about a free hand and no conscience; she claimed, on the contrary, that the test of a really good cook is to contrive appetizing meals at minimum cost and never, never to waste a single scrap. I confess that I greatly enjoy the free-handed method, and the New Englander who can suppress the traditional—and inherent—conscience generally seems to me a much more genial companion than the one who cultivates it. But Ina's Spartan methods were certainly never obvious to anyone unacquainted with them; and without the curb which she put on my flights of fancy, I doubt whether the family budget—or what corresponded to one at that time—would have even approached balance.

Some of the recipes on the following pages had already been evolved by Ina when she lived with my mother, from very old

Southern cookbooks which the latter had collected during the six years that she lived at the University of Virginia. Among these are Ellie's Eclaire, which bears no resemblance whatsoever to an éclair as we generally use the term; and the Rose Cream Cake, which I still use for my birthday parties and other special occasions. (Once, omitting the rose coloring, I used it for a wedding breakfast at my house in Alexandria, Virginia.) Some recipes came from New England sources unknown to me, though where I do know them, I have tried to give them proper credit; and some are due to my experiments with recipes found in newspapers and magazines long since lost, and to the ideas which I had gleaned during two sojourns in Europe, each of a year's duration, before my marriage. Among the latter are *Pêches à la Condé* and Rock Rice with Hot Raspberry Sauce. I had no recipes for these until I concocted them myself, but I had eaten both dishes many times at Continental tables d'hôte, and I had been brought up to regard rice as a staple, whether combined with gravy and served as a vegetable or combined with sugar and served as a dessert. Properly, it is one of the best foods on earth; and I shudder when it comes on someone else's table, resembling library paste more nearly than anything else, or when it is served with scrambled eggs or fish—for instance—as I have seen it appear at a very good Northern club; it must have either gravy or sugar to bring out its flavor. Curried eggs with rice are, of course, delicious, because the curry performs the service I have just mentioned to perfection; the juices from seafood will do the same, when the rice is served with seafood à la Newburg; and the dish of Shrimps with Rice and Green Peas, served on hot saltine crackers, which is one of my own inventions, owes much of its excellence to the fact that cold boiled rice is mixed with thick, well-seasoned cream and thoroughly stirred while it is reheated. But unflavored boiled or steamed rice, unmixed with any other ingredient, is a sorry dish, even when it is fluffy rather than soggy.

At my mother's house, we always had cherry bounce with our Thanksgiving and Christmas dinners and wine jelly when we were ill. Sherry added a semi-occasional note of elegance to a party or an emergency and champagne was regarded as a proper accessory for weddings and christenings. The apples which were not eaten fresh or made into jelly were taken to Cousin Henry's cider mill—Cousin Henry was Cousin Ellen's husband—and all the youngsters of the neighborhood gathered around to watch the primitive process of manufacture, and to drink as much as they chose when the cider came fresh from the press. We drank it that way at home, too; but after it became "hard" we were not supposed to do so, though we occasionally sampled the product which our elders concocted, with the addition of raisins, yeast and so on, and consumed with evident pleasure and sometimes hilarious results. When in Europe, my mother mixed wine with her water, and so did I; but whereas her mixture, being half and half, was a beautiful crimson, mine, being at least four-fifths water, was pale pink, and I was never taught anything about vintages. Male guests at Pine Grove Farm were offered whiskey in the den, but they drank it unobtrusively, though not secretly; and highballs were never served in the living room to men and women alike, nor were cocktails or even wine, except on rare occasions, though champagne did become a regular feature at my birthday parties.

Ina was a strict Prohibitionist, and therefore the years spent under her influence were almost entirely unproductive of recipes for food or drink flavored with alcohol in any form. There were two notable exceptions, however: Frozen Pudding and Fruit Punch. I evolved the recipes for both of these myself, and was permitted to serve them, the pudding because Ina considered that part of the curse had been removed since it was not a drink, the punch on condition that I would always mix and pour it myself. Both were immensely popular. The recipe for punch was often doubled and redoubled in the course of a party; and after the remains of a large moulded pudding, which had been the *pièce de résistance* at dinner, had been repacked and placed down cellar in the freezer, a group of merrymakers would descend and dig it out, for a supplementary midnight snack!

The First World War brought rationing problems, shortages and strikes, now almost forgotten in the light of the later and more serious ones. Our beautiful white bread and rolls vanished from our tables, and we found new uses for the coarser flours. We were told that these could not be shipped to France because they were too perishable and because the French did not know how to use them. The first reason we accepted philosophically and unquestioningly; we were challenged by the slogan, "Food Will Win the War!" and overawed by the list of rules and regulations, surmounted by a grim likeness of Herbert Hoover, then Food Administrator, which was prominently displayed in every kitchen, and besides, we were sincere in our wish that our allies should have the best we could offer them; but we did not quite grasp why, if we could learn to use them—as we could and did—the French could not do so also. However, in spite of our puzzlement, we persevered, with very good results, except that these coarser flours played havoc with some delicate digestions, especially in the case of young children. One of my most vivid memories about my last winter at Pine Grove Farm, before we went to Washington, is that of sitting before the living room fire, with my youngest son in my arms, wondering how I was going to keep him warm and nourished until spring. For the most part, we had only green wood to burn, as we had expected to be in Concord, and the usual systematic cutting in our timberlands had been done with absence in view; but it had proved impossible to stretch a gubernatorial salary of $3,000.00 a year to include house rent and I had remained at home with the children. Coal was sent up from Boston in twenty-five pound lots, by express, when there was any coal and any express; but this meager supply did not go very far in a house that normally consumed at least a ton a week during cold weather, and there were six weeks on end when the thermometer at our front door did not go up to zero. Meanwhile, there was not enough rice flour, barley flour, or potato flour to make the substitutes which the little boy could tolerate. However, spring came at last, we managed somehow, and most of my memories of this management are happy ones. A substitute cake, invented by one of my Newbury friends, Clara Worthen, was one of our most successful experiments. I am proud to include it among the recipes for the dishes which were prepared with a free hand and no conscience!

Breads, Muffins, etc.

BREAD, WHITE

(Mary Phillips—my favorite recipe)

1 yeast cake	3 teaspoons salt
6 cups warm milk	12 cups flour
¼ cup sugar	

Soften the yeast in the lukewarm water. Scald the milk and pour it into a large mixing bowl. Stir in the sugar and salt, and cool to lukewarm (80–85° F.). Add 3 cups of the flour, stirring well, then add the softened yeast. Stir in the remaining flour, cover and place in a warm spot to rise overnight. In the morning stir the dough down, and work in about 6 more cups flour, or enough to make a dough that is light but does not stick to the hands. Turn the dough out onto a lightly floured board, and knead for a few minutes until the dough is smooth and elastic. Mold the dough into loaves and put the loaves in greased bread pans. The dough should fill the pans two-thirds full. Cover with a damp cloth and let the loaves rise for about 1½ hours, or until double in bulk. Bake the loaves in a moderately hot oven (400° F.) for 50 minutes.

If the modern cook prefers, on general principles, to use a little shortening, or if she has reason to believe that the milk we used was richer than she can command (though milk from Holstein cows is what we used and this is not as rich as that from Jerseys) 4 tablespoonfuls may be added.

N.B.—(Almost fifty years later!) "Molding" meant that enough of the dough to make a dozen "cloverleaf"—or, as we first called them "pincushion rolls"—went into one pan, enough for a dozen breadsticks into another and the rest into regular bread loaves—three or four. There was no change in the mixture for the rolls and the breadsticks, but they were lightly brushed over the top with butter after they had risen and before they went into the oven, and the loaves were not.

BREAD, WHITE

(Ina Danforth)

2 *cups milk*	1 *tablespoon sugar*
2 *cups lukewarm water*	1 *teaspoon salt*
½ *yeast cake, crumbled*	12 *cups flour*

Scald the milk and cool to lukewarm. Add the water, yeast, sugar and salt and mix well. Stir in as much of the flour as possible with a wooden spoon, cover and let rise in a warm place overnight. In the morning, stir the dough down and turn it out on a floured board. Work in the remaining flour, or enough to make a dough that is light but does not stick to the hands. Shape the dough into loaves and put the loaves in greased bread pans. Cover and let the loaves rise for about 1 hour in a warm place until double in bulk. Bake in a moderately hot oven (400° F.) for 50 minutes.

Gluten bread may be made by this same recipe, using gluten flour in place of white flour.

BREWIS

(Mary Phillips)

1 *tablespoon butter*	1 *cup crumbled brown bread*
1 *cup rich milk*	*Pinch of salt*

Scald the milk and butter. Add the brown bread and salt and simmer over boiling water for about 30 minutes, or until the liquid is absorbed.

NUT BREAD

(Mrs. G. E. Cummings)

1 cup whole wheat flour	1 teaspoon salt
5 teaspoons baking powder	½ cup chopped nuts
1½ cups white flour	1 egg, beaten
¼ cup sugar	1 cup milk

Mix the dry ingredients and stir in the nuts. Combine the egg and milk and stir into the dry mixture. Turn the batter into a buttered bread pan and let stand for 20 minutes. Then bake in a moderate oven (350° F.) for 45 minutes.

BOSTON BROWN BREAD

1 cup whole wheat flour	1½ teaspoons soda
1 cup rye flour	1 cup sour milk
1 cup yellow corn meal	¾ cup molasses
1½ teaspoons salt	1 cup sweet milk

Combine the whole wheat flour, rye flour, corn meal and salt. Stir the soda into the sour milk. Stir the sour milk, molasses and sweet milk into the dry ingredients and mix well. Fill 1-pound, round coffee cans two-thirds full, cover tightly and steam for 3½ hours. Remove the covers and bake the bread in a moderate oven (350° F.) for 30 minutes.

MUFFINS, PLAIN

2 cups sifted flour	1 egg, well beaten
⅓ cup sugar	1 cup milk
Pinch of salt	1 tablespoon melted butter or
2 teaspoons baking powder	cream

Sift the dry ingredients into a mixing bowl. Combine the egg and milk and pour all at once into the dry ingredients. Stir briskly until all the flour is moistened. Do not beat until smooth. The batter should look lumpy. Lightly stir in the butter or cream and fill buttered muffin tins two-thirds full. Bake in a hot oven (400° F.) for 25 minutes and serve piping hot.

Cakes, Icings, Cookies and Desserts

LADY CAKE

(Ina Danforth)

½ cup butter
1½ cups sugar
2 cups sifted flour
½ teaspoon soda

1 teaspoon cream of tartar
¾ cup milk
1 teaspoon vanilla
4 egg whites, stiffly beaten

Cream the butter and sugar together thoroughly. Sift the dry ingredients and stir them into the butter-sugar mixture alternately with the milk. Stir in the vanilla and fold in the stiffly beaten egg whites. Bake in a buttered square or rectangular pan in a moderate oven (375° F.) for about 25 minutes, or until a cake tester inserted in the center comes out clean. Turn the cake out onto a rack to cool. Frost with Lady Baltimore Frosting.

I have found the best results are obtained by slicing fruit cake very thin when serving, and all other cakes very thick. For example, a slice of Sultana Cake should be as thin as it can conveniently be cut, and a slice of Angel Cake cut less thin than two or three inches wide becomes almost tasteless.

LADY BALTIMORE FROSTING

(Ann Seranne)

3 cups sugar
1 cup water
¼ teaspoon cream of tartar

3 egg whites, stiffly beaten
½ cup chopped walnut meats
6 figs, chopped

Combine the sugar, water and cream of tartar, bring to a boil and boil rapidly until the syrup spins a long thread. Pour the syrup in a fine stream into the beaten egg whites, beating constantly. Set aside half the frosting for the top and sides of the cake. Add the nuts and figs to the rest to use as filling between the layers.

WHITE CAKE

(Ina Danforth)

¼ cup butter	1 teaspoon baking powder
1 cup sugar	½ cup milk
1½ cups flour	4 egg whites, stiffly beaten

Cream the butter and sugar together thoroughly. Sift the dry ingredients and stir them into the butter-sugar mixture alternately with the milk. Fold in the stiffly beaten egg whites. Bake in a square or rectangular pan in a moderate oven (375° F.) for about 25 minutes, or until a toothpick inserted in the center comes out clean. Turn cake out onto a rack to cool.

DELICATE CAKE

(Ina Danforth)

½ cup butter	1 cup water
1½ cups sugar	1 teaspoon vanilla
3 cups sifted flour	5 egg whites, stiffly beaten
3 teaspoons baking powder	

Cream the butter and sugar together thoroughly. Sift the dry ingredients and stir them into the butter-sugar mixture alternately with the water. Stir in the vanilla and fold in the stiffly beaten egg whites. Bake in a buttered square or rectangular pan in a moderate oven (375° F.) for about 25 minutes, or until a cake tester inserted in the center comes out clean. Turn the cake out onto a cake rack to cool. Frost with your favorite frosting.

RIBBON CAKE

(Ina Danforth)

⅔ cup butter	1 teaspoon molasses
2 cups sugar	1 tablespoon flour
3 eggs	½ cup currants
3 cups flour	½ cup raisins
1 teaspoon cream of tartar	1 teaspoon cinnamon
1 teaspoon baking soda	1 teaspoon nutmeg
1 cup milk	1 teaspoon cloves

Cream the butter and sugar together thoroughly. Beat in the eggs one at a time. Sift the dry ingredients and stir them into the butter-sugar-egg mixture alternately with the milk. Turn two-thirds of this batter into two oblong baking pans and to the remaining batter stir in the rest of the ingredients. Pour the spiced batter into another oblong baking pan and bake the three layers in a moderate oven (350° F.) for 25 to 30 minutes, or until the layers test done. Put the layers together, while they are still warm, with jelly. When the cake is cool, frost with Chocolate Frosting.

CHOCOLATE FROSTING
(Very rich)

(Mary Phillips)

1½ squares bitter chocolate	½ teaspoon melted butter
⅓ cup scalded cream	1 teaspoon vanilla
Pinch of salt	Confectioners' sugar, sifted
1 egg yolk	

Melt the chocolate over hot water and beat in the cream gradually. Stir in the salt, egg yolk, butter and vanilla. Then stir in enough confectioners' sugar to make the frosting the right spreading consistency.

ORANGE CAKE

(Ina Danforth)

3 tablespoons butter	½ teaspoon soda
2 cups sugar	½ tablespoon hot water
5 egg yolks, well beaten	Juice and grated rind of 1
3 cups flour	orange
1 teaspoon cream of tartar	3 egg whites, stiffly beaten
1 cup water	

Cream the butter until soft, add the sugar gradually and cream until the mixture is fluffy. Stir in the egg yolks. Sift the flour and cream of tartar and stir in the dry ingredients alternately with the water. Stir in the soda, dissolved in the hot water, and one half the orange juice and rind. Fold in the beaten egg whites. Turn the batter into a buttered square or rectangular pan and bake in a moderate oven (350° F.) for about 25 minutes, or until a cake tester inserted in the center comes out clean. Turn the cake out onto a cake rack to cool. Frost with Boiled Frosting made with remaining orange juice instead of water.

BAILEY CHOCOLATE CAKE

(Clara Bailey Worthen—A World War I "Substitute" Cake)

1½ squares bitter chocolate	1 egg yolk
2 tablespoons fat	1 cup corn syrup
1½ cups barley flour	¼ cup water
3 teaspoons baking powder	1 teaspoon vanilla
¼ teaspoon soda	1 egg white, stiffly beaten

Melt the chocolate and fat over hot water and beat until smooth. Sift together the flour, baking powder and soda three times. Beat the egg yolk, add the corn syrup and water, and beat well. Combine the liquid and dry ingredients, stir in the melted chocolate and the vanilla, and fold in the beaten egg white. Turn the batter into a buttered cake pan and bake in a moderate oven (350° F.) for about 30 minutes, or until a cake tester inserted in the center comes out clean. Turn out onto a cake rack to cool and frost with White Mountain Cream.

WHITE MOUNTAIN CREAM

(Boiled Frosting)

1 cup sugar   1 egg white, stiffly beaten
¼ cup water

Dissolve the sugar in the water, bring to a boil and boil rapidly until the syrup spins a long thread. Pour the syrup in a thin stream into the egg white, beating constantly. Continue to beat until the frosting stands in peaks.

ELLIE'S ECLAIRE

(Old Southern Recipe)

4 egg yolks   4 cups scalding milk
6 tablespoons sugar   3 layers of sponge cake
3 tablespoons cornstarch

Beat the egg yolks and beat in the sugar and cornstarch. Gradually stir in the hot milk and cook over boiling water, stirring constantly, until the mixture is thick. Cool. Spread the filling between the layers of cake and frost the cake smoothly with Chocolate Frosting.

ROSE CREAM CAKE

(Old Southern Recipe, always used for my birthday cake)

1 cup butter	1 cup milk
3 cups sugar	2 teaspoons vanilla
4 cups sifted flour	Red vegetable color
4 teaspoons baking powder	10 egg whites, stiffly beaten

Cream the butter until soft, gradually stir in the sugar and beat until the mixture is fluffy. Sift the flour and baking powder and stir into the butter-sugar mixture alternately with the milk. Stir in the vanilla and enough red coloring to make the batter a delicate pink. Fold in the beaten egg whites. Turn the batter into three graduated, buttered layer cake pans and bake in a moderate oven (325° F.) until a cake tester inserted in the center comes out clean. Turn the layers out immediately on cake racks to cool and, when cool, frost with Boiled Frosting. For a cake this size, you will need twice the quantity of icing.

SULTANA CAKE

(Old Southern Recipe)

½ cup butter	1½ teaspoons cinnamon
1½ cups sugar	½ cup rich milk
4 eggs, separated	½ teaspoon baking soda
2 cups flour	½ tablespoon hot water
1 teaspoon cream of tartar	1 cup Sultana raisins
1½ teaspoons nutmeg	

Cream the butter until soft. Gradually add the sugar and cream together until the mixture is fluffy. Beat in the egg yolks. Mix and sift the flour, cream of tartar, nutmeg and cinnamon and stir in these dry ingredients alternately with the milk. Stir in the soda, dissolved in the hot water, and add the raisins.

Turn the batter into a buttered cake pan and bake in a moderate oven (350° F.) for 45 minutes. Turn out onto a cake rack to cool and frost with Boiled Frosting.

WALNUT CAKE

(Old Southern Recipe)

½ cup butter
1 cup sugar
2 eggs, separated
1½ cups flour
2 teaspoons baking powder

½ cup milk
2 teaspoons vanilla
½ cup chopped raisins
½ cup chopped walnut meats

Cream the butter and sugar together until the mixture is fluffy and beat in the egg yolks. Sift the flour and baking powder and stir the dry ingredients into the butter-sugar-egg mixture alternately with the milk. Stir in the vanilla, raisins and walnuts. Beat the egg whites until stiff and fold them into the batter. Turn the batter into a loaf pan, lined with oiled paper, and bake in a moderate oven (350° F.) for 40 minutes, or until a cake tester inserted in the center comes out clean. Turn the cake out onto a cake rack to cool and frost with Boiled Frosting. Decorate with walnut halves.

SOFT GINGERBREAD

1 cup molasses
1 egg, beaten
½ cup melted butter
3 cups flour

1 teaspoon soda
1 tablespoon ginger
Pinch of salt
1 cup milk

Combine the molasses, egg and melted butter. Sift together the flour, soda, ginger and salt and stir the dry ingredients into the molasses mixture alternately with the milk. Beat well, turn into a shallow buttered pan and bake in a moderate oven (350° F.) for about 40 minutes.

HARD GINGERBREAD

1 cup butter	1 teaspoon soda
3 cups sugar	1 cup sour cream
3 eggs, beaten	Flour
1 tablespoon ginger	

Cream the butter and sugar and stir in the ginger, soda and sour cream. Stir in enough flour to make a very stiff dough. Roll out the dough thinly on a lightly floured board and cut it into squares. Bake the squares in a hot oven (425° F.) for about 8 minutes.

BLUEBERRY CAKE

2 cups flour	1 egg, beaten
1 teaspoon soda	1 cup milk
2 teaspoons cream of tartar	2 cups blueberries
1½ cups sugar	2 tablespoons melted butter

Mix and sift the flour, soda and cream of tartar. Gradually stir the sugar into the beaten egg. Stir in the sifted dry ingredients alternately with the milk. Add the blueberries and stir in the melted butter. Turn the batter into a buttered loaf pan and bake in a moderate oven (375° F.) for about 30 minutes, or until a cake tester inserted in the center comes out clean. Turn out onto a cake rack to cool.

PLAIN CAKE

½ cup butter	3 teaspoons baking powder
1 cup sugar	1 cup milk
2 eggs, beaten	1 teaspoon vanilla
2¾ cups flour	

Cream the butter until soft and gradually stir in the sugar. Beat in the eggs. Sift the flour and baking powder and add the dry ingredients alternately with the milk. Stir in the vanilla. Turn into a buttered square or rectangular cake pan and bake in a moderate oven (375° F.) for about 25 minutes, or until a cake tester inserted in the center comes out clean. Turn out on a cake rack to cool and frost with Maple Sugar Frosting.

MAPLE SUGAR FROSTING

(Ina Danforth)

¾ cup grated maple sugar   ¼ cup water
¼ cup white sugar   1 egg white, stiffly beaten

Combine the maple sugar, white sugar and water; bring to a boil, and boil until the syrup spins a long thread. Pour the syrup in a thin stream into the beaten egg white, beating vigorously. Continue to beat until the frosting stands in stiff peaks.

ANGEL CAKE

1 cup flour   Pinch of salt
1½ cups sugar   1 teaspoon cream of tartar
11 egg whites (1⅓ cups)   1 teaspoon vanilla

Sift the flour and ¼ cup of the sugar four times and set aside. Sift the remaining sugar five times and set aside. Put the egg whites in a large bowl and add the salt. Beat the whites with a rotary beater until they are foamy. Add the cream of tartar and continue beating until the whites are just stiff enough to form a peak when the beater is withdrawn. Sprinkle over them 2 tablespoons of the sugar and, still using the rotary beater, beat just enough to blend. Repeat this process until all the sugar has been added. Lightly beat in the vanilla and put the rotary beater aside.

With a wire whisk or wooden spoon start to fold in the flour.

Sift about ¼ cup of the flour over the mixture and fold it in. Sift another ½ cup of the flour over the mixture and repeat the folding until all the flour has been incorporated. Pour the batter into a 9-inch tube pan, letting it sheet from the mixing bowl. Run the blade of a knife through the batter to remove any large air bubbles and bake in a moderate oven (325° F.) for 40 to 60 minutes, or until the cake is delicately browned on top. Invert the pan over three upturned teacups to cool for 1 hour before removing the cake from the pan.

GOLDEN CAKE

(Made with the egg yolks left over from the Angel Cake)

¼ cup butter	1 teaspoon baking powder
½ cup sugar	¼ cup milk
5 egg yolks, beaten	1 teaspoon orange extract
⅞ cup flour	

Cream the butter and sugar together thoroughly and beat in the egg yolks. Sift the flour and baking powder and add the dry ingredients alternately with the milk. Stir in the flavoring. Turn the batter into an angel cake pan and bake in a moderate oven (375° F.) for about 30 minutes, or until a cake tester inserted in the center comes out clean. Turn out the cake onto a cake rack to cool.

DOUGHNUTS

(Ina Danforth)

4 cups flour	2 eggs
2 teaspoons baking soda	1½ cups sugar
1 teaspoon cream of tartar	1¼ cups sour milk or
2 teaspoons salt	buttermilk
2 teaspoons nutmeg	1 tablespoon melted butter

Mix and sift the flour, baking soda, cream of tartar, salt and nutmeg. Beat the eggs until thick and pale in color, gradually beat in the sugar, and then stir in the milk or buttermilk mixed with the melted butter. Gradually stir in the flour mixture, blending until almost smooth. Turn out on a floured board and roll out ¼ inch thick. Cut with a floured cutter and fry in hot deep fat (360° to 370° F.) until golden. Drain on absorbent paper.

LITTLE SOUR CREAM CAKES

1 cup sugar	1 cup chopped raisins
1 egg, beaten	1 teaspoon cinnamon
1 cup thick sour cream	1 teaspoon nutmeg
1 teaspoon baking soda	1 teaspoon cloves
Pinch of salt	2 cups flour

Cream the butter and sugar and stir in the egg and sour cream in which the soda has been dissolved. Add the salt, raisins and spices and stir in just enough flour to make a soft dough. Drop the dough by spoonfuls on a buttered cooky sheet and bake in a moderate oven (350° F.) for about 12 minutes.

OATMEAL MACAROONS

3 eggs, separated	½ teaspoon salt
1 cup sugar	1 teaspoon vanilla
3 cups rolled oats	3 tablespoons melted butter
2½ teaspoons baking powder	

Beat the egg yolks until they are thick and pale in color and beat in the sugar. Stir in the rolled oats mixed with the baking powder and salt. Stir in the vanilla and melted butter. Beat the egg whites until stiff and fold them into the batter. Drop the batter by spoonfuls on buttered cooky sheets and bake in a slow oven (300° F.) for about 25 minutes, or until macaroons are golden.

MERINGUES

3 egg whites, stiffly beaten *1 teaspoon vanilla*
1 cup sugar

Beat about half the sugar, 2 tablespoons at a time, into the egg whites until the meringue is thick and glossy. Then carefully and gradually fold in the remaining sugar. Fold in the vanilla. Drop the meringue by spoonfuls on baking sheets lined with wax paper and bake in a slow oven (250° F.) for about 30 minutes.

MAPLE MOUSSE

(F.P.K.'s Own Invention)

4 eggs   *2 cups heavy cream, whipped*
1 cup hot maple syrup

Beat the eggs slightly and stir in the maple syrup. Cook over simmering water until the custard thickens. Cool and fold in the whipped cream. Turn into a mold and cover tightly. Pack in a mixture of 4 parts cracked ice to 1 part rock salt and freeze for 3 hours.

PLAIN MOUSSE

(F.P.K.'s Own Invention)

1 cup sugar   *1 tablespoon gelatin softened*
⅓ cup water   *in 2 tablespoon hot water*
3 drops lemon juice *2 cups heavy cream, whipped*

Combine the sugar, water and lemon juice, bring to a boil and boil until the syrup spins a long thread. Stir in the gelatin, cool to lukewarm and fold in the whipped cream. Turn the mixture into a mold and seal tightly. Pack the mold in a mixture of 4 parts cracked ice to 1 part rock salt and freeze for 3 hours. Unmold and serve with any desired dessert sauce.

FROZEN PUDDING

(F.P.K.'s Own Rule)

1 cup chopped candied fruits of all kinds	2 eggs
	2½ cups hot milk
Brandy	1 cup heavy cream, whipped
1 cup sugar	½ cup rum
⅛ teaspoon salt	

Soak the fruits in brandy to cover for several hours. In a saucepan beat the sugar, salt and eggs until smooth and stir in the hot milk. Cook the mixture over simmering water until the custard coats a spoon, strain into a bowl and cool. Fold in the cream and rum. Fill a mold with alternate layers of the cream and brandied fruits. Seal the mold tightly and pack in a mixture of 4 parts cracked ice to 1 part rock salt. Freeze for 2 hours.

ROCK RICE

(F.P.K.'s Own Invention)

½ cup rice	1 tablespoon gelatin
1 cup milk	2 tablespoons cold water
¾ cup sugar	1 cup heavy cream, whipped

Wash and drain the rice and put it in a saucepan with the milk. Bring to a boil and cook over boiling water for about 30 minutes, or until the rice is very tender and has absorbed most of the milk. Add the sugar and the gelatin softened in the cold water and stir until the sugar and gelatin are dissolved in the rice. Cool and fold in the whipped cream. Turn into a mold and seal tightly. Pack the mold in a mixture of 4 parts cracked ice to 1 part rock salt and freeze for 3 hours. Serve with hot raspberry sauce.

HOT RASPBERRY SAUCE

Beat 1 egg until stiff. Add gradually 1 cup warm raspberry syrup, beating constantly. Any other syrup may be used in place of raspberry.

PLUM PUDDING ICE CREAM

(Adapted by F.P.K. from rule found in an old newspaper, and always served at Christmas dinner)

½ cup raisins	½ cup sugar
¼ cup currants	2 squares bitter chocolate
Brandy	¾ teaspoon ground cloves
1 cup milk	¾ teaspoon ground cinnamon
1 cup cream	1 teaspoon vanilla

Soak the raisins and currants in brandy to cover for several hours. Scald the milk and cream. Add the sugar and chocolate and stir until they are thoroughly dissolved. Add the fruit mixture and the spices and cool. Stir in the vanilla. Freeze until stiff in a hand freezer, using 3 parts ice to 1 part rock salt. Pack into a mold, seal tightly and pack the mold in a mixture of 4 parts cracked ice to 1 part rock salt. When ready to serve unmold the cream on a cold platter and surround with whipped cream slightly flavored with brandy.

PEACHES WITH RICE
(Pêches à la Condé)

(F.P.K.'s Own Rule)

2 cups milk	2 tablespoons sugar
½ cup rice	Pinch of salt
1 egg, beaten	

Scald the milk, add the rice and cook over boiling water for about 45 minutes, or until the mixture is thick and the rice is tender. Stir in the egg, sugar and salt, turn into a mold, and chill until the pudding is firm. Unmold on a chilled serving platter and surround with canned peaches.

LEMON SPONGE PUDDING

1 cup sugar	2 eggs, separated
2 tablespoons flour	Juice of 2 lemons
3 tablespoons melted butter	1 cup milk
Pinch of salt	

Mix the sugar and flour thoroughly. Add the butter, salt and egg yolks and beat until smooth. Stir in the lemon juice and milk and fold in the stiffly beaten egg whites. Turn into a buttered deep baking dish and bake in a moderate oven (350° F.) for about 40 minutes.

GRAHAM PUDDING

1 egg	1 cup graham flour
1 cup molasses	1 teaspoon soda
1 cup milk	1 teaspoon salt
1 cup all-purpose flour	1 cup chopped raisins

Beat the egg and stir in the molasses and milk. Sift the all-purpose flour, graham flour, soda and salt and stir the dry ingredients gradually into the molasses mixture. Stir in the raisins and turn the batter into a buttered mold. Steam for 2½ to 3 hours and serve with the following sauce.

SAUCE FOR GRAHAM PUDDING

¼ cup butter	½ cup heavy cream, whipped
½ cup sugar	1 teaspoon vanilla
2 eggs, separated	

Cream the butter and sugar. Beat the egg yolks thoroughly and stir them into the butter-sugar mixture. Just before serving beat the egg whites until stiff and fold them and the whipped cream into the sauce. Stir in the vanilla.

INDIAN PUDDING

4 cups milk	½ cup molasses
½ cup corn meal	¼ teaspoon salt
1 tablespoon butter	

Bring 2 cups of the milk to a boil, stir in the cornmeal and cook, stirring, for 5 minutes. Remove the meal from the fire and stir in the butter, molasses, salt, and the remaining 2 cups milk. Turn the batter into a buttered baking dish and bake in a slow oven (250° F.) for 3 hours.

MARMALADE PUDDING

1 cup butter	2 cups flour
1 cup sugar	4 eggs, well beaten
1 cup marmalade	1 teaspoon baking soda

In a saucepan combine the butter, sugar and marmalade, and heat, stirring constantly, until these ingredients are melted and well blended. Remove from the heat and stir in the flour. Stir in the beaten eggs and, finally, the soda. Turn the batter into a buttered mold and steam for 2 hours. Serve with wine sauce.

MINCEMEAT

(My Mother-in-law's Rule)

3 *pounds round steak*
6 *pounds apples, chopped*
1½ *pounds suet, ground*
1 *cup chopped citron*
1 *pound raisins*
1 *pound currants*
2 *cups boiled cider**
½ *tablespoon ground mace*

½ *tablespoon ground cloves*
1 *tablespoon ground cassia*
2 *pounds brown sugar*
2 *teaspoons salt*
¾ *cup apple jelly*
Juice of 1 orange
Juice of 1 lemon
1 *cup brandy*

Cook the meat in boiling water to cover until tender, and cool in the broth. Put the meat through a food chopper and return it to the broth with all the rest of the ingredients except the brandy. Bring to a boil and simmer for 1½ to 2 hours, stirring frequently. Cool, add the brandy, and seal in glass jars.

* Boiled cider is cider that is boiled until it is reduced by half its original quantity.

Main Dishes

CREAMED SHRIMP WITH RICE

2 cups cold boiled rice
2 cups heavy cream
1 pound freshly cooked
    shrimp, shelled and
    deveined

Salt and pepper to taste
Saltine crackers
Green peas

In a saucepan combine the rice and cream. Cook over boiling water for about 30 minutes, stirring frequently, until the mixture is smooth and hot. Add the shrimp and salt and pepper and cook for 10 minutes longer. Serve piping hot on toasted crackers, surrounded by cooked green peas. A little grated onion and curry powder may be added to the rice and cream.

CODFISH BALLS

1 pound salt codfish
6 potatoes
Hot milk

3 tablespoons butter
2 eggs, well beaten
Salt to taste

Soak the codfish in cold water overnight. In the morning drain and cover with fresh cold water. Bring the water to a boil and simmer the codfish until tender. Let the codfish cool in the water and meanwhile boil the potatoes in water to cover well until tender. Drain and mash the potatoes with enough hot milk to make them light and fluffy. Beat in the butter. Flake the codfish and combine the fish and mashed potatoes. Stir in the eggs and beat well. Season with salt if necessary and roll the mixture into small balls. Fry the balls in hot deep fat (370° F.) until golden brown and drain on absorbent paper.

BOSTON BAKED BEANS

2 cups navy beans
½ teaspoon baking soda
¼ pound salt pork
2 teaspoons salt

⅛ teaspoon dry mustard
¼ cup molasses
Boiling water

Wash and pick over the beans, cover with cold water and let stand overnight. In the morning drain the beans, cover them with fresh cold water, add the soda and bring the water to a boil. Simmer the beans, covered, until the skins burst. Test by taking a few up in a spoon and gently blowing on them. If the skin loosens and turns back, they are ready for the oven. Turn both beans and water into a bean pot and bury the salt pork in the center. Mix the salt, mustard and molasses with about 1 cup of boiling water and pour the mixture over the beans, adding additional water, if necessary, to cover them. Cover the bean pot and bake the beans in a slow oven (250° F.) for about 8 hours. Remove the cover during the last half hour of baking.

SALMON LOAF

1 pound can of salmon
½ cup soft bread crumbs
1 tablespoon melted butter

1 tablespoon lemon juice
4 eggs, beaten

Pick over and flake the contents of the can of salmon and combine the fish with the bread crumbs, melted butter and lemon juice. Stir in the beaten eggs and turn the mixture into a buttered loaf pan. Bake in a moderate oven (350° F.) for about 35 minutes. Unmold and serve with hot tartar sauce.

RISOTTO FOR 4 PERSONS

4 tablespoons butter
1 small onion, minced
1 cup rice
Pinch of saffron

Hot beef or mutton stock
1 cup grated Parmesan
   cheese

Heat the butter in an iron skillet and in it sauté the onion until it is golden and transparent, but not brown. Wash the rice in several changes of cold water, rubbing the grains between the hands to remove the excess starch. Add the rice and cook slowly, stirring constantly, for about 5 minutes, or until the kernels of rice are deep yellow. Add a pinch of saffron if desired. Gradually stir in about 1½ cups of the hot stock until the kernels are well moistened and the rice is covered with the stock. Cover the skillet and cook slowly for 15 minutes, or until the rice is tender. Stir in the cheese and cook, stirring, for 3 minutes longer. Serve very hot.

BAKED HOMINY

1 cup hominy grits
1 cup boiling water
½ teaspoon salt

2 cups milk
2 tablespoons butter
1 egg, well beaten

Pour the grits gradually into the boiling salted water, stirring constantly, and boil for about 2 minutes. Stir in 1 cup of the milk and cook over boiling water for 30 minutes. Remove the grits from the fire and stir in the remaining cup of milk, the butter and the egg. Turn the mixture into a buttered baking dish and bake in a moderate oven (350° F.) for 30 to 40 minutes.

Dressings, Relishes, Punch and Candy

FRENCH DRESSING

(I. F. Keyes—My sister-in-law)

¼ teaspoon salt
¼ teaspoon dry mustard
½ teaspoon sugar
1 teaspoon walnut ketchup
1½ teaspoons tomato ketchup

1 tablespoon vinegar
4 tablespoons olive oil
A little grated onion or
   slivered olives

Combine the dry ingredients, add the walnut and tomato ketchup and mix well. Beat in the oil and vinegar and add the onion or olives to taste.

MAYONNAISE

2 egg yolks
1 teaspoon dry mustard
½ teaspoon salt
¼ teaspoon cayenne pepper

2 cups olive oil
2 tablespoons vinegar
2 tablespoons lemon juice

In a mixing bowl beat the egg yolks well. Add the mustard, salt and cayenne and mix thoroughly. Beat in 1 tablespoon of the vinegar, then begin to add the oil a few drops at a time, beating constantly. Whenever the mayonnaise thickens too rapidly add a little of the remaining vinegar and the lemon juice. Toward the end the oil may be added more rapidly. Do not add all the oil unless it is necessary to bring the mayonnaise to the desired consistency, for the exact amount needed will depend on the size of the egg yolks used.

PEPPER RELISH

(F.P.K.'s Own Invention)

24 red peppers, seeded and chopped	24 onions, peeled and chopped
	6 cups vinegar
24 green peppers, seeded and chopped	4 tablespoons salt
	2 cups sugar

In a preserving kettle mix the peppers and onions. Cover with boiling water, let stand 5 minutes and drain. Then add the vinegar, salt and sugar. Bring to a boil and simmer for 5 minutes. Pack the relish into hot sterilized jars, seal while hot and store in a dark cool spot.

SOUR PICKLE

1 cup sugar	4 quarts vinegar
1 cup salt	Small green cucumbers,
1 cup dry mustard	freshly picked

In a stone jar combine the sugar, salt and mustard and stir in the vinegar. Fill the jar with the washed cucumbers. Cover the jar and place it in a cool dark place for several weeks before using the pickles.

PICCALILLI

4 quarts chopped green
  tomatoes
¾ cup salt
2 teaspoons pepper
3 teaspoons dry mustard
3 teaspoons cinnamon
3 teaspoons allspice

3 teaspoons cloves
½ cup white mustard seed
2 quarts vinegar
4 green peppers, seeded and
  sliced
2 onions, peeled and chopped

Sprinkle the tomatoes with the salt and let stand overnight. In the morning drain well. In a large kettle combine the spices and vinegar and bring to a boil. Add the tomatoes, peppers and onions, bring again to a boil and simmer for 15 minutes. Pack into hot sterilized jars, seal and store.

SWEET CUCUMBER PICKLE

8 pounds ripe cucumbers
Alum
4 pounds brown sugar

1 quart vinegar
1 cup mixed whole spices tied
  in a bag

Peel the cucumbers and cut them into strips. Cover them with cold water, adding ¼ ounce of alum to each quart of water used. Let stand overnight. In the morning bring the cucumbers and liquid to a boil, drain immediately and plunge the cucumbers into cold water until cold.

In a kettle combine the brown sugar and vinegar. Add the spice bag and bring the syrup to a boil. Add the cucumbers and simmer for about 10 minutes, or until the cucumbers are tender. Pack the cucumbers in hot sterilized jars. Continue to boil the syrup for 5 minutes longer, then fill the jars to overflowing with the syrup and let stand for 24 hours. The next day, drain the syrup from the jars, bring to a boil and boil for 5 minutes. Again fill the jars and let stand for 24 hours. Repeat this draining and boiling process on the following morning. On the last day seal the jars while hot and store.

MUSTARD PICKLES

1 quart large cucumbers, chopped	Salt
	6 tablespoons dry mustard
1 quart small cucumbers or gherkins	1 tablespoon turmeric
	2 tablespoons ground celery seed
1 quart green tomatoes, quartered	
	1 cup sugar
1 quart tiny onions, peeled	1 cup flour
2 large cauliflowers, cut into pieces	2 quarts vinegar

Combine the vegetables in a large bowl. Add 1 tablespoon salt to each quart of boiling water needed to cover the vegetables, pour the salted water over the vegetables and let stand overnight. In the morning drain thoroughly and put the vegetables into a preserving kettle. Mix the dry ingredients with enough of the vinegar to make a smooth paste, gradually stir in the rest of the vinegar and pour the mixture over the vegetables. Bring slowly to a boil, stirring constantly. Turn into hot sterilized jars and seal at once. Store in a dark cool spot.

PUNCH

(F.P.K.'s Own Rule)

Juice of 10 lemons	2 cups dry red wine
2 lemons, sliced	½ cup rum
Juice of 6 oranges	¼ cup brandy
Juice from 1 can of pineapple	Sugar

In a large punch bowl combine the fruit, fruit juice, wine and liquor and stir in sugar to taste. When ready to serve place a large chunk of ice in the center of the punch bowl and spoon the liquid over the ice until it is diluted and well chilled.

MOLASSES CANDY

(Carrie Southard's Recipe)

2 cups molasses	1 tablespoon vinegar
1 cup sugar	1 cup boiling water
2 tablespoons maple syrup	2 tablespoons soft butter
½ teaspoon soda	Peppermint flavoring
1 teaspoon cream of tartar	

In a 4-quart saucepan combine the molasses, sugar, maple syrup, soda, cream of tartar, vinegar and boiling water. Bring slowly to a boil, stirring until the sugar is thoroughly dissolved. Then boil rapidly to the soft-ball stage, or to 242° F. on a candy thermometer. Add the butter, a little at a time, and continue to cook the syrup to 252° F. on a candy thermometer, or until a little of the syrup dropped into cold water forms a ball which is hard enough to hold its shape. Stir frequently toward the end of the cooking to prevent scorching. Remove from the stove and let the syrup stand until it stops boiling, then pour it onto an oiled marble slab or large china plate to cool. As the syrup cools, turn the edges toward the center several times to keep the candy at an even temperature. When cool enough to handle, add a little peppermint flavoring and pull the candy until it turns light in color. Pull part of it at a time into a rope about ¾ inch in diameter and cut into pieces.

WHITE CANDY

2 cups sugar	½ teaspoon cream of tartar
1 cup boiling water	Pinch of salt
¼ teaspoon soda	1 teaspoon vanilla

Combine all the ingredients except the vanilla in a 2-quart heavy saucepan, bring to a boil and cook rapidly until the syrup reaches the soft-ball stage, or to 238° F. on a candy thermometer. Remove the syrup from the heat and pour it at once onto a cool wet marble slab or china plate. Let the syrup cool for a few minutes, then with a rubber scraper, work the syrup in a circle until it becomes white. When cool enough to handle, knead the candy until it becomes creamy. Store in a tightly covered jar for 2 days before using. Then melt the fondant over boiling water and flavor it to taste with vanilla. Drop the hot melted fondant from the tip of a tablespoon onto a lightly oiled cooky sheet to cool and set.

Part Two

THE WASHINGTON HOSTESS

MY PLEASANT GARDEN

My garden's just a grassy square
A picket fence encloses,
But bridal wreath blooms early there
And violets, and roses.

Along the walks of mellowed brick
Are rows of sturdy box,
And near the purple iris, thick
Gay rows of hollyhocks.

And there are trees—yes, four of these,
To shield me from the street:
A sycamore spread wide before
The terrace where I eat,

And two magnolias which stay
Green all the winter through—
(Their lovely flowers come in May
And fall in June, it's true,

But if I grieved because of this
It would be thankless folly,
In summertime I do not miss
The berries on my holly!)

So I have these, my pleasant trees,
And furthermore, by dint
Of Heaven's grace upon the place
A bed of pleasant mint.

And when my daily work is done,
A julep's goodly cheer,
With friends who know that everyone
I love is welcome here.

The garden at "Tradition"
Alexandria, Virginia

QUEEN ANNE'S LACE was the first of my novels to attain much of a sale, and readers and reviewers alike leaped to the conclusion that it was autobiographical—indeed, some of them went so far as to congratulate me on my successful rise from a sordid background and sorry beginnings, and were greatly embarrassed when they discovered that their assumptions had been erroneous. I was amused, but by no means disconcerted by this widespread mistake; as a matter of fact, it was very helpful to me, for it enabled me to write reams of thinly disguised autobiography thereafter, quite unsuspected of so doing, except by my sons, from whom, especially the eldest, I have never been able to keep a secret successfully. The truth is there are only two entire chapters in *Queen Anne's Lace* which are almost straight autobiography: the one in which the new senator's wife receives on the occasion of her first "At Home" and the one in which the wife of the same senator—by this time up for re-election—takes the returns over the telephone, which her husband will not touch. There are, however, a few near-auto-biographical passages here and there and among them are the following, the first describing my heroine's initial attempts at entertaining after her marriage, and the second the first dinner she attends—at the home of another senator—after she goes to Washington as a senator's wife:

"The Sunday dinner which Anne set before her family-in-law was neither elaborate nor original—tomato bisque soup; roast chicken, mashed potatoes, onions and string beans, accompanied by light rolls and her new grape jelly; fruit salad; vanilla ice cream with chocolate sauce, sponge cake and coffee. . . . Then the Thanksgiving feast took place at the younger Conrads', and it *was* a feast, for Anne outdid herself. . . . They began to ask in Neal's friends, young lawyers and their wives who had been swift to offer hospitality to the bride and groom; the Mayor and his sister, the minister and his two married daughters. This meant shaded candles on the table, salted nuts, chilled celery and olives, more elaborate courses. It meant extra work, too. Still the labor was nothing, absolutely nothing. Anne laughed at that. But those bills! The figures began to dance before her eyes."

*   *   *   *

"Two servants in purple livery entered, bearing silver trays, laden with frosty cocktails, and tiny savory sandwiches. Senator Lassiter offered his arm to the Ambassadress, and advanced, with her beside him, at the head of the procession which wound its way to the strains of music from an unseen organ through a second great drawing room, across a galleried hall, and into a long, paneled dining room flanked with great carved sideboards. The table was covered with a lace cloth; golden vases filled with poinsettias alternated with golden *épergnes* filled with smooth, glowing fruit, down its stately length; at each place was a golden service plate, golden knives and forks, thin stemmed goblets of fine Venetian glass. The liveried men servants—six of them in evidence now—were offering caviar, resting in the carved hollows of great blocks of ice. This was followed by a clear green turtle soup, lobster Newburg in 'horns of plenty' made of fluffy pastry, a saddle of mutton with multitudinous vegetables, a molded gelatine salad accompanied by cheese soufflé, white balls of ice cream, rolled in shredded cocoanut and resting on illuminated spun sugar, tiny candy-like cakes. There was sherry to drink, claret, sauterne and champagne, though Anne touched none of it, and after the ladies had returned to the drawing room, there was coffee, dark brandy, colorless cointreau and emerald-colored

crème de menthe poured slowly from bulky bottles into infin-
itesimal glasses. Anne, feeling as if she had been suddenly
transported to one of Monte Cristo's banquets, hoped that she
was successfully concealing the swimming sensation which almost overcame her. . . . She must, it seemed, completely reor-
ganize her ideas about entertaining."

To be sure, my outlook was never as limited as my heroine's
before she went to Washington and my own entertaining thereafter was never as lavish as the dinner which altered her viewpoint. Nevertheless, a change undeniably took place, less in the
number of persons who broke bread with me than in what I
thought would pass muster as such.

The recipes which had been evolved at Pine Grove Farm
formed the nucleus of the Washington regime, and some of
them quickly became favorites of my newfound friends. Shrimps
with rice and peas, cucumber cream salad and rose cream cake
were among these favorites. Mary Phillips and Ina Danforth had
both left me to be married, but Scotch Cathie Argo had come to
live with me the day Ina departed and, in turn, had married
Henry Deming, the hired man at Pine Grove Farm. When my
husband and I went to Washington, the Demings went, too;
and though Cathie hated to cook—or claimed that she did—she
could feed more people well on less notice than anyone else I
have ever seen, and still do an immense amount of general house-
work on the side. I had no one else to help me in the early years
in Washington, except an occasional accommodator; and while I
am staggered now at the memory of the amount and kind of
cleaning and laundry that was done in my enormous house at
Pine Grove Farm when I was first married, I am still more
staggered at the memory of the amount of cooking done in the
small, rather nondescript apartment where I lived when I first
went to Washington. Later, when we moved to a larger, more
convenient and more attractive apartment and my modest staff
was augmented by the arrival of Clara Wilson, who is still with
me, it ceased to be so much of a miracle. But looking back from
this distance of time and space, it seems little short of that.

One aspect of the situation was, however, of immense help to me: up to then, my ideas of what constituted good cooking and adequate menus would have been bounded by the New England conception of these, had it not been for the years I spent abroad, and the happy accident of my birth in Virginia, which gave me the great good fortune of a foothold in that state. I do not mean to imply that this conception was not excellent, as far as it went; and I am still stoutly prepared to maintain, against all comers, that there are no better cooks anywhere in the world than in Newbury, Vermont. But it was undeniably a broadening, as well as a new experience, to meet women from every state in the Union, and to sample the specialties which they had transplanted from their own natural habitats to the Capital.

The luncheons of the Ladies of the Senate afforded the best possible means of acquainting me with these specialties. This organization, which was started during the First World War primarily for the purpose of doing Red Cross work, and which has now more or less reverted to its original status, was, between the two world wars, largely social in character. Every Tuesday, a group of senatorial ladies, appointed to do this by the president of the organization, provided the luncheon for which a large caucus room in the Senate Office Building was put aside. Waiters from the Senate restaurant set and cleared away the tables, and coffee, rolls and butter could be secured from this restaurant, too. Otherwise, everything was done by the hostesses of the day, from providing the food to serving it. We were limited as to menus—that is, we were allowed to have only one hot and one cold main dish, and cake or pastry for dessert. But we were encouraged to show originality in the dishes we did provide, and nothing was said against the addition of some small extra, like my frosted fudge, for instance. One dish after another, hitherto strange to me, came in swift succession within my delighted ken. We were all proud of our recipes and made no secret of them; in fact, we were glad to "swap." The result in my case, and I am sure in many others, was a greatly enlarged personal cookbook. I have carefully kept the names of the women who helped in this expansion, and am glad to record them, along with their recipes.

Prohibition was in full force during my early years in Washington and, though I distrusted the efficacy of the "noble experiment" from the beginning, I did feel that it really *was* a noble experiment and, being naturally law-abiding, besides having an inherent horror of intemperance, never once served alcohol in any form at my own table from the time the law was passed until it was repealed. In any case, teas and not cocktail parties were the order of the day in Washington: *thés dansants* for the young and the not so young, if the latter were merrily inclined; formal teas as the standard manner of mass entertaining for ladies in official life; quiet fireside teas for families and familiar friends. I still feel that something has been lost, in Washington and elsewhere in the United States, with the blessed exception of Boston, because teas have now been so generally by-passed. The youngsters and the lively young matrons and men about town had carefree frolics at their *thés dansants* and no headaches or befuddlement afterward. The official At Homes, when tea was often supplemented by coffee and hot chocolate and always complemented by delicious sandwiches and cakes, had a dignity and elegance which I have never seen a cocktail party attain, for the candle-lighted tea tables were always beautifully decorated with flowers and ladies of great distinction were always chosen as pourers and came dressed in their best "bib and tucker." Moreover, these parties took place sufficiently early—usually from four to six, less often from five to seven—so that one's appetite for an eight o'clock dinner—also an affair of beauty, dignity and elegance—was not spoiled. As for the quiet family tea, I do not think that its praises have ever been sufficiently sung, and this was very generally served—just as a highball is now—when the only guests were "droppers-inners" or when there were none at all.

One of my proudest moments, as an official hostess, was the

one in which I was told I served the best tea in Washington! Of course, this was not strictly true—few compliments are; there were many other hostesses whose tea was just as good. But its outstanding merit, in their case as in mine, lay largely in the matter of preparation. The tea was brewed with freshly boiled water, in an earthen teapot which had been thoroughly rinsed and heated with freshly boiled water; and, after a few minutes, the brew was transferred to another hot teapot—it could be, and generally was, silver this time—so that it would not become bitter or overstrong. It was renewed, according to this formula, at frequent intervals; and a second jug of freshly boiled water always stood close to the teapot, so that those who liked their tea weak would not have to drink it full strength. The secret of my wonderful tea lay in nothing more or less than this meticulous care; plenty of persons could afford a more expensive brand than I could; but it was casually made, allowed to stand indefinitely, and replenished from time to time merely by the addition of water which might be hot, but which was quite frequently tepid, and which was all too seldom freshly boiled.

Over a long period of years, my good tea was the mainstay of my mass entertaining. (I use the term "mass entertaining" with considerable feeling, even after this lapse of years, since in those days it was no unusual thing for a senator's wife to be called upon to receive anywhere from a hundred to five hundred guests, many of them total strangers to her, on her weekly day at home! True, I had given as many as 350 persons at a time a light supper at Pine Grove Farm without the help of a caterer; but this had been only on isolated occasions and not as a regular practice.) When it became legally permissible to serve beverages with alcoholic content again, I made the happy acquaintance of three, with which I had hitherto been only vaguely familiar, and speedily added these to my items of entertainment.

The first was the mint julep, as it was served at Wakefield, the hospitable country home of General and Mrs. George Barnett, near Front Royal, Virginia. I have since heard that the last instructions which a Kentucky colonel traditionally mur-

murs, on his deathbed, to his son and heir, run like this: "Never insult a decent woman; never bring in a horse hot to the stable; and never crush the mint in a julep." Perhaps some of the long-standing feuds between Kentucky and Virginia may be laid to this advice, for in Virginia we *do* crush the mint in a julep. (I venture to say "we" because, though a New Englander by ancestry and upbringing, I am a Virginian by the happy accident of birth, by the deliberate choice of this wonderful state as a winter residence over a longish period of years, and by many ties of affection with *real* Virginians!) That is, we crush the mint which goes into the bottom of the silver goblet—it must be silver, for otherwise it will not frost properly—into the warm fresh syrup of sugar and water—or, for those who prefer their juleps unsweetened, into the warm water—which is sparingly poured over it, to extract its delicate flavor. Next goes in a tablespoonful of the best brandy, and then very dry ice, enough to fill the goblet. I know only one way to have the ice sufficiently dry, and that is to put it in a canvas bag and to pound it into small pieces with a wooden mallet; the canvas absorbs the excess moisture in a way that no mechanical metal crusher can ever do. When the goblet is full of ice, except for the crushed mint and the syrup and the brandy nestling underneath, then it is time to stir in the bourbon, slowly and without measuring; and when the frost on the outside of the goblet is so thick that you need a knife, or strong fingernails, to scrape it off, *then* it is time to add a sprig of mint, which is *not* crushed, to the top! This sprig is not merely for decoration; you inhale its fragrance all the time you are sipping your julep; and a mint julep should be sipped very slowly, just as it should be prepared very carefully, and for these two reasons is most suitably served, in my opinion, only to small groups of congenial friends, who have no other engagement staring them in the face. The minute it is hastily put together, or tossed off like a cocktail, it loses its savor.

As I have said, it was Lelia Barnett who taught me to make mint juleps the way they should be made; but that was many years ago, and since then, they have become such an integral part of my own housekeeping and entertaining, that I have felt their concoction should be described at length among my experiences, as well as treated more briefly among my recipes. Traditionally, juleps form a hot weather beverage; but I honestly believe this is because it is something of a feat to grow mint in a cold climate; and—praise be!—the climate south of the Potomac is seldom so cold that mint will not flourish in it outdoors. But there is now a mint bed at the Oxbow in Newbury, Vermont, where mint can be nursed along from May to October, and then transplanted in the window boxes of a sunny kitchen, where chives for quite other purposes also belong. There was also one at "Tradition"—of which more hereafter—when I lived in Alexandria; and now there is one in the patio at Beauregard House in New Orleans and one in the garden at Compensation in Crowley which require no nursing; so for a long time, I have been pretty sure of a julep every night when at home, summer or winter, not only for myself, but for as many friends as drop in casually to bear me company; and every now and then I give a mint julep party. But only once have I asked more than twenty persons to such a party, and that was when Lelia Barnett's cousin, the Duchess of Windsor, came with the Duke to Beauregard House. All things being equal, I consider from six to a dozen the best number; and I have also learned that if a guest himself does not automatically stop at the second julep, it is best not to offer him any more. It is such a soothing, pleasant beverage, when properly prepared and served, that the uninitiated are apt to forget that it is also a powerful one; and my viewpoint on limiting the number of drinks, as well as the number of guests, was strengthened and cemented when a gentleman, who admitted to four and who had probably imbibed six, followed me from the garden to the drawing room—where I had gone to light the candles—when I was living in Alexandria and, after glancing about him, told me he thought it would make a wonderful place for a wedding; and sure enough, within a week, he had arranged to be married there, and I had another party, considerably larger than the first he had attended, on my hands!

Though I do limit the number of drinks and the number of guests, I try to make up for this stringency by seeing that no one goes hungry at a mint julep party. In the first place, I firmly subscribe to the theory that drink, like ink, needs a blotter; in the second, I believe that food adds to the sense of leisure, as well as to the sense of well-being which I am eager to create. Miss Clara has always excelled in the making of small puffs and, instead of using whipped cream or custard as a filling, has used shrimps and mayonnaise. I think these have been more popular than any other single offering at our mint julep parties, though her ribbon sandwiches and her cream cheese balls, rolled in finely diced dried beef, have likewise always had their advocates. We have always had one or more hot offerings, too: biscuits fresh from the oven as long as anyone wanted them, split, buttered hot and put together with any preferred filling; olives wrapped in bacon and skewered; toasted cheese sandwiches; and when we have known beforehand that even a few guests would settle down for the entire evening, we have had an alligator pear loaf, an angel cake, a sunshine cake and coffee.

Next, after mint juleps, in my new order of entertaining, after the repeal of Prohibition, indubitably came eggnog as this was, and still is, served in Washington and adjacent parts of Maryland and Virginia during the Christmas holidays. Its proper and usual complements always have been and probably always will be coffee, beaten biscuit stuffed with country ham, chicken salad sandwiches and, of course, fruitcake. The eggnog party, like the mint julep party, should, in my opinion, be leisurely; and though it is not infrequently a daytime affair, taking place either before midday dinner, or beginning in the morning and lasting until evening, I personally enjoy it most when it takes the place of supper and comes at the end of a day's activities rather than when they are still staring you in the face, though there are several schools of thought about this. I have enjoyed so many eggnog parties in so many different settings that I hesitate to single any out for mention; but those at the beautiful old Taylor house in Alexandria will certainly always be associated in my mind with glowing open fires, fragrant Christmas greens, shining brass and silver, beautiful old family portraits and the warmest sort of a welcome; while the recipe that I have finally settled on as the best among the many excellent ones offered me came to me through the generosity of Miss Susan Kintner of Washington, a *cordon bleu* if there ever was one, though real estate is actually her vocation!

Probably the third alcoholic beverage which has stood me in good stead for many years can also be traced to Susan Kintner, for I drank it first at the wedding reception of Ordway Whitford, whose elder sister, Harriet, then my secretary, later married Susan's brother, Edwin; and as Harriet and Edwin were already a "courting couple," and as the Kintner family was delighted with Harriet, it is quite likely that she already had access to Susan's culinary secrets! As I have said before, I had been brought up to regard champagne as the proper, indeed almost the inevitable, drink at weddings and christenings; but champagne served on the scale necessary to slake thirst in Washington was quite beyond my purse, if offered undiluted. Therefore, I was naturally thankful to be introduced to a punch in which it was, to be sure, an outstanding ingredient, but by no means the only ingredient, and in which any good domestic champagne would serve the purpose as well as one of imported vintage. Moreover, the recipe for punch, as originally given me, has been subject to all sorts of pleasant variations; and by the time we reached the third generation of christenings in my family, I was nowhere nearly as restricted as to a suitable choice of beverage for my guests as was my mother.

After serving eighteen years in the Senate, my husband decided that he did not wish to run again, but to retire to Pine Grove Farm, which, all his life, he had loved better than any other place on earth. I understood his feeling and sympathized with it: he had held public office ever since graduating from college. He had been selectman in our home town for many years; he had served several times in the state legislature; he had been first treasurer and then chairman of the state excise board; and he had been governor of New Hampshire throughout American participation in the First World War, immediately before entering the Senate. All this represented great stress and strain and it was natural that he should crave respite from it. But while it also bespoke confidence in his ability and respect for his character, it represented very little money. The governor's salary at that time was three thousand dollars a year, a senator's seventy-five hundred; with three sons to educate, it had been hard to make both ends meet, and I was thankful that my writing had helped. Now, as I saw it, this must help still more, for there would be no senatorial salary after my husband's retirement, and none from any other source; moreover, Pine Grove Farm had long since ceased to operate as a profitable dairy. We discussed ways and means and it was finally decided that he should fulfill his wish of going home, but that I would remain in Washington, and commute between there and New Hampshire, since the Capital offered far more opportunities for me, as a writer, than the country. A few years before this, we had given up our Washington apartment and moved to a pleasant house we were able to rent in Alexandria, an arrangement which had suited us both, since to me it meant getting back into Virginia, even if only just over the border, and to my husband living in the place which, as Chairman of Public Buildings and Grounds, he had helped make into a convenient suburb, through the creation of the Memorial Highway. It was a wrench to leave it, especially for me. But I found a small apartment in an unfashionable part of town, edited a magazine by day, worked on my novels by night, went on speaking tours in what would otherwise have been time off from the magazine, and got to the Farm when and as I could.

It was a stiff program and it makes me tired now when I think of it; at the time, it was all the harder to endure because it was subject to misinterpretation. There was a rumor that my husband and I had separated, that I had been unwilling to leave the excitement of Washington for the quiet of the country. Of course our close friends realized there was no truth in this, and so did everyone else thoughtful enough to consider that there is not much pleasurable "excitement" in working eighteen hours a day; so the rumor never spread very far. Nevertheless, it hurt. But the stiff program served its purpose: my husband spent his last years as he wanted to spend them and I proved my ability to support myself and to contribute to the welfare of others dear to me.

Meanwhile, generally speaking, Sunday was the day when I could accomplish the most at my desk, because it was the day everyone else gave over to relaxation and pleasure, after (or instead of) churchgoing. But it was also the only day when I could possibly entertain, because on week days I was at my office by nine-thirty, taking a basket lunch with me, and usually not returning home until seven; then, as soon as I had eaten my supper, I settled down to work on the current novel. Once or twice a week I went to a late afternoon reception or to a dinner; but it was practically impossible for me to prepare for either one in my own apartment. It was then that I hit upon the idea of giving Sunday breakfasts—not only because they were feasible from the standpoint of my working time, but because they were very, very inexpensive!

Cathie and Henry Deming had returned to New Hampshire with my husband, but Clara had stayed staunchly with me and did all the work, including most of the washing, in the little apartment. We talked over the Sunday breakfasts, and decided that, for these, we must get in two accommodators, but that we would have them come just in time to help with the serving and stay only long enough to help wash the dishes. Then we mapped out the general plan which was afterward followed with little or no variation: on the sideboard we placed two pitchers of fruit juice, which we varied, but which we tried to keep original—that is, we avoided orange juice, not for any lack of appreciation, but because it was offered everywhere, and went in for berry juices, grape juices and combinations of the two; the guests poured these beverages out for themselves. At one end of the dining room table were the home-cooked baked beans and fish balls; at the other end, the carefully brewed coffee; these were served by two friends to whom I assigned the responsibility beforehand. On either side of the table were the home-cooked brown bread, doughnuts and applesauce and to these, also, the guests helped themselves. Then they were seated at card tables, already laid with linen, silver and glass, and scattered through the apartment. Everyone sat down to eat, everyone was comfortable and everyone, apparently, was happy. At all events, no formal dinners that I ever gave received more praise, and just as many high officials and visiting firemen as ever were my guests. These breakfasts took place at twelve, so that anyone who wanted to go to church beforehand would have time to do that, and everyone who wanted to play golf afterward would have time to do that, too. But very often the twelve o'clock guests were still around at five or six. The atmosphere seemed conducive to friendly arguments, to off-the-record disclosures, and to general geniality. If lingerers were still there at the cocktail hour, they were given suitable refreshments in moderation; but no alcoholic beverages were served with the breakfasts; and Clara and I discovered, to our delight, that we could feed twenty-five persons our New England breakfast for fifteen dollars, and that this sum included the accommodators' charge, so that I could afford to entertain once a month!

Soon after my husband died, I resigned my editorship and began to devote practically all my working hours to creative writing which, by then, was the way I preferred to use them. I also wanted very much to return to Alexandria and eventually, with the proceeds of my book, *The Great Tradition*—most of which had been written after office hours—I acquired the title to another old house there, on which I had been keeping my eye for some time. It had gone completely to rack and partially to ruin, but it had a great tradition of its own, and the two circumstances combined to give it the name I bestowed upon it. At various times, members of the Washington and Lee families had occupied it; in the double drawing rooms beautiful twin chandeliers, never converted from long disused gas to non-existent electricity, still bore mute and almost pleading witness to their days of gracious living. So did an equally beautiful mirror—probably too cumbersome for convenient removal—that still gleamed through the gloom of the long-shuttered entrance hall. In the beginning, the house had been an appendage of the famous Gadsby's Tavern; many distinguished guests had been quartered there in preference to the larger place, as being more private and more select; and some of the most important con-ferences regarding the strategies of the American Revolution had taken place in the large room, which originally ran straight across the front of the second story and which had fine paneling and a lovely carved mantel of Italian marble. This room had been divided up with beaverboard into cubicles for the far less distinguished guests who later on became its casual lodgers and finally inhabited, in the one heated corner, by a poor lonely old lady who was waiting to be taken away to a rest home. The house had been on the market for a long time and no one had been interested in it. But when I was taken to see it by Susan Kintner—the enterprising young realtor hitherto mentioned in connection with Christmas eggnog and wedding punch—I visual-ized the historic assembly room, restored to its pristine order and spaciousness, as the ideal study, and the double drawing rooms, on the ground floor, with the wide French doors between them flung open again, as the perfect setting for the kind of parties I wanted to give. To be sure, the house had no central heating and practically no lighting or plumbing, and the kitchen and onetime buttery were in a state of deplorable dirt. But their condition left me undaunted; and when I stepped out into the side yard, overgrown with rank grass, cluttered with broken brick, and separated from the street only by a decrepit railing of weather-beaten boards, I saw how this yard might look, too: the bricks could be shaped into a terrace, shaded by a sycamore tree —the one remaining object of beauty in the wreckage; the rank grass could be disciplined into smooth lawns, bordered by box and old-fashioned flowers; the broken railings could be used for kindling wood and supplanted by a white picket fence. Without more ado, I told Susan that if we could persuade the owners to sell the place for half the modest sum I had available and a contractor to restore it for the other half, she had made a sale. But, when I said, "I acquired the title," rather than that "I bought the house," I did so advisedly, for I had to mortgage it very heavily and mortgage my own time far ahead, too! However, acquire it I did; then I restored it, carefully and lovingly, rented it profitably during the months when I was traveling or at home in New England; and, finally, when it became evident that Louisiana was the most logical writing center for me in the wintertime, I sold it at a profit. Meanwhile, I spent five happy years as its owner and these years marked the third period of my experience as a Washington hostess.

The house was blessed, at a simple but impressive ceremony, in which solemnity gradually merged into festivity; after that, came many other gatherings, diversified in character. I gave formal dinners again, the first of these in honor of Mrs. Roosevelt, then the President's wife, and herself the most gracious, thoughtful and hospitable hostess to preside over the White House during the years I spent in and near Washington. The Chinese Ambassador, Dr. Hu Shih, and the Minister of Guatemala and Señora Recinos were among the Chiefs of Missions who were also honor guests at dinner early in my occupancy of Tradition. Occasionally, I gave formal luncheons, too, for I was no longer so hard pressed for either time or money as to make these impossible. Two weddings, two coming-out parties, various "benefits" and innumerable receptions took place in the double parlors. But it is to the mint julep parties in the small garden, the eggnog parties in the holly-decked house and the informal suppers in both places to which I look back with the greatest pleasure of all. Miss Clara could prepare spaghetti with a sauce that I have never seen surpassed outside of Italy; this, with a big wooden bowl of green salad, red wine, and some light sweet accompanied by strong coffee constituted a supper that I was not ashamed to set before anyone and, little by little, it became

my standby, and was served more often than the New England
Sunday breakfasts—I offered it, for instance, to the Society of
Woman Geographers when this met with me, and to many other
equally select groups. On Sunday evenings, when Miss Clara
was out, the supper was cold and there was no one to help me
serve it; but if callers dropped in, during the later afternoon, as
they were apt to do, we had a party just the same. I remember,
for instance, a Sunday when Dr. and Señora Alfaro came to
call. He had been the Minister of Panama in the early twenties
and afterward, when that country achieved an Embassy to the
United States, the Panamanian Ambassador. Later, he became
Panama's President and, though he retired temporarily to private
life, his fame as an international lawyer did not permit him to
remain in anything like seclusion. Eventually, he became a
member of the Permanent Court of Justice at the Hague, Chief
of Mission of UNRRA to Caribbean and Central American
Republics, Delegate of Panama to the United Nations Confer-
ence on International Organizations at San Francisco and the
recipient of many other varied and well-deserved honors.
Throughout all these changes both he and his wife—a woman
who combines every spiritual with every social grace—remained,
and still remain, my very good friends; but hitherto the entertainment we exchanged had been of a somewhat studied and
formal order. On the occasion of the Sunday call to which I
have referred, I remembered that I had been fortunate enough
to secure some especially fine Amontillado, which I knew Dr.
Alfaro would appreciate. After offering this, along with the
sandwiches Miss Clara had prepared for my supper and left in
the refrigerator, I also remembered that I had made hardly a
dent in the roast of beef which had constituted the mainstay of
my Sunday dinner, and that there was an exceptionally good
cheese and a fresh angel cake in the house. I asked my distinguished visitors if they would not stay and share these with me
and presently, altogether, we were carrying plates and silverware
and glasses out to the rustic table in the garden. We did not
leave it until midnight.

A refugee rabbi and his wonderful wife, several editors and

publishers who came down unexpectedly from New York, senators and congressmen from "the Hill," diplomats from the far-flung corners of the earth, Washingtonians and Virginians without number and representing almost every known profession, were among the others who contributed to the enjoyment of my al fresco feasts. But the record for lingering on to the wee sma' hours occurred when a French captain, with whom I had made a perilous trans-Atlantic crossing after the outbreak of World War II, and who was later assigned to convoy duty in the African Theatre, telephoned to say that he was in Washington for one evening and that, if agreeable and convenient, he would like to spend it at my house. There was no time to assemble much of a group; but I did get hold of two congenial spirits who lived nearby and, after dinner, we embarked on a game of bridge, of which the captain was very fond and which he played extremely well, though three no trumps was invariably his bid, whatever he held for cards. The game, which had begun in suitable silence, became more and more conversational, as we gradually persuaded the captain to talk about his war experiences. Once really launched, he went on and on, and the rest of us laid down our cards and listened with fascination. I had no idea what time it was when the party broke up; but my neighbors happened to glance at the clock on a nearby bank as they were going home: the hands pointed to five minutes of five.

In New England, while I had always been used to having a good many guests, both in my mother's house and in my husband's, it was company with a capital C, so to speak; the earlier period in Washington itself, and the first period in Alexandria had involved a trend to more rather than less formality; but in the little apartment of G Street and then at Tradition, I found out that entertaining does not need to be expensive to be delightful and to be appreciated, and that frequently the party which has not been planned at all tops all the others, as far as both hostess and guests are concerned. The tardy acquisition of this knowledge proved the best possible preparation for the unexpected role that was still ahead of me—that of the Southern writer.

NUT BREAD

Susan B. Spender

(Mrs. Aeldon P. Spender, Missouri)

1 egg, beaten	1 teaspoon salt
1 cup sugar	3 teaspoons baking powder
1 cup chopped pecan meats	1½ cups milk
3 cups flour	

Combine the egg, sugar and pecans. Sift together the dry ingredients and stir them into the egg mixture alternately with the milk. Turn the batter into a buttered loaf pan, let stand for 30 minutes, then bake in a slow oven (325° F.) for about 45 minutes, or until a cake tester inserted in the center comes out clean. Turn the loaf out onto a rack to cool.

CHOCOLATE NUT BREAD

Lidia Norbeck

(Mrs. Peter Norbeck, South Dakota)

½ cup sugar	4 cups (2 pounds) plain
½ teaspoon salt	bread dough
1 teaspoon cinnamon	Flour
2 tablespoons cocoa	1 cup walnut meats
1 tablespoon shortening	1 cup raisins
1 cup milk	

Mix the sugar, salt, cinnamon, cocoa, shortening and milk into the bread dough until the batter is doubled in bulk. Mix in enough flour to make a dough that is light but does not stick to the hands. Knead in the walnut meats and raisins, divide the dough in half and form each half into a loaf. Bake the loaves in buttered bread tins or on baking sheets in a hot oven (425° F.) for 15 minutes. Reduce the oven temperature to 350° F., and continue to bake for about 40 minutes longer, or until the bread is browned.

FLOUR MUFFINS

Julia Wheeler Harris

(Mrs. Wm. J. Harris, Georgia)

1½ tablespoons lard	2 eggs, beaten
2 teaspoons sugar	2 cups flour
Pinch of salt	4 teaspoons baking powder
1 cup milk	

Cream the lard until it is fluffy and stir in the sugar and salt. Stir in the milk and eggs, then the flour, sifted with the baking powder. Fill muffins pans two-thirds full and bake in a hot oven (400° F.) for 25 minutes.

POTATO ROLLS

(Mrs. Richard P. Ernst, Kentucky)

7 cups flour	1 cup milk
½ cup vegetable shortening	2 eggs, well beaten
1 cup mashed potatoes (cold)	1 cake yeast dissolved in
1 teaspoon salt	½ cup lukewarm water
½ cup sugar (scant)	

Sift 1 cup of the flour three times. Add the shortening to the sifted flour and cut it in thoroughly with two knives. Then add the potatoes, salt and sugar and stir in the milk, eggs, and dissolved yeast. Let the batter stand in a warm place for 3 hours, then add enough sifted flour (from 5 to 6 cups) to make a soft dough. Put the dough in a warm place to rise for 3 hours, knead the dough down and shape it into small rolls. Arrange the rolls on greased baking sheets, brush the tops with melted butter and let rise for 30 minutes. Bake the rolls in a moderate oven (350° F.) for 20 to 25 minutes, or until lightly browned. Serve hot.

WAFFLES

Florence Kling Harding

(Mrs. Warren G. Harding, Ohio)

2 eggs, separated	2 cups milk
2 tablespoons sugar	3 cups flour
1 teaspoon salt	3 teaspoons baking powder
2 tablespoons butter, melted	

Beat the egg yolks and stir in the sugar, salt and melted butter. Stir in the milk and enough of the flour to make a thin batter. Just before baking stir in the baking powder and fold in the egg whites, stiffly beaten. Bake in a hot waffle iron.

LEMON BUTTER FOR TEA BISCUITS

Natalia S. Jones

(Mrs. Andrieus Jones, New Mexico)

Dissolve 1 tablespoon cornstarch in ¼ cup cold water and stir this into 1 cup boiling water. Cook, stirring, until the mixture is clear and thickened. Stir in ½ cup sugar, the juice of

2 lemons, ½ cup butter, and 3 egg yolks and 1 whole egg beaten with a little of the hot sauce. Cook, stirring constantly, over simmering water for 3 minutes. Remove from the heat and stir in 1 teaspoon grated lemon rind. Use to spread on hot biscuits.

VEAL BIRDS

Florence C. Capper

(Mrs. Arthur Capper, Kansas)

Wipe 2 thin slices of veal cutlet (about 1½ pounds) and pound the slices until they are very thin. Cut the meat into pieces about 4 inches square. Chop the trimmings finely and mix the trimmings with 1 cup bread crumbs, ¼ teaspoon celery seed, and salt and pepper to taste. Spread the veal squares with this filling, roll them up like tiny jelly rolls and secure them with toothpicks. Roll the veal "birds" in flour and sauté them in butter over a gentle flame for about 40 minutes, turning them occasionally to brown on all sides. A few minutes before serving heat 1 cup heavy cream and stir in 1 tablespoon flour mixed to a paste with 1 tablespoon butter. Cook, stirring, for 5 minutes and pour the sauce over the "birds."

CHILE CON CARNE

Lucille S. Sheppard

(Mrs. Morris Sheppard, Texas)

1 cup Mexican frijoles (*pink beans*) or kidney beans
1 pound round steak, chopped
2 medium onions, minced
2 tablespoons bacon drippings
2 cups water
2 large tomatoes, *peeled and quartered*
1 teaspoon salt
½ teaspoon pakrika
2 tablespoons chile powder mixed with 1 cup hot water

Soak the beans overnight in water to cover and, in the morning, drain. Sauté the steak and onions in the bacon drippings, stirring constantly, until the onion is soft and yellow. Turn the mixture into a saucepan and add the water, beans, tomatoes, salt and spices. Bring the liquid to a boil and simmer for 3 hours, adding a little more water from time to time if necessary.

BEEFSTEAK SPANISH

Elizabeth Y. Ashurst

(Mrs. Henry F. Ashurst, Arizona)

Broil a beefsteak in the usual way. In a saucepan heat ½ can of tomatoes, 3 large onions, chopped, and 1 tablespoon chile powder, and cook, stirring frequently, until the onion is tender. Stir in bit by bit 1 tablespoon flour mixed to a paste with 1 tablespoon soft butter and cook, stirring, until the sauce is slightly thickened. Correct the seasoning with salt and pour the hot sauce over the broiled steak.

CHICKEN PIE

Florence Kling Harding

(Mrs. Warren G. Harding, Ohio)

1 plump stewing chicken	1 teaspoon salt
12 small potatoes, peeled	4 teaspoons baking powder
1 onion, peeled	4 tablespoons lard
4 cups flour	Water

Simmer the chicken in salted water to cover until the meat falls from the bones. Strain and reserve the chicken stock and cut the chicken meat into small pieces. Cook the potatoes and onion in stock to cover until tender.

Sift the flour, salt and baking powder into a mixing bowl and cut in the lard. Stir in enough water to make a soft dough that cleans the bowl. Line a baking dish with a thin layer of the dough and bake in a hot oven (450° F.) for about 15 minutes, or until the crust is lightly browned. Fill the crust with the chicken, onion and potatoes and a little of the chicken stock, cover with a thin layer of dough and bake in a hot oven for another 12 to 15 minutes, or until the top crust is browned. To the remaining chicken broth stir in bit by bit a paste made of equal amounts of flour and butter until the broth is slightly thickened. Correct the seasoning with salt and pepper and serve this sauce with the hot pie.

PRESSED CHICKEN

Ida M. Cameron

(Mrs. Ralph H. Cameron, Arizona)

Cover 2 plump stewing hens with boiling water and simmer them for about 1 hour. Add salt to taste, cover and continue to cook until the birds are tender. Remove the chickens from the stock to cool. Cut the meat from the bones, return the bones and the skin of the chickens to the stock and simmer for at least 30 minutes longer. Strain 1 quart of the stock into a saucepan, cool and discard the fat that rises to the surface. Add 2 tablespoons gelatin which have been softened in ¼ cup cold water and heat, stirring, until the gelatin is thoroughly dissolved.

Put the chicken meat through the fine blade of a meat grinder and mix it with 1 cup chopped green olives, 1 cup chopped walnut meats and 1 small can pimientos, chopped. Season the mixture well with salt and pepper and stir in the stock. Press the mixture firmly into a mold and chill in the refrigerator until firm.

LOUISIANA BAKED FISH CREOLE

Olive Ransdell

(Mrs. Joseph E. Ransdell, Louisiana)

Poach a 4 to 5 pound fish in salted water to cover for about 30 minutes, or until the flesh flakes from the bones. Drain and put the fish in a buttered ovenproof dish. Cover the fish with Sauce Creole and bake in a moderate oven (325° F.) for about 20 minutes, basting frequently. Remove the fish from the oven and garnish it with 3 hard-cooked eggs, sliced. Serve with cooked rice.

SAUCE CREOLE

2 tablespoons bacon drippings
    or lard
2 onions, coarsely chopped
2 tablespoons flour
1/4 cup water or fish stock

1 can tomatoes
1 clove garlic, minced
Salt, cayenne pepper and
    black pepper to taste

In a heavy skillet heat the bacon drippings or lard and in it sauté the onions until they are delicately browned. Stir in the flour and cook, stirring, until the flour is golden brown. Add the remaining ingredients and cook over a gentle flame for 30 minutes.

SHAD ROE SOUFFLÉ

Mary Chandler Hale

(Mrs. Eugene Hale, Maine)

1 shad roe
3 eggs, separated
1/2 cup milk

1/2 teaspoon salt
Pinch of pepper

Simmer the roe in water to cover for 15 minutes. Drain, remove the membrane covering it and mash the roe thoroughly.

Beat the egg yolks lightly and stir in the milk, mashed roe and salt and pepper. Beat the egg whites until stiff and fold them into the yolk mixture. Turn the batter into a soufflé dish and bake in a hot even (450° F.) for 20 to 25 minutes.

WASHINGTON VEGETARIAN LOAF

Mary F. Henderson

(Mrs. John Henderson, widow of late Senator from Missouri)

1 large onion, minced	1 cup blanched ground
2 tablespoons butter	almonds
1 cup tomato sauce	4 eggs, beaten
1 cup soft bread crumbs	3 hard-cooked eggs, sieved

Sauté the onion in the butter until it is transparent and mix it into the tomato sauce, bread crumbs and almonds. Stir in the beaten eggs and lastly stir in the sieved hard-cooked eggs. Turn the mixture into a buttered baking dish, place the baking dish in a shallow pan of hot water and bake in a slow oven (325° F.) for about 1 hour. Remove the dish from the water and bake for 10 minutes longer. Unmold on a serving dish and serve with hollandaise sauce.

This loaf is generally made a day or more before serving, to be reheated, or cut into slices and served cold.

FRUIT SALAD

Mary M. Overman

(Mrs. Lee S. Overman, North Carolina)

1 tablespoon gelatin	1 can pineapple, diced
2 tablespoons cold water	1 can pears, diced
¼ cup boiling water	1 can apricots, diced
Juice of 6 oranges	1 can white cherries, pitted
Juice of 3 lemons	4 grapefruit
3 cups sugar	

Soak the gelatin in the cold water for 5 minutes, add the boiling water and stir until the gelatin is thoroughly dissolved. Stir the gelatin into the juice of the oranges and lemons and stir in the sugar. Add the pineapple, pears, apricots and cherries. Peel the grapefruit, break it into segments and free the segments of membrane and seeds. Add the grapefruit to the salad mixture, turn it into a mold rinsed in cold water and chill in the refrigerator overnight. Serve on lettuce with any desired dressing.

CHEESE AND FRUIT SALAD

Mary M. Overman

(Mrs. Lee Overman, North Carolina)

2 cups heavy cream, whipped
5 ounces soft cream cheese
2 cups mayonnaise
2 cups seeded Malaga grapes, chopped
1 can sliced pineapple, diced

Fold the whipped cream into the cream cheese and stir in the mayonnaise. Add the fruit, mix well and turn into individual salad molds. Chill in the refrigerator until set and unmold on beds of lettuce leaves.

APRICOT SALAD

Mary M. Borah

(Mrs. Wm. E. Borah, Idaho)

Whip 1 cup heavy cream and mix it well with 3 tablespoons mayonnaise. Stir in 10 marshmallows, cut into small pieces, and ½ cup chopped black walnuts. Arrange apricot halves on crisp lettuce leaves and garnish with the whipped cream dressing.

UTOPIAN SALAD

Olive Ransdell

(Mrs. Joseph E. Ransdell, Louisiana)

4 eggs, beaten	6 oranges
2 tablespoons sugar	1 pineapple, shredded
2 tablespoons water	1 cup minced pecan meats
3 tablespoons butter	1 bottle maraschino cherries,
2 cups heavy cream, whipped	halved

In a saucepan combine the eggs, sugar and water. Place the saucepan in a skillet containing 1 inch of simmering water, and cook, stirring constantly, until the custard is hot and coats the spoon. Stir in the butter and cool. When cold fold in the whipped cream and keep in the refrigerator.

Peel the oranges, break them into segments and free the segments of membrane and seeds. Cut the flesh into small pieces and combine the orange with the pineapple, pecans and cherries. Chill and when ready to serve, arrange the fruit and nut mixture on individual salad plates lined with lettuce leaves. Serve with the cream dressing.

CHEESE JELLY

Catherine Calder

(Mrs. Wm. M. Calder, New York)

½ tablespoon gelatin	Salt and pepper to taste
¼ cup cold water	6 green olives, finely chopped
3 ounces cream cheese	2 tablespoons chopped pecan
3 ounces pimiento cheese	meats
½ cup heavy cream, whipped	

Soak the gelatin in the water for 5 minutes and turn into a saucepan. Stir, over boiling water, until the gelatin is dissolved. Cream together the cream cheese and the pimiento cheese until the mixture is light and fluffy and set aside. Combine the whipped cream and the dissolved gelatin with a little salt and pepper, the olives and pecan meats, and stir the combination into the cheese mixture. Beat well, turn the mixture into a mold rinsed in cold water and chill in the refrigerator overnight. When ready to serve, turn the jelly out onto a cold plate and garnish with lettuce leaves, stuffed olives and whole pecan meats and serve with mayonnaise.

TOMATO ASPIC

Vera King

(Mrs. Wm. H. King, Utah)

1 large can tomatoes	Salt, pepper and sugar
2 onions, chopped	1 tablespoon gelatin
3 stalks celery with the leaves, chopped	1 cup cold water
	Juice of 1 lemon

Combine the tomatoes, onions and celery and season the mixture to taste with salt, pepper and sugar. Bring to a boil, simmer until the vegetables are tender and press through a fine sieve. While the liquid is still hot, add the gelatin softened in the cold water, and stir until the gelatin is thoroughly dissolved. Stir in the lemon juice, pour into molds rinsed in cold water and chill in the refrigerator until set. Unmold on lettuce leaves and sprinkle with chopped celery. Serve with mayonnaise.

GRAHAM PUDDING

Clara C. Lenroot

(Mrs. Irvine L. Lenroot, Wisconsin)

2 *teaspoons soda*	1 *teaspoon ground cloves*
1 *cup molasses*	1 *teaspoon ground cinnamon*
1 *cup milk*	*Pinch of salt*
2 *cups graham flour*	1 *teaspoon vanilla*
1 *cup chopped seeded raisins*	

Stir the soda into the molasses and stir in the milk. Gradually stir in all but ¼ cup of the flour and dredge the raisins with this reserved flour. Stir the spices, salt and vanilla into the batter and fold in the floured raisins. Turn the batter into a pudding mold, cover the mold tightly and steam for 3 hours. Serve the pudding with the following sauce.

SAUCE

Cream together 1 cup sugar and ½ cup soft butter. Beat in 3 egg yolks and fold in 3 stiffly beaten egg whites. Flavor to taste with vanilla and chill thoroughly. Beat well before serving.

NUT PUDDING

Mary M. Borah

(Mrs. Wm. E. Borah, Idaho)

¾ *cup butter*	1 *teaspoon soda*
1¾ *cups sugar*	1 *cup chopped nut meats*
2 *eggs, lightly beaten*	½ *cup jam*
2¼ *cups flour*	

Cream together the butter and sugar and beat in the eggs. Sift the flour and soda and stir the dry ingredients gradually into the egg mixture. Stir in the nuts and jam and turn the batter into a pudding mold. Cover the mold tightly and steam the pudding for 2 hours. Turn out and serve with hard sauce or whipped cream.

CARAMEL PIES

Amelia C. Glass

(Mrs. Carter Glass, Virginia)

1 cup butter	1 cup pitted Damson plum
1 cup sugar	preserves
5 eggs, separated	1 teaspoon vanilla

Cream together the butter and sugar and beat in the egg yolks one at a time. Beat the egg whites until stiff and fold them into the yolk mixture. Fold in the Damson preserves and the vanilla.

Fill tart pans lined with rich pie dough with the mixture and bake the little pies in a hot oven (425° F.) for 10 minutes. Reduce the oven temperature to 350° F. and continue to bake for 15 to 20 minutes longer or until the crust is golden.

LEMON PIE

Grace Coolidge

(Mrs. Calvin Coolidge, Massachusetts)

1 cup sugar	2 eggs, separated
1½ tablespoons flour	1 tablespoon butter, melted
Juice of 1 lemon	1 cup milk

Combine the sugar and flour and stir in the lemon juice, beaten egg yolks and butter. Stir in the milk and fold in the egg whites, stiffly beaten. Line a pie plate with rich pie dough and bake it in a hot oven (450° F.) for about 10 minutes, or until the crust is set. Add the filling and bake in a slow oven (325° F.) for about 35 minutes, or until the filling is set.

CHESS CAKE

Mrs. Sarah Lee Phillips

(Mother-in-law and hostess of Senator Edge, New Jersey)

3½ cups sugar	4 eggs, beaten
¼ cup butter	1 cup milk
1 tablespoon sifted flour	Grated rind of 1 lemon

Line a pie plate with rich pie dough and bake it in a hot oven (450° F.) for about 10 minutes to set the dough to keep the bottom crisp.

Cream the sugar and butter and beat in the flour. Stir in the beaten eggs, milk and lemon rind and turn the mixture into the partially baked pie shell. Bake the pie in a moderate oven (325° F.) for about 35 minutes, or until the custard is set.

CHOCOLATE LOAF CAKE

Jennie M. McCumber

(Mrs. Porter J. McCumber, North Dakota)

2 cups sugar	4 eggs, separated
¾ cup butter	⅔ cup milk
2 squares (ounces) bitter chocolate melted with 5 tablespoons hot water	1¾ cups sifted flour 1 teaspoon baking powder Flavoring to taste

Cream together the sugar and butter until the mixture is light and fluffy. Stir in the melted chocolate and the beaten egg yolks.

Stir in the milk, then gradually stir in the flour sifted with the baking powder. Add flavoring to taste and fold in the stiffly beaten egg whites. Turn the batter into an oiled loaf pan and bake in a moderate oven (350° F.) for 45 to 50 minutes, or until a cake tester inserted in the center comes out clean. Turn the cake out of the pan onto a cake rack to cool.

CREAM CAKE

(Mrs. Wesley L. Jones, Washington, D.C.)

⅞ cup sugar	2 teaspoons baking powder
¼ cup butter	⅞ cup milk
2 eggs	1 teaspoon vanilla
2 cups sifted flour	

Cream together the sugar and butter and beat in the eggs. Sift the flour and baking powder together and stir them into the sugar-butter mixture alternately with the milk. Stir in the vanilla. Bake the batter in 4 buttered layer cake pans in a moderate oven (350° F.) for about 20 minutes, or until a cake tester inserted in the center comes out clean. Turn the layers out onto cake racks to cool and put together with whipped cream sweetened and flavored to taste.

FRUITCAKE

Hattie W. Carraway

(Mrs. T. H. Carraway, Arkansas)

2 cups brown sugar	1 nutmeg, grated
2 cups (1 pound) butter	1 teaspoon allspice
10 eggs	½ teaspoon cinnamon
Grated rind and juice of 1 lemon and 1 orange	½ cup dark molasses
	¼ teaspoon salt

1 cup milk
2 pounds mixed English
   walnuts and pecans in their
   shells
2 pounds seeded raisins

1 pound currants
½ pound citron, slivered
¼ pound candied cherries
½ pound blanched almonds
2 cups flour

Cream the sugar and butter together until the mixture is light and fluffy. Beat in the eggs, one by one. Stir in the fruit rind and juice, the spices, molasses, salt and milk. Crack the nuts, pick out the meats and chop coarsely. Mix the nut meats, fruit and flour together and add them to the sugar-butter mixture. Turn into a fruitcake pan lined with oiled heavy paper and cook in a fireless cooker for 5 to 6 hours, or in a slow oven (250° F.) for 4 to 5 hours.

FRUITCAKE*

Inez H. Stanfield

(Mrs. Robert N. Stanfield, Oregon)

2 cups (1 pound) brown
   sugar
2 cups (1 pound) butter
12 eggs, separated
4 cups (1 pound) flour
1 pound citron, slivered
1 pound candied orange,
   slivered
1 pound currants

1 pound raisins
2 pounds chopped walnut
   meats
1 teaspoon each of ground
   cloves, cinnamon, mace
   and nutmeg
½ cup each of brandy and
   sherry, or coffee and apple
   cider

Cream together the sugar and butter until the mixture is light and fluffy. Beat in the egg yolks, two at a time. Sift 1 cup of the flour over the fruit and nuts and mix well. Sift the remaining

* Mrs. Stanfield's mother—Anne Terry Hill—brought this fruitcake recipe from Tennessee to Oregon.

flour with the spices gradually into the batter, mixing well after each addition. Stir in the liquid and the fruit and nuts and fold in the stiffly beaten egg whites. Turn the batter into a fruit cake pan lined with oiled heavy paper and bake in a slow oven (250° F.) for 5 hours. Turn out onto a cake rack to cool and, when cool, store in a closely covered tin box with a fresh apple, cut into halves.

LEMON JELLY CAKES

Mary Chandler Hale

(Mrs. Eugene Hale, Maine)

1 cup butter	⅔ cup milk
2 cups sugar	1 teaspoon essence of vanilla,
5 eggs, beaten	lemon, bitter almond or
3 cups flour	orange
2 teaspoons baking powder	

Cream the butter and sugar and beat in the eggs. Sift the flour and baking powder and stir in the dry ingredients alternately with the milk. Add flavoring to taste.

This cake requires a great deal of beating to make it light. Bake in round tins, putting just enough batter in the tins to cover the bottom. Bake in a moderate oven (350° F.) for about 12 minutes, or until the layers are done. Put the layers on a plate, trim the edges neatly and spread jelly filling between them.

JELLY FILLING

Grate 2 lemons and squeeze out the juice. Combine the rind and juice with ¾ cup sugar, 3 tablespoons butter and 2 eggs, well beaten. Cook the mixture over simmering water, stirring constantly, until the filling is thick.

POUND CAKE BY MEASURE

Olive Ransdell

(Mrs. Joseph E. Ransdell, Louisiana)

1 cup sweet butter	5 eggs
1⅔ cups fine granulated sugar	2 cups flour
	Lemon extract

Cream the butter until it is light and fluffy. Gradually add the sugar, beating vigorously after each addition. Beat in the eggs one at a time, again beating vigorously. Fold in the flour carefully a little at a time and flavor the batter with lemon extract to taste. Line a loaf pan with buttered paper, turn the batter into the pan and bake in a slow oven (300° F.) for 50 to 60 minutes, or until the cake tests done. Turn the cake out onto a cake rack to cool.

SILVER CAKE

(Mrs. Charles A. Culberson, Texas)

1 cup butter	6 teaspoons baking powder
2 cups sugar	1 cup milk
3 cups flour	10 egg whites, stiffly beaten

Cream together thoroughly the butter and sugar. Sift together the flour and baking powder and add the dry ingredients alternately with the milk. Fold in the egg whites. Turn the batter into two buttered cake pans and bake in a moderate oven (350° F.) for about 35 minutes, or until the layers test done. Turn the cakes out onto cake racks to cool and when cool, fill and frost with marshmallow icing.

MARSHMALLOW ICING

2 cups sugar
Dash of lemon juice
1 cup water
4 egg whites, stiffly beaten

½ pound marshmallows,
   cut into pieces
Chopped pecans
Maraschino cherries

Combine the sugar, lemon juice and water, bring to a boil and boil rapidly until the syrup spins a long thread. Cook for 1 minute longer, then pour it in a thin stream into the beaten egg whites, beating constantly. Add the marshmallows and fill and frost the cake. Sprinkle with the chopped pecans and cherries.

SPONGE CAKE

Mary B. Pomerene

(Mrs. Atlee Pomerene, Ohio)

8 eggs, separated
2 cups sugar

2 cups flour
6 tablespoons cold water

Beat the egg yolks and sugar until the mixture is thick and pale in color. Stir in the flour and water. Beat the egg whites until stiff and fold them carefully into the yolk mixture. Turn the batter into a tube pan and bake in a slow oven (325° F.) for about 1 hour. Remove the cake from the oven and invert over cups until the cake is cool.

BOILED SPONGE CAKE

(Mrs. Edwin F. Ladd, North Dakota)

1¼ cups sugar
Dash of lemon juice
1 cup water
6 eggs, separated

1 teaspoon vanilla
1 cup sifted flour
1 teaspoon cream of tartar
Pinch of salt

In a saucepan combine the sugar, lemon juice and water, bring to a boil and cook rapidly until the syrup spins a fine thread. Beat the egg whites until stiff, gradually beat in the syrup and continue to beat until the meringue is cool. Beat the egg yolks and vanilla and fold the egg yolk mixture into the meringue. Sift together the flour, cream of tartar and salt and fold the dry ingredients gradually into the batter. Turn into a tube pan and bake in a slow oven (300° F.) for about 1 hour. Let cool for 5 minutes in the pan, then turn out onto a cake rack to cool.

NUT AND DATE CAKE

Nannette L. Townsend

(Mrs. Charles E. Townsend, Michigan)

1 cup sugar
3 eggs, separated
1 cup chopped walnut meats
1 cup chopped pitted dates

¾ cup sifted flour
1 teaspoon baking powder
1 teaspoon vanilla

Beat the sugar and egg yolks for 15 minutes, then stir in the nuts and dates. Sift together the flour and baking powder and stir them into the egg mixture. Beat the egg whites until stiff and fold them into the batter. Stir in the vanilla and turn the batter

into a buttered loaf pan. Bake in a moderate oven (350° F.) for
40 to 50 minutes, or until the cake tests done.

DATE TEA CAKES

Lidia Norbeck

(Mrs. Peter Norbeck, South Dakota)

1½ cups brown sugar	1 teaspoon salt
1 cup butter	1 teaspoon cinnamon
3 eggs, well beaten	¼ teaspoon baking powder
1 teaspoon soda dissolved	1 teaspoon vanilla
in ½ cup water	1 teaspoon lemon extract
1¾ cups flour	1 pound pitted dates, chopped

Cream together the sugar and butter, add the eggs and beat
well. Stir in the soda. Sift together the flour, salt, cinnamon and
baking powder and stir the dry ingredients into the egg mixture.
Beat thoroughly, then add the vanilla, lemon extract and the
dates. Fill small muffin pans two-thirds full with batter and bake
in a moderate oven (350° F.) for 10 to 20 minutes, depending
on the size of the pans.

FILLING FOR APPLE–LEM–CO CAKE

Josephine Minter Dial

(Mrs. Nathaniel B. Dial, South Carolina)

2 cups sugar	1 large tart apple, peeled
2 cups water	and grated
Pinch of cream of tartar	Grated rind of 1 lemon
1 egg white, stiffly beaten	1 fresh coconut grated

Combine the sugar, water and cream of tartar. Bring to a boil
and boil rapidly until the syrup spins a long thread. Pour the
syrup in a thin stream into the beaten egg white, beating con-

stantly. Stir in the apple, lemon rind and grated coconut. Spread the filling thickly between two layers of light white cake. The apple and lemon give the filling a rare flavor and the cake keeps fresh and delicious longer than any other I know.

CHOCOLATE COOKIES

Charlotte R. Pepper

(Mrs. George Wharton Pepper, Pennsylvania)

6 egg whites, stiffly beaten	½ cup sifted flour
1 cup sugar	6 tablespoons cocoa

Beat the sugar gradually into the beaten egg whites, then fold in the flour sifted with the cocoa. Drop the batter by the spoonful onto a greased cookie sheet and bake in a slow oven (250° F.) for about 30 minutes, or until the cookies are crisp.

FIG COOKIES

(Mrs. Edwin Broussard, Louisiana)

¾ cup butter	2 teaspoons almond extract
1 cup sugar	2 cups sifted flour
1 egg, beaten	

Cream the butter and sugar until the mixture is light and fluffy, stir in the egg and almond extract. Sift in the flour gradually, mixing well after each addition, and roll the dough out ⅛ inch thick on a floured board. Cut the dough into circles about 2 inches in diameter. Put a spoonful of the fig filling in the center of a circle, moisten the edge and cover with another circle of dough. Press around the edge with the tines of a fork to enclose the filling and continue until all the filling and dough has been used. Put the cookies on a buttered cookie sheet and bake in a moderate oven (350° F.) for about 15 minutes, or until browned.

FIG FILLING

½ pound dried figs, chopped   ⅓ cup boiling water
   or ground   1 tablespoon lemon extract
⅓ cup sugar

Combine the ingredients in a saucepan and cook over boiling water, stirring constantly, for about 20 minutes, or until the filling is thick.

SUGAR COOKIES

Nannette L. Townsend

(Mrs. Charles E. Townsend, Michigan)

1½ cups sugar, half brown   1 teaspoon soda
1 cup butter   Dash of nutmeg
2 eggs, beaten   Flour
⅔ cup buttermilk   Hickory nuts, chopped

Cream the sugar and butter and stir in the buttermilk, soda and nutmeg. Stir in enough flour to make a soft dough. Roll the dough out thinly on a lightly floured board and cut into rounds. Place the rounds on an oiled baking sheet, sprinkle them with granulated sugar and chopped hickory nuts and bake in a moderate oven (350° F.) for about 12 minutes, or until lightly browned.

CORNFLAKE MACAROONS

(Mrs. Edwin F. Ladd, North Dakota)

1 cup sugar   1 cup shredded coconut
4 egg whites, stiffly beaten   1 cup chopped walnut meats
3 cups cornflakes

Beat the sugar gradually into the beaten egg whites, then fold in the cornflakes, coconut and walnuts. Drop the batter from a spoon onto a cookie sheet lined with wax paper and bake in a slow oven (250° F.) for 20 to 30 minutes.

NUT DATE STRIPS

(Miss Alice Page, Vermont)

3 *eggs*	½ *teaspoon each of salt and*
2 *tablespoons warm water*	*cinnamon*
1 *cup flour*	½ *teaspoon vanilla*
1 *teaspoon baking powder*	1 *cup chopped walnut meats*
1 *cup sugar*	1 *cup chopped pitted dates*

Beat the eggs until light, add the warm water and continue to beat until the eggs are thick and lemon colored. Gradually beat in the sugar and stir in the flour sifted with the baking powder, salt and cinnamon. Stir in the vanilla, nuts and dates. Turn the batter into a large square baking pan, buttered, and bake in a moderate oven (350° F.) for 30 minutes, or until the top has a dull crust. While hot, cut into strips, sprinkle with sugar and lift the strips out onto a cake rack to cool.

FROZEN PEARS

Eula W. Kendrick

(Mrs. John B. Kendrick, Wyoming)

Pack a can of pears in cracked ice, using 3 parts ice to 1 part rock salt, and let stand for at least 3 hours. When ready to use, cut the top off the can and slip out the frozen pears and syrup. Cut in slices and serve with whipped cream.

JELLIED APPLES

Mary M. Borah

(Mrs. Wm. E. Borah, Idaho)

Peel large, firm tart apples and remove the cores without cutting through the bottom of the apples. Fill the centers with preserved ginger and sprinkle with sugar and lemon juice. Put the apples in a buttered baking pan with ½ cup hot water and bake in a hot oven (400° F.) for about 30 minutes, or until the apples are tender, basting frequently with the juices in the pan.

RICE IMPERIAL

Margaret R. Phipps

(Mrs. Lawrence C. Phipps, Colorado)

Whip 2 cups heavy cream and stir in 1 cup confectioners' sugar, 1 teaspoon vanilla or sherry, and 1½ cups freshly cooked rice. Soften 2 tablespoons gelatin in ½ cup water and stir the mixture over hot water until the gelatin is completely dissolved. Stir the gelatin into the rice mixture, mix well and turn it into a decorative pudding mold. Chill in the refrigerator until set. When ready to serve, turn out the pudding on a chilled serving plate and serve with shredded fresh pineapple.

CHILI SAUCE

(Mrs. Joseph I. France, Maryland)

25 red tomatoes, *peeled and chopped*

6 *sweet green peppers, peeled and chopped*

6 *sweet red peppers, peeled and chopped*

12 *onions, peeled and chopped*

1 *tablespoon celery seed*	5 *tablespoons salt*
1 *tablespoon mustard seed*	14 *tablespoons sugar*
1 *tablespoon cloves, tied in a*	7 *cups vinegar*
bag	

Combine all the ingredients in a preserving kettle, bring to a boil and simmer for 1 hour, or to the desired consistency. Discard the spice bag, pour into hot sterile jars and seal.

CURRANT RELISH

Catherine J. Ball

(Mrs. L. Heisler Ball, Delaware)

3 *pounds currants*	*Grated rind of 3 lemons*
3 *pounds sugar*	*Grated rind of 2 oranges*
1 *pound raisins*	

In a kettle combine the currants, sugar and raisins. Bring slowly to a boil, stirring until the sugar is melted, and boil for 10 minutes. Add the fruit rinds, bring again to a boil, then seal in hot sterilized jars.

ORANGE MARMALADE

Lulu Pain Fletcher

(Mrs. Duncan U. Fletcher, Florida)

1 *orange*	*Water*
1 *grapefruit*	*Sugar*
1 *lemon*	

Remove the peel from the fruit and put it in a saucepan with water to cover. Bring the water to a boil, simmer the peel for 45 minutes and drain. Repeat this process twice more. Then grind half the peel in a meat grinder and cut the other half into thin strips with kitchen scissors. Break the fruit into segments and discard the membranes and seeds. Combine the fruit and peel and weigh. Cover the fruit with 3 times its weight in water, bring to a boil and boil for about 1 hour. Measure the fruit and liquid and add an equal amount of sugar, bring again to a boil, and boil rapidly until the syrup is the consistency of thick honey and is amber in color. Put the marmalade into jars, cover with melted paraffin and, when cold, seal.

Breads and Muffins

SALLY LUNN

(Clara E. Wilson)

1 cake yeast	4 cups sifted flour
2 cups milk, scalded and	2 eggs, well beaten
cooled to lukewarm	1 teaspoon salt
4 tablespoons butter, melted	1 tablespoon sugar

Soften the yeast in the lukewarm milk. Add the butter, flour, eggs and salt and beat until the batter is smooth. Pour the batter into a buttered tube pan, cover and put in a warm spot, free from drafts, for about 1½ hours, or until the batter doubles in bulk. Sprinkle with the sugar and bake in a hot oven (450° F.) for 20 to 30 minutes.

MUSH ROLLS

(Clara E. Wilson)

4 cups water	1 cup lard
½ teaspoon salt	1 cake yeast dissolved in ¼
1¼ cups corn meal	cup lukewarm water
1 cup sugar	Flour

Bring the water to a boil and add the salt. Stir in the corn meal, cool a little, then stir in the sugar and lard. Let the mixture stand until it is lukewarm, then stir in the dissolved yeast. Set the batter in a warm place to rise for about 3 hours, or until light. Work in enough flour to make a stiff dough and let the dough rise in a warm place until double in bulk. Punch the dough down and shape it into rolls. Let the rolls rise until double in bulk, then bake in a moderate oven (350° F.) for 20 to 25 minutes, or until lightly browned.

CORN BREAD

(Clara E. Wilson)

¼ cup sifted flour	1 tablespoon sugar
1½ cups yellow corn meal	2 eggs, well beaten
4 teaspoons baking powder	1¼ cups milk
1 teaspoon salt	¼ cup shortening

Mix and sift the dry ingredients. Combine the eggs and milk, add gradually to the dry ingredients and stir until the batter is smooth. Melt the shortening in a square pan. Cool and swirl the pan to coat the sides and bottom evenly. Stir the excess shortening into the batter, turn the batter into the prepared cake pan and bake in a hot oven (450° F.) for 35 to 40 minutes.

DOUGHNUTS

(Clara E. Wilson)

4 cups flour	2 eggs
4 teaspoons baking powder	1 cup sugar
1 teaspoon salt	1 cup milk
1 teaspoon cinnamon	1 teaspoon melted butter
¼ teaspoon nutmeg	

Mix and sift the dry ingredients. Beat the eggs until thick and pale in color, gradually beat in the sugar, and then stir in the milk and butter. Gradually stir in the dry ingredients, blending until almost smooth, and adding additional flour if necessary to make a light dough that does not stick to the bowl. Turn the dough out on a floured board and roll it out ¼ inch thick. Cut with a floured doughnut cutter and fry a few rounds at a time in hot deep fat (370° F.) until golden brown. Drain on absorbent paper.

Main Dishes and Curry Sauce

LOBSTER CHOWDER

(Clara E. Wilson—adapted from a newspaper recipe)

4 2-pound lobsters
4 cups milk
2 cups cream
1 small onion
1 clove garlic
1 tablespoon flour

4 tablespoons butter
1 teaspoon Worcestershire
 sauce
Salt and pepper to taste
2 crackers, rolled into fine
 crumbs

Cook the lobsters in simmering salted water for one hour. Split the lobsters and crack the claws. Remove the meat from the body and claws, reserving the livers, and set aside. Crush the shells, cover them with 1 cup boiling water, and simmer for 10 minutes.

Put the milk and cream in a large saucepan. Add the water from the lobster shells, the onion and the garlic. Scald the liquid, keep hot over simmering water for 30 minutes, and strain. Return the liquid to the saucepan and stir in bit by bit the flour mixed to a smooth paste with the butter and the reserved lobster livers. Add the Worcestershire sauce, salt and pepper to taste, and the lobster meat, cut into small pieces, and cook over simmering water for 30 minutes. Just before serving stir in the cracker crumbs.

SPANISH OMELETTE

(Clara E. Wilson)

6 eggs, separated
2 tablespoons water
Salt and pepper

1 tablespoon butter
Spaghetti meat sauce (see Index)

Beat the egg whites until stiff. Beat the egg yolks lightly and beat in the water and a little salt and pepper. Fold the two mixtures together carefully. Heat the butter in a large frying pan. Swirl the pan to coat the sides and bottom evenly with the melted butter and pour in the soufflé batter. Cook over gentle heat until the omelette is set and lightly browned on the bottom. Use a spatula to lift the omelette to see when it starts to brown. Then set the pan in a hot oven (450° F.) until the omelette is well puffed and golden. Fold the omelette in half on a heated platter, putting a few spoonfuls of spaghetti meat sauce between the folds. Cover the omelette with a blanket of spaghetti meat sauce and serve immediately.

SPAGHETTI WITH MEAT SAUCE

(Clara E. Wilson)

2 cloves garlic, crushed
2 tablespoons olive oil
1 small onion, chopped
½ green pepper, seeded and chopped
½ pound ground beef
1 large can tomatoes

1 can tomato paste
Water
1 teaspoon salt
½ teaspoon pepper
½ teaspoon sugar
¾ pound spaghetti

Brown the garlic in the oil and discard. Add the onion and

green pepper to the oil and sauté until they are golden brown. Remove and set aside the onion and pepper and to the oil remaining in the pan add the beef and cook, stirring, until the beef is brown. Turn the beef into a saucepan and add the tomatoes and tomato paste. Fill the tomato paste can with water and add it along with the reserved onion and green pepper. Season the sauce with salt, pepper and sugar and cook over a low fire for about 2 hours.

Cook the spaghetti in rapidly boiling salted water for about 15 minutes, or until just tender. Drain in a colander and rinse well with hot water to remove the excess starch. Put the spaghetti into a serving dish and pour the sauce over it. Serve with grated Parmesan cheese to six.

RICE AND CHEESE FONDUE

(Clara E. Wilson)

Heat 1 cup milk and add 1 tablespoon butter, ½ teaspoon salt, ¼ teaspoon paprika, 1 cup cooked rice, and ½ cup diced cheese. Stir in 1 egg, lightly beaten, and mix well. Turn the mixture into a buttered baking dish and bake in a moderate oven (350° F.) for 30 minutes.

FRIED CHICKEN À LA MARYLAND

(Clara E. Wilson)

2 frying chickens, cut into serving pieces	3 cups bread crumbs
	½ cup butter
Salt and pepper	2 tablespoons water
3 eggs, lightly beaten	Cooked rice
¼ cup flour	Bacon slices, cooked crisp

Sprinkle the pieces of chicken with salt and pepper and dip them in the beaten egg. Mix together the flour and bread crumbs, coat the chicken well with the mixture, and fry in hot deep fat (370° F.) until the pieces are lightly browned.

Put the chicken in a baking pan with the butter and water and bake in a moderate oven (350° F.) for about 1 hour, or until tender, basting frequently.

Serve the chicken on rice with crisp bacon, and cover with a rich cream gravy. Garnish the serving platter with corn fritters.

CORN FRITTERS

Mix 2 cups corn, fresh or canned, with ¾ teaspoon salt, ¼ teaspoon pepper and 1 egg, lightly beaten. Add 2 teaspoons melted butter and ½ cup milk and mix well. Stir in 2 cups flour sifted with 1 teaspoon baking powder. Beat well and drop by the spoonful into deep hot fat (370° F.). Fry a few fritters at a time until golden and drain on absorbent paper.

HAM À LA BRECK

(Clara E. Wilson)

Cooked macaroni
1 cup chopped ham
1½ cups milk
4 eggs, lightly beaten
½ teaspoon salt

⅛ teaspoon pepper
1 tablespoon prepared
   mustard
A few drops onion juice

Fill a baking dish three-quarters full with cooked macaroni and sprinkle the macaroni with the ham. Combine the remaining ingredients and pour them into the baking dish. Bake in a moderate oven (350° F.) for about 30 minutes, or until the sauce is bubbling and the surface is lightly browned.

SQUAB AND MUSHROOMS UNDER GLASS

(Clara E. Wilson)

For each serving, roast a squab until nicely browned and tender. Put each bird on a separate ovenproof dish. Peel and remove the stems from 6 mushrooms for each bird. Arrange the mushrooms around the birds, sprinkle with salt and pepper, and pour over each bird 2 tablespoons heavy cream. Dot generously with butter and cover each bird and its garnishings with a glass bell. Cook in a hot oven (450° F.) for about 20 minutes, or until the mushrooms are done, and serve each squab under its covering of glass.

CHICKEN MOUSSE

(Catherine A. Deming)

½ package lemon jello
1 cup boiling chicken stock, free of fat
1 cup coarsely chopped chicken meat
1 cup finely chopped celery
1 tablespoon vinegar
1 cup finely chopped pimiento
½ teaspoon salt
Dash of cayenne pepper
½ cup heavy cream

Add the lemon jello to the hot chicken stock and stir until it is thoroughly dissolved. Stir in the chicken meat, celery, vinegar and pimiento and season the mixture with salt and cayenne pepper. Cool and fold in the cream, whipped. Turn the mixture into a mold rinsed in cold water and chill in the refrigerator until ready to serve.

CURRY SAUCE

(Clara E. Wilson)

2 *tablespoons butter*	1 *can consommé*
2 *tablespoons flour*	½ *teaspoon curry powder*

Melt the butter and flour together and gradually stir in the consommé. Cook, stirring, until the sauce is slightly thickened and flavor with the curry powder, which has been dissolved in a little hot water.

Salads and Salad Dressings

CREAM OF CUCUMBER SALAD*

2 teaspoons gelatin

2 tablespoons cold water

¼ cup hot milk

1 cucumber, cut into small cubes

1 cup heavy cream, whipped

½ sweet pimiento, chopped

1 teaspoon tarragon vinegar

Salt and lemon juice to taste

Soften the gelatin in the cold water, add the hot milk and stir until the gelatin is dissolved. Add the remaining ingredients and mix well. Turn the salad into a mold and chill in the refrigerator for 12 hours. Serve on lettuce leaves with French dressing.

FRENCH DRESSING

(Catherine A. Deming)

½ teaspoon dry mustard

½ teaspoon salt

¼ teaspoon sugar

Pinch of cayenne pepper

Juice of 1 lemon

¼ cup tarragon vinegar

1 cup olive oil

Combine the spices, lemon and vinegar. Beat in gradually about 1 cup olive oil or olive oil to taste.

* This salad dates back to my New England bride days. I took it to the Senate luncheon when we entertained for Cabinet Ladies, and everyone said it was the best salad ever served there. I had so many requests for this recipe that I had it printed on cards and gave it away for Christmas greetings.

Puddings, Pies, Cakes, Cookies, Desserts and Candy

PICKET FENCE PUDDING

(Catherine A. Deming)

2 squares (ounces) bitter chocolate

2 tablespoons confectioners' sugar

4 eggs, separated

4 tablespoons hot water

1 dozen ladyfingers

Whipped cream

Melt the chocolate over hot water and stir in the sugar. Add the egg yolks and water and beat well. Cool and fold in the stiffly beaten egg whites. Line a serving dish with ladyfingers and turn the chocolate mixture into the center of the bowl. Fill the bowl with whipped cream, sweetened and flavored with vanilla to taste.

HOT CABINET PUDDING

(Clara E. Wilson)

Stale cake

½ cup finely cut figs

2 cups milk

2 eggs, lightly beaten

½ cup sugar

1 teaspoon vanilla

Butter a baking dish and fill it with layers of stale cake, cut into small squares, sprinkling each layer with some of the chopped figs. Combine the milk, eggs, sugar and vanilla. Pour the mixture into the baking dish and bake the pudding in a moderate oven (350° F.) for about 35 minutes. Serve hot with whipped cream.

MOLASSES CRUMB PIE

(Clara E. Wilson)

¾ cup flour
½ cup brown sugar
¼ teaspoon salt
½ teaspoon cinnamon
⅛ teaspoon each of nutmeg, ginger and cloves

2 tablespoons butter
½ cup molasses
1 egg yolk
½ teaspoon soda dissolved in ¾ cup boiling water
Pastry

To make the crumbs: Combine the flour, sugar, salt and spices and cut in the butter to make a crumbly mixture.

To make the filling: Combine the molasses, egg yolk and soda and beat well.

Line a pie pan with rich pie dough and in it put alternate layers of the crumbs and filling, making the top layer crumbs. Bake the pie in a hot oven (450° F.) for about 15 minutes, or until the edges begin to brown. Reduce the heat to moderate (350° F.) and continue to bake for 20 to 30 minutes longer, or until the filling is set. Serve with whipped cream.

PRALINE PUMPKIN PIE

(Clara E. Wilson)

1 cup brown sugar
4 tablespoons flour
1 teaspoon cinnamon
½ teaspoon cloves
½ teaspoon salt
2 eggs

1 egg yolk
1 cup milk
1 cup cooked pumpkin purée
¼ cup butter
¾ cup chopped pecans

In a saucepan combine the sugar, flour, cinnamon, cloves and salt. Beat the eggs and egg yolk and stir them into the flour mixture. Stir in the milk and cook over boiling water, stirring constantly, until the custard falls in thick drops from the end of the spoon. Add the pumpkin, butter and pecans and mix well. Turn into a baked pie shell and cool. When cool, cover with whipped cream and garnish with pecans.

BOSTON CREAM PIE

(Clara E. Wilson)

3 *eggs, separated*	2 *teaspoons baking powder*
1 *cup sugar*	2 *tablespoons milk*
1½ *cups flour*	*Vanilla*

Beat the egg yolks and sugar until the mixture is thick and pale in color. Sift together the flour and baking powder and stir the dry ingredients into the egg and sugar mixture. Stir in the milk and vanilla to taste. Turn the batter into two buttered and floured layer cake pans and bake in a moderate oven (350° F.) for about 30 minutes, or until the layers test done. Cool the cakes on cake racks and put together with the following filling. Dust the top of the cake with sifted confectioners' sugar.

FILLING

3 *tablespoons sugar*	1 *tablespoon vanilla*
3 *cups milk*	1 *egg, beaten*
2 *tablespoons cornstarch*	

Combine the sugar and 2 cups of the milk. Stir this gradually into the cornstarch, then add the remaining milk, the vanilla, and beaten egg. Cook, stirring constantly, until the filling is thick, being careful not to let it boil. Cool.

JAM CAKE

(Clara E. Wilson)

½ cup butter
1⅓ cups brown sugar
2 eggs, separated
⅔ cup strawberry jam
⅔ cup chopped nuts
⅔ cup seedless raisins

2⅔ cups flour
1 teaspoon salt
4 teaspoons baking powder
1 teaspoon each of cinnamon
and nutmeg
⅔ cup milk

Cream the butter and sugar and stir in the egg yolks. Add the jam and mix well. Toss the nuts and raisins mixed with ½ cup of the flour and add to the batter. Sift the remaining flour, salt, baking powder and spices and add the sifted dry ingredients alternately with the milk. Fold in the stiffly beaten egg whites. Turn the batter into a buttered tube pan and bake in a moderate oven (350° F.) for about 45 minutes, or until the cake tests done. Turn the cake out onto a rack to cool.

BURNT SUGAR CAKE

(Clara E. Wilson)

1½ cups sugar
1 cup hot water
1 cup butter

2 eggs, separated
2½ cups flour
2 teaspoons baking powder

Put ½ cup of the sugar in a heavy skillet and heat until it smokes and really burns to a dark caramel color. Remove from the fire and stir in the water to make a syrup. Cool. Cream together the sugar and butter and stir in the egg yolks, syrup, and the flour sifted with the baking powder. Lastly fold in the stiffly beaten egg whites. Turn the batter into two layer cake pans and bake in a moderate oven (350° F.) for 30 to 35 minutes, or until a cake tester inserted in the center of a layer comes out clean. Turn the layers out onto cake racks to cool.

ICE BOX COOKIES

(Clara E. Wilson)

1 cup sugar	2 cups flour
¾ cup butter	½ teaspoon salt
2 eggs	1 teaspoon baking powder
½ cup chopped nut meats	

Cream together the sugar and butter and beat in the eggs, one at a time. Stir in the nuts and the flour sifted with the salt and baking powder. Shape the dough into a roll and wrap in wax paper or aluminum foil, or press the dough into a buttered pan and cover. Put the dough in the refrigerator overnight. It may remain in the refrigerator for as long as three weeks. When ready to bake, slice the dough thinly, put the slices on a buttered baking sheet and bake in a moderate oven (375° F.) for about 8 minutes, or until the cookies are lightly browned.

QUICK COCONUT MACAROONS

(Clara E. Wilson)

1 teaspoon vanilla	2½ cups grated coconut
⅔ cup condensed milk	2 egg whites, stiffly beaten

Add the vanilla to the milk and stir in the coconut. Add the beaten egg whites and blend well. Drop the batter from a spoon onto a greased baking sheet and bake in a moderate oven (350° F.) for about 15 minutes.

DATE ROLL

(Catherine A. Deming)

24 graham crackers, rolled   1 package pitted dates,
   into fine crumbs   chopped
24 marshmallows, finely cut   ½ cup chopped nut meats
                                   ½ cup heavy cream

Set aside ½ cup of the cracker crumbs and mix the rest of the
ingredients thoroughly. With the hands form the mixture into
a long roll, roll the roll in the reserved crumbs and wrap in wax
paper or aluminum foil. Chill in the refrigerator for several
hours, or overnight. Slice and serve with whipped cream.

PEPPERMINT REFRIGERATOR ICE CREAM

(Clara E. Wilson)

2 cups milk   1 cup peppermint candy,
2 teaspoons gelatin   crushed
½ cup cold water   2 cups heavy cream, whipped

Put the milk into a saucepan, add the gelatin softened in the
cold water and the peppermint candy, and stir over low heat
until the candy is thoroughly dissolved. Cool, turn into a freezing
tray and freeze until the mixture is thick and mushy. Fold in
the cream and freeze again until mushy. Turn the cream into
a chilled bowl and beat until it is smooth, but not melted.
Return to the freezing tray and freeze for 2 hours. Makes 1
quart ice cream. Serve with chocolate sauce.

CHOCOLATE SAUCE

(Clara E. Wilson)

1 cup sugar   1 teaspoon butter
2 squares chocolate, melted   1 teaspoon vanilla
⅓ cup boiling water

Combine sugar, chocolate and water. Bring to a boil and add butter. Let boil for five minutes. Add vanilla.

FROSTED FUDGE

(Catherine A. Deming)

1 cup cream   1 cup cocoa
2 cups sugar   ¼ cup butter

In a saucepan combine the cream, sugar and cocoa and bring to a boil. Add the butter and boil until a little of the syrup dropped into cold water forms a soft ball. Remove from the heat and beat until the fudge begins to harden. Pour into a buttered pan and cool. When cold pour over the fudge white boiled frosting made in exactly the same way as for cake frosting. (See Index.) Let the frosting set for half an hour, then cut the fudge into squares.

Hors d'Oeuvres

SHRIMP PUFFS

(Clara E. Wilson)

½ cup butter
1 cup boiling water
1 cup flour
4 eggs

1 package frozen shrimps
Mayonnaise
Salt and pepper
Lemon juice

Stir the butter and water over a gentle flame until the butter is melted. Add the flour all at once and stir vigorously until the mixture leaves the sides of the pan in a smooth ball. Remove from the fire and beat in the eggs, one at a time. Drop the batter from a teaspoon onto a buttered baking sheet and bake in a hot oven (400° F.) for about 20 minutes, or until the puffs are brown and dry.

Cook the shrimp in simmering water for about 20 minutes. Cool and remove the shells and dark veins down the backs. Mix the shrimp with enough mayonnaise to coat each one well. Season with salt and pepper and a little lemon juice. Split the puffs almost through and insert one shrimp in each puff.

AVOCADO LOAF

(Clara E. Wilson)

4 ripe avocados
1 teaspoon lemon juice
½ teaspoon salt
1 small onion, grated

1 loaf unsliced bread
2 hard-cooked eggs
Stuffed olives

Press the avocado flesh through a fine sieve and beat it thoroughly with the lemon juice, salt and grated onion. Cut the crusts from the loaf of bread and slice it lengthwise into three layers. Reform the loaf with a layer of the avocado mixture between the layers. Cover the top and sides of the loaf with the remaining avocado mixture and garnish all around the loaf with slices of the hard-cooked egg whites and olives. Put the egg yolks through a sieve and sprinkle them in the center.

RIBBON SANDWICHES

(Clara E. Wilson)

3 *slices white bread* *Peanut butter*
3 *slices whole wheat bread* *Pimiento cheese spread*

Spread peanut butter on a slice of white bread. Cover with a slice of whole wheat bread and spread with pimiento cheese spread. Put on another slice of white bread and spread with peanut butter. Repeat until all the bread is used, alternating the breads and the spreads, leaving the top slice plain. Cut off the crusts and slice in half-inch slices. Cut the slices in half.

Beverages

EGGNOG

(Susan Kintner)

12 eggs, separated
1½ cups sugar
1 quart heavy cream

1 pint milk
1 quart rye whiskey
2 ounces rum

Beat the egg yolks and 1 cup of the sugar until thick and pale in color. Beat the egg whites until stiff and gradually beat in the remaining sugar. Whip the cream lightly and combine the eggs, cream and milk. Gradually stir in the rye and rum.

CHAMPAGNE PUNCH

(Susan Kintner)

1 pint orange ice
1 pint lemon ice
2 bottles sauterne
3 bottles champagne

3 quarts club soda
Fruit for garnish
½ cup green curaçao

Combine all the ingredients in a punch bowl and add a large block of ice. Garnish the punch with fruits such as cherries, strawberries, orange and lemon slices. Makes 7½ quarts.

MINT JULEPS

(Lelia Montague Barnett)

Break 3 or 4 mint leaves into a mint julep cup. Add ¼ tea-spoon sugar, if desired, and 1 tablespoon brandy and muddle this with the mint and sugar. Fill the cup with ice which has been crushed in a canvas bag. (This is done to absorb any excess moisture.) Fill the cup with bourbon whiskey and stir until the cup frosts. Decorate with sprigs of mint.

Part Three

THE SOUTHERN WRITER

ONLY THE FOUNTAIN SPEAKS

*It is so quiet you would never guess
That just beyond the tall brick walls which rise,
Above the live oak and crepe myrtle trees,
The tumult of a busy city street
Rises and falls, but never wholly stops.
Surely the patio is the best of all
The legacies Spain left us; it is only here
That we can really find tranquillity,
When all around us there is stress and strain.
It is our place of refuge from a world
Otherwise too much with us. Our retreat
From all that complicates and meddles and intrudes.*

*It is not empty, it is only still:
The waxen white camellias come to bloom
Amidst their glossy leaves, and fall and leave
A snowy carpet underneath the shrubs
Bordered with box and brilliant, later on,
With many-hued azaleas, whose luxuriance
Reaches beyond the box and falls across
The flagstone walks in rainbow-tinted sprays.
But when the day is over, and the night
Comes closing down to meet the tall brick walls,
Only the fountain speaks.*

*No ghostly footsteps sound across those stones—
Why should they, when the fountain tells the story
Of those who built and planted, lived and died,*

Who wept and laughed and worked and loved
Within these walls, when this still place was Spain,
And later France and later still, half Ireland and half France,
Before it was the very core and breath
Of the Confederacy?

The fountain speaks so undemandingly
That you need never hear, against your will
The story of the Spanish architect—the convent bred
French girl married to an Irish judge—
Their son, who made the world aware of a child champion,
Winning games of chess, not only here, among Orleanians,
But at the Courts of England and of France.

You thought the murmur stopped? No, that was only
Because the man who all too soon would give
The signal to fire on Fort Sumter,
And shatter quietude throughout the South,
Was telling us, through the fountain, about that interlude,
So brief and blessed, when he brought his bride
To live here—and then left for war.
Strange—it was she who died, he who survived.
No wonder there are pauses now and then,
Or that the fountain's voice seems somehow hushed.

Well, it is very late. The crescent moon
That rocked above the tall crepe myrtle trees
Has disappeared. The stars are growing dim
Above the white camellias, and the walls
Seem closer to the skies than when the sun
Shone on the flagstones where no footfall sounds.
The lights in other houses on the street
Were put out long ago. Now mine can be put out.
The work that kept me at my desk so late
Is finished. I can peacefully lie down,
Knowing that I have left no task undone,
And when my prayers are said can go to sleep,
Mindful, with my last waking thought, of all those others
Who here, before me, did their work, and thankful
That in this place, pervaded with their presence,
Only the fountain speaks.

The Beauregard House, New Orleans, Louisiana

WHEN I first went to Louisiana to write, it was with no idea that the move was a permanent one. A friend of mine, a retired diplomat, who had first known me when I was ranging the world and writing about international affairs, had urged me for years to attempt a work of non-fiction on the political scene in his native state and I had steadfastly refused. I had practically been weaned on a ballot, and I had commented on the political scene all the way from Patagonia to Persia and back again without committing, as far as I am aware, any serious errors; but I knew when I was licked; politics in Louisiana were something I had never understood and I felt sure I never would. I did not change my mind or alter my position. But eventually this gentleman persuaded me to visit New Orleans during Carnival and, incidentally, took me to the French Market for coffee and doughnuts—an experience no visitor should miss—and introduced me to a Gin Fizz as this beverage is prepared in the Crescent City —not more or less in the form of a Tom Collins, as elsewhere, but as a concoction of rich cream, orange-flower water and various other mysterious and more heady ingredients. Though I enjoyed these regional delicacies, I have good coffee and doughnuts at home; and the best Gin Fizz I have ever tasted, no matter how concocted, is not to be compared, in my book, with a good Mint Julep. So probably, I should have continued to spend my time contentedly in Washington, nearby Virginia and New England, with occasional trips to Europe and semi-occasional ones elsewhere, if, at the first ball which my host and I attended together, the idea for a novel with the Carnival theme had not entered my head. It did not require much persuasion on his part to convince me that I should return to Louisiana the following year to write it; and, before I had finished it, I had another idea for a novel with a Louisiana setting—not one with a Carnival theme this time, but with the River Road as its *mise en scène*. Somewhat aghast at this unexpected turn of events, I went back to Alexandria, and spent a year writing a book with more familiar settings—namely Washington and New England—meanwhile thinking the other matter over. But in the end I succumbed to the inevitable: it was all too clear that a whole series of Louisiana novels was ahead of me, and that I might as well make up my mind to live there part of each year.

My first winter in New Orleans was spent in a charming house of the raised cottage type, which had originally belonged to the Claiborne family—famous for having given Louisiana its first Anglo-Saxon governor—but which was then the property of Mr. and Mrs. Mortimer Favrot. A suite of pleasant rooms was set aside by them for my occupancy and that of Jean Darling, the friend from Newbury who accompanied me; but for once I had no housekeeping responsibilities and worked at top speed, in quarters suggesting the fulfillment of an architect's dream, while Mrs. Favrot ordered the meals, superintended the servants and, in short, continued to run the establishment. She had an excellent colored cook named Roberta, whose Oysters Rockefeller could bear comparison with those served in any restaurant, whose gumbos and *daubes glacées* were of the first order and whose Truites Marguery actually surpassed any I have eaten elsewhere. These constituted my delightful introduction to Creole cookery; but since it did not occur to me that such delicacies would have more than passing interest for me, I did not concern myself with the mysteries of their concoction until later. In fact, it was not until two years afterward, when I went to live in the so-called "Cottage"—of twenty rooms!—on the River Road that the dishes of the Deep South began to take on real meaning to me, and that I realized, as the little booklet by the Vingt-Quatre Club of

Lafayette so aptly puts it, that, "Louisiana cooking has many sources of heritage . . . the French, both Acadian and Creole (Spanish and French). English, German and Irish settlers more or less adopted Louisiana cooking, while Italian immigrants have clung to the olive oil and pastries of their native land. Mexican cooking has drifted up to us through Texas with many variations of seasoning of their staple foods, corn and bean products. Combined, all these go to make up Louisiana cooking."

Housekeeping, at the point when I began to be conscious of this, was not without its difficulties and its drawbacks. The kitchen in The Cottage had a floor of bricks which might have been evenly laid in the first place, but which by then were in a state of crumbling undulation; it would have been impossible to scrub them in the old-fashioned way, because no woman could possibly have knelt to do so without risk of barking her knees; and "passing the mop"—which I soon learned was the usual local substitute for scrubbing—was completely ineffective. There was a picturesque kitchen fireplace, hung with pots and kettles, and a lovely view from the windows of a small orange grove. But the dining room was inaccessible except through the rear gallery, which involved going up and down two flights of steps; and the only item of semi-modern equipment was a very small stove, which had sufficed the owners on the rare occasions when they returned to their beautiful ancestral home for more than a few hours. I secured their permission to lay a wooden floor over the bricks and cover this with linoleum; to install a supplementary range, an up-to-date sink and two refrigerators, one for block ice and one operated by electricity; and to cut a door through into a small storeroom through which, in turn, a door could be cut through into the dining room. This storeroom, which was filled with junk and did not even have brick over the dirt which formed its floor, I divided in half, making one half into a modern pantry and the other half into a modern laundry. All this took time and money, for the improvements were, of course, made under my supervision and at my expense; collecting materials and rounding up workmen cut badly into my writing time, which of course meant that my earning powers decreased proportionately. But we finally achieved a unit designed for efficiency.

We had by no means reached the end of our problems, however. We had no telephone and no Rural Free Delivery and we were eight miles from our source of supplies—Baton Rouge—nor was the intervening stretch of the River Road always passable. Miss Clara, who had faithfully accompanied me, chafed under the impossibility of calling up the corner grocery half a dozen times a day, if she felt like it. Moreover, as we were frequently reminded, quite superfluously, by the local tradespeople, there was a war on. Not only were meats, butter and sugar rationed, but so was gasoline; therefore, if some commodity were left off a list of grocery shopping, we could not dash back to Baton Rouge and get it, even if provender for the next meal seemed at the moment more important than progress on the next chapter of the current book.

It was especially hard to plan, as much—I might say most—of my company was unexpected, and gradually I was obliged to make a radical change in my eating habits. Callers who dropped in between six and seven were perfectly satisfied if served with coffee or bourbon or both, as they had eaten a hearty noonday dinner; but they were frequently still there at eight or nine, and by this time I was starving, after having lunched on an egg, a green salad and a cup of tea, usually quickly consumed from a tray, so that my writing day would be interrupted as little as possible. Of course, I would have been delighted to ask these chance visitors to dine informally with me, if I had been possessed of the ample provisions which had made the garden suppers in Alexandria so delightful. But alas! I was not. The climax came after two old friends arrived without notice and I did ask them to stay, when I had made a swift calculation on the possibilities of stretching supplies. Just as we were about to leave the library for the dining room, eight total strangers came to make their first call; even such visits are apt to be leisurely in Louisiana and at nine-thirty the newcomers were still contentedly sipping bourbon and chatting of this and that, while I grew hungrier and hungrier, for no amount of optimism could enable me to visualize enough dinner for eleven persons when I had provided for one. The next morning I told Miss Clara that henceforth we would have a two o'clock dinner, and keep a soup kettle on the stove, into which every sort of scrap could go, after the French fashion. (No knuckle of veal and shin of beef as a matter of course now, the way it was in those bygone days at the Oxbow; and no kindly Mr. Greenleaf coming with his welcome cart to the back door and insisting that he could not charge for such "innards" as sweetbreads and liver!) I also told her that we must likewise keep on hand pounds and pounds of shrimp for salad. With these two mainstays some sort of a supper could always be provided; and we would plan ahead for a small dinner party once a week, allowing enough leeway in our planning so if guests, other than those who had been invited, appeared on the scene, we could ask them to stay. Squab, like shrimp, were nearly always obtainable; and though they represented more of a strain on the budget, they were our best bet for the weekly dinners. In our efforts to provide enough, we frequently provided too many, and then of course we had to eat them the next day. I was thankful enough for those squab then; but never since have I ordered one when a menu was a matter of choice.

I have never been able to make any of my French friends believe that Americans took rationing seriously, either in the First or the Second World War. They are hard to convince (1) that there was any such thing; and (2) that we conscientiously observed the rules and regulations laid down for us. Above all, they are inclined to laugh incredulously at the idea that sugar did not appear as abundantly as ever on the tables of those who lived in the heart of the sugar country, whether they raised it themselves or not. I am proud to say that I do not know of a single infringement of the law, either on my own table or that of any friends and neighbors; but I am also happy that my early acquaintance with maple sugar—and with those who made it!—stood me in good stead during those difficult days at The Cottage. It was maple sugar that went into the juleps of those who wanted their drinks sweetened; and it was maple sugar that flavored the pies made from Louisiana's "lagniappe crop" of dewberries. I have always thought Miss Clara's pies were delicious: the chicken pies that are an integral part of our Christmas and Thanksgiving feasts; the meat pies in which left-over scraps of beef or lamb are combined at all seasons with potatoes, carrots and onions in a deep baking dish and cooked with a top crust, but no bottom crust; the apple pies which finish off any kind of a meal. But none of her pies has ever tasted so good to me as those she made from the dewberries that grew wild along the River Road and were skillfully blended with the maple sugar that came down from Vermont.

Gradually the pattern of entertaining at The Cottage fell into more or less acceptable form; the droppers-inners were fed substantially, if inelegantly, on soup and shrimp, the invited guests on squab, supplemented with whatever else we could find. In either case, the table was set with all the best linen and silver and lighted by tall tapers, except when we decided to use the ancient punkah, which still hung overhead, and which created so much breeze that we had to choose between that and candlelight. There were nearly always flowers in abundance, for I had given the same care and thought to reclaiming the garden and grounds that I had to renovating and modernizing the house; and the setting was almost automatically restful and distinctive, for none of the famous old houses in which I have been privileged to live could surpass The Cottage in essential charm. So we hoped all this would make up for some of the deficiencies in the menus and I believe it did.

But difficulties of one sort or another continued to beset us: the dairy where we were at first able to get plenty of milk was closed by official order, because of unsanitary conditions; it took an appeal to the governor to secure drums of water, sent out from town, for kitchen, laundry and bathroom use, while all drinking water was transported from an urban source in immense jugs. As I was trying to write at top speed, and as I was ill a great deal of the time, all these handicaps would have worn me down, even more than they did Miss Clara, if it had not been for Creacy who, at this point, entered my life.

When I first became aware of her existence, she was living, with her husband, King, in a small shack on the edge of the property I had rented. It had no plumbing and no electricity and the roof leaked so badly that, whenever it rained, Creacy and King were obliged to move their bed from one corner of the shack to another, in order to avoid being deluged. As the ground between the shack and The Cottage was undrained, rainstorms also meant that Creacy was obliged to come to work in rubber boots and the rest of her attire was in keeping; but come she did, rain or shine. In the beginning this was merely to do house cleaning and laundry work; but before long she had become an excellent waitress and chambermaid and I discovered that she could ply a needle with great skill. Then finally I made the still more gratifying discovery that Creacy could cook.

I do not remember whether this was when Miss Clara fell and broke a rib and had to take things easy for a few days, though she never really gave up; or whether it was when I found that I had to go to New Orleans about once a month, to get medical treatment, secure source material and seek editorial advice, and that it would be cheaper, more convenient and much pleasanter to have some sort of a *pied-à-terre* of my own there rather than to grapple with the hotel situation, which was almost as discouraging as the housekeeping situation at The Cottage. (It will be remembered that during the war five-day limits were put on the occupancy of hotel accommodations in most cities, that lodgings were limited even if obtainable at all and that room service was next to non-existent.) At all events, when I secured quarters at historic Beauregard House, which had been saved from destruction by a small band of patriotic women and temporarily divided into apartments, it was logical that Miss Clara should be in charge there, rather than at The Cottage; and as the whole of Beauregard House and its dependencies gradually came within my province,* the logic of this arrangement was more and more apparent. Creacy took the helm at The Cottage and when the book about the River Road was finished and I left it for "Compensation," the house in Crowley, Louisiana, that I had acquired, Creacy and King went with me. They have been there ever since and it is due to Creacy that I can include in this book some of the Southern recipes which have pleased me most and which now appear most frequently on my table.

Crowley is more Anglo-Saxon in background and habit than most of the neighboring towns and cities in southwestern Louisiana. I chose it as a winter residence because it calls itself, not without reason, "The Rice Capital of the World," and, at the time of the choice, it appeared that such a setting would have great advantages for me. In spite of the long delay in carrying out my original purposes in going there, I have never regretted my decision, for I have grown extremely fond of it. However, when it comes to a question involving the expansion of my personal cookbook, I must confess that, except for the addition of more and more dishes with rice as a basis, I have gleaned more from Lafayette, which lies twenty-four miles east of Crowley, and which is still the most thoroughly French of any city in that region, just as Crowley is the least so.

Lafayette is essentially Catholic as well as essentially French and, by nature, gregarious and gay no less than devout. Churches are crowded for all Masses, but after Mass—no matter which has been attended—congenial gatherings are the order of the day and Absinthe Frappé is the favorite beverage. A master hand at making it is the prominent architect, Fred Nehrbass, who, though a mid-Westerner by birth, married into the Mouton family, one of the most outstanding of the locality, and now

* Since this book went to press, Beauregard House Inc. has ceded the property to the Keyes Foundation, which has acquired and restored the original side garden, adding this to the main house, patio and slave quarters. Frances Parkinson Keyes, though herself only a member of the advisory committee, has been designated as caretaker by the officers of the Foundation, so Beauregard House is now more than a mere residence for her.

seems no less of a Louisianian than his lovely wife, Marie. They
are both naturally "given to hospitality" and are never happier
than when dispensing it. Fred claims that the superlative excellence of his Absinthe Frappé is due to the fact that he uses
White Rock in his mixture instead of plain water. "I put a one-
ounce jigger of absinthe for each drink in a cocktail shaker,"
he says. "Then I put one chunk of ice in the shaker and drip
White Rock over it—one and a half to two ounces for each
ounce of absinthe, stirring with a spoon. (If the drink is to be
consumed rapidly, more White Rock should be used.) Next, I
add about one half spoonful of sugar for each drink, in the form
of a simple syrup. (I make the syrup by putting six spoonsful of
sugar in hot water, using as little water as possible in the mixture.) Finally, I fill the glasses with finely chopped ice and pour
the absinthe over it."

After you have spent a leisurely hour or so sipping Absinthe
Frappé—or anything else you may prefer, though you make a
great mistake if you do not choose Fred's special brand—they
will lead you to a table gleaming with silver and crystal, lavishly
decorated with camellias or roses, according to the season, and
literally groaning with good food, whatever the season. Personally, I consider that, when I have given my guests a good wild
goose gumbo or a good crayfish bisque, they should expect
nothing else besides a light salad or a light sweet. But a gumbo
or a bisque is only the beginning of a meal for Fred and Marie;
a *Daube Glacée* is almost sure to follow, or a mammoth ham,
beautifully glazed and supplemented with slices of pineapple
and peaches, which serve both as a flavoring and a decoration.
Then come a salad and a sweet. The salad may simply be of
the type known as *fatiguée*, where lettuce, cucumbers and so on
are allowed to stand in their French dressing for some time
before the dish is served; but it is more likely to be one of
molded gelatin, with Roquefort cheese conspicuous among its
carefully blended ingredients. The sweet will probably be an
immense cake, a feast to the eyes as well as the palate, and it
will take a different form practically every time you go there:

the shape of a dome when a young architect with modernistic leanings is among those present; a boat for a sailor, a book for an author and, on or about the 19th of March, a cross. At other times, it may be variously designated or patterned; but when the feast day of one of the most beloved saints on the calendar rolls around, it is always in the form of a cross and it is always called St. Joseph's Cake. Each course will be accompanied by the wine best calculated to emphasize its special merits and afterward there will be Café Brulôt or rich, strong black coffee with a variety of liqueurs.

St. Martinville is another charming nearby city where the French influence still prevails, and here a hostess to whom I owe many ideas, as well as many good times, is Mrs. Lester Montegut, *née* Carmen Bulliard, whose family manufactures the famous Evangeline Sauce.

Merry Hebert, who has lived in White Castle since her marriage, but who grew up in Plaquemine, is another friend who has helped to expand my cookbook, especially through her recipes for Puff Pudding and Pralines; and Gertrude Munson of Napoleonville is still another. There are so many *spécialités de la maison* at the Munsons' hospitable home, Glenwood Plantation House, that it is hard to choose among them; but I have selected a few which seem to me outstanding.

If you go to New Orleans from Crowley via Lafayette, St. Martinville, White Castle and Glenwood, you are well on your way by the time you leave Napoleonville; and, in the Crescent City, the persons who have contributed most to my knowledge of the culinary art are Edna Landry, Helene Adams and Hermann Deutsch. Mrs. Landry has won several prizes for her recipes and no wonder; she is, perhaps, most renowned for her preparation of crayfish, but everything she makes is delicious. Mr. and Mrs. Adams have what to my mind is the most attractive small house in New Orleans—at least among those I have been privileged to see. The furniture in the dining room is French, the wine cabinet and other side pieces authentic Seignouret, the dining table of solid cherry with a beautiful carved

border and legs, and the matching chairs all in the Seignouret
style. The chandelier above this magnificent table, the *corbeille*
which forms its centerpiece, the clock, candelabra and vases on
the mantel, are all of Sèvres porcelain, with turquoise blue as
their predominating color; and on a stand in one corner is a
liqueur set of fine embossed crystal, which once graced the
banquets of Governor Roman. An Irish note is introduced by
Mr. Adams' collection of Waterford glass decanters and goblets,
one of the finest in the South; an English note by the antique
butler's tray, and the egg-shaped covered dish of Sheffield plate
which adorns the sideboard.

The food is as distinctive as its setting. Mrs. Adams is one of
those who has been most insistent to a New Englander that
there is a difference between Oyster Stew and Oyster Soup and
she proves it in the most effective possible way. Other dishes in
which she excels are Chicken Gumbo Filé, Seafood Okra Gumbo,
Green Salad, Garlic Bread and Plum Pudding with Hard Sauce.
Either of the gumbos, followed by the Green Salad and the
Garlic Bread, and in turn, by the Plum Pudding, makes a feast
fit for the gods. As a matter of fact, this is true of any of Helene
Adams' menus; and since she has generously contributed no less
than nineteen recipes to my (?!) cookbook, the gentle reader
will have ample opportunity to make a selection. Mrs. Adams
herself suggested, when I was discussing the subject with her,
that the inexperienced housekeeper would probably do well to
begin with Fool's Cake. "Fool's Cake?" I echoed, somewhat
mystified. "Yes—any fool can make that," Mrs. Adams explained
somewhat condescendingly.

Sazerac Cocktails with "tidbits" generally precede a meal at the
Adams; and either red or white wine—according to which gumbo
is served—goes with it. Afterward, the coffee cannot possibly be
too strong and liqueurs are superfluous.

I should not forget to add, in passing, that besides being
indebted to Perry and Helene for many feasts in their own
house, no one has been more helpful in acquainting me with
the small, intimate and very delightful type of "neighborhood"

restaurant which, but for them, I probably never would have found at all. Among these is Liuzza's, run on matriarchal lines, with grandmother, mother and daughter all taking an active part in its management. (Father does, too, but he does not have quite as large a male contingent of relatives to help him!) And there is now a little great-grandaughter who will, no doubt, soon be equally helpful. Liuzza's is not stylish as to either location or equipment, but it is clean, attractive and—in summer—delightfully cool; and the great frosted glasses, in size and shape reminiscent of those formerly associated with Berlin white beer, in which beer is prodigally served, add to the general impression of refreshment, as great rows of these are shoved into sight through the window between the bar and the restaurant proper. There is an à la carte menu, from which it is possible to order almost anything within reason; but the client who is really in the know will probably select a table d'hôte menu, keeping in mind the specialty of the day. Liuzza's Meatballs with Spaghetti, Baked Eggplant, Zucchini, Green Salad and a sweet could certainly not be improved upon as to quality at any price, and the helpings are enormous; and, believe it or not, you get all this for seventy-five cents! Of course, if you wish to go higher, you can have Boiled Smoked Sausage with "all the fixin's" for eighty-five cents or Breaded Pork Chops—likewise amply complemented —for ninety-five cents. As for me, I follow the Adams' advice and stick to the meatballs, a decision I shall never regret.

Hermann Deutsch, Associate Editor of the New Orleans *Item,* claims that anyone who can read can cook. I do not agree with him; I think that cooks are born, not made, as Cathie Deming always claimed that ladies are. Some persons can never learn to drive cars, some can never learn to play the piano and some can never learn to trim hats; in like measure, some, in my opinion, can never learn to cook. But I will admit that, given a spark of God-given talent to start with, much can be achieved through experience, effort and interest in all of these directions. I think Hermann Deutsch had the talent for cooking, among many others, from the beginning; but he certainly has gone to infinite pains to develop it, and will spend hours perfecting a meal that he wishes to have superlatively good. He is skilled in the use of herbs, and his sauces are marvels of blended seasoning, while his menus, as a whole, show great originality; it was at his house, for instance, that I first saw reedbirds served with a crescent-shaped side dish of salad. He is also most ingenious in the matter of adaptations. For instance, a few years ago, he was invited, as a member of the New Orleans Chapter of the *Confrerie de Chevaliers du Tastevin,* to dine aboard the French cargo, *Sieur de Bienville,* which has a galley staff that would bear comparison with that of any vessel afloat. Preparations for the feast had begun even before the *Sieur de Bienville* left France, and one of the items on the menu was entered there as *Les Filets de sole Normande.* Actually, the filets had been rolled into *paupiettes* and, for perfectly obvious reasons, Hermann wheedled the recipe out of the culinary Corot who had confected them. Since fresh-caught *Roches de Grandcamp* sole is not so readily come by at Schwegmann Bros. Super Market, and mussels grown on strings let down from barges in the Gironde Estuary are another scarcity item in the New Orleans area, he took the liberty of substituting filets of Pass Manchac catfish for the one, and plump, March-harvested Louisiana oysters for the other. The result was acclaimed by the masters of *La Société des Escargots Orléannais*—the most exacting group of gourmets north or south of any given point. He calls it *Paupiettes de Catfish Manchacoise* and gives the following directions for serving four:

"Wipe eight rather small filets of fish—approximate dimensions 1½ inches by 5—and sprinkle them lightly with salt. Roll them into short cylinders (a caper may be rolled up in the center of each if desired, or a blanched almond or a whole half pecan). Secure the cylinders by skewering them with a toothpick or by tying them with white thread. Poach them lightly in a sound white wine—the better the wine, the better the result—being very careful not to overcook them; a trifle underdone is best.

"Transfer the *paupiettes* to a heated platter, reserving the wine. To two tablespoons butter in a saucepan add one tablespoon grated onion and a little sweet basil (about two fresh leaves or their equivalent) very finely minced. Add to this a generous cup of the wine in which the *paupiettes* were poached, and simmer for about ten minutes, being careful not to let the mixture get hot enough to darken the butter.

"During the simmering (or before) set a dozen and a half oysters to drain, and add the liquid (though not more than half a cup) to the wine-butter-onion sauce. Let it return to the simmering temperature and then add a whole beaten egg, a little at a time, stirring madly to prevent curdling; or drop the egg into an electric blender and add the hot liquid in a slow trickle to achieve a smooth blend. Return the mixture to the fire to let it thicken, stirring constantly. Gradually add the contents of a can of sliced (or stems and pieces) mushrooms and, last of all, the drained oysters. Correct the seasoning at this point, return the pan to the fire very cautiously and only long enough to let the 'beards' of the oysters curl, pour the sauce over the *paupiettes* and serve at once."

Another example of Hermann's ingenuity is revealed in his adaptation for *antecuchos*. He says that, in Lima, Peru, at the gracious home of Frank Achilles of Panagra, he was initiated into the twin pleasures of these and *El Zapo,* to companion the pre-luncheon beverages. "It is doubtful whether the necessary bronze *El Zapo* castings are obtainable in this country," he goes on to relate. "It is a game of skill on which money can be wagered, but *antecuchos* are an appetizer. The recipe was written down for me by Señora Mercedes Neira Cuenca, native of an Ecuadorian village, after she had finished her tour of duty preparing them before a charcoal brazier. According to her, the secret of *antecuchos* lies in the preparation of the three sauces which collaborate in producing a wonderful flavor. Doña Mercedes used cubed beef heart as a foundation, but any red, lean meat, cut into approximately one-inch cubes will do. She also used a bundle of green corn husks as a swab to dab on the glazing sauce, and sharp splinters of split green bamboo for skewers. But a kitchen brush and metal skewers will serve just as well.

"The three sauces are first the marinade, next the glazing sauce, and finally a 'dip' for the finished product. Here they are:

"No. One—the marinade: Combine a cup of vinegar, a teaspoon of salt, a quarter teaspoon of chili powder, a teaspoon of cumin, a tablespoon of finely minced bell peppers, one clove of crushed garlic. When the ingredients are well mixed, put the cubed meat into the sauce, stirring them around in it from time to time, as it stands in the refrigerator for a minimum of two hours.

"No. Two—the glaze: To half a cup of olive oil, add half a teaspoon of arnotto or *achote* seeds, or a quarter teaspoon of turmeric, half a teaspoon of cumin, a tablespoon of prepared mustard, a little finely minced bell pepper and a quarter cup of vinegar. Blend thoroughly. Spit three marinated meat cubes on each skewer, dip them into the glazing sauce, and lay them on a grille over glowing charcoal. Turn the skewers two or three times during the course of the broiling process and dab on a little more of the glazing sauce during each turn.

"No. Three—the dip: To three tablespoons of minced onion and two cloves of garlic, minced, add a quarter cup each of vinegar and olive oil. Season to taste with salt and olive oil, and purée it smoothly with an electric blender. Serve in a separate bowl, so that guests may dip their broiled *antecucho* skewers into it, before plucking off the meat and eating it."

Like most Louisianians of my acquaintance, Hermann enjoys barbecues, which I must admit are not among my own favorite forms of entertainment, as the mosquitoes nearly always arrive at the same time as the *pièce de résistance;* but I am willing to put up with the pests for the sake of barbecued chicken as Hermann serves it. He also specializes in underground cooking, somewhat in the Hawaiian manner. It is a sight worth seeing to behold a mammoth turkey emerge from a deep hole, smoking and tender, and well wrapped in cabbage leaves which have absorbed much of its flavor.

While Hermann and I disagree about many other things, we are in almost complete accord as to what constitutes good cooking. Our opinion as to the ways in which rice may be properly served is a notable exception. He claims that it should never appear on any table except in a soup or as a vegetable with a complement of good gravy. I claim that New England rice puddings, whether a "poor man's" or one made with custard and raisins; numerous cold rice puddings like *Pêches à la Condé* and Rock Rice with Raspberry Sauce, that I learned to know on my first trip to Europe; and the wonderful Spanish desserts made with rice, which I learned to know later, not to mention the *riz au lait* of southwestern Louisiana, are all well worthy of any gourmet's attention.

I should be very remiss if I did not mention the contribution made by several clubs and restaurants to my knowledge of the culinary art, as practiced in the Deep South. The Village, on the bypass just outside Baton Rouge, specializes in Italian food of impeccable quality. *Manicotti,* which can be had any day, and *Lasagna,* which is a Sunday special, are perhaps the most famous, but all are worth sampling and, once ordered, are sure to prove irresistible. I was not surprised, the last time I went there, as the fortunate guest of Lewis Gottlieb and Cecil Bird, to find that The Village—which, of course, is not a village at all, but a restaurant—had almost doubled in size; the ever growing number of satisfied patrons must have made this enlargement imperative.

The Hoo-Shoo-Too Club, also near Baton Rouge, where I have likewise been several times as the guest of Lewis Gottlieb, specializes in a Turtle Stew that is superlative in quality. This soup is also very good at Roussel's Restaurant, which is owned and operated by members of the family invariably associated with the manufacture and distribution of the unique product of that region—perique tobacco—and which is conveniently located at La Place, on the Airline between Baton Rouge and New

Orleans; but even more outstanding at this restaurant, as far as I am concerned, are the soup made of river shrimp and lima beans and the Chicken Georgine. In Opelousas there is a small restaurant called Didee's, run by a colored family, which offers only a few different dishes and specializes in gumbos and roast chicken—or, as it is called here, baked hen—with rice dressing; but the lack of variety does not seem to matter, for all ingredients are of the best and everything is perfectly seasoned. The Bar-None Ranch on the River Road, owned and operated by Mr. and Mrs. Ad Given Davis—the former as famous for his palomino horses, which have won prizes here, there and everywhere, and his superb riding equipment as he is for his wonderful food—is another restaurant to which the acid test of excellence can be safely applied.

In the Crescent City there is an *embarras de richesses* as far as good places to eat are concerned, whereas elsewhere in the state there are surprisingly few—or, if there are many, I have not been able to discover them, nor have the compilers of those guide books which make a business of surveying gastronomical possibilities in a region and recommending those which have won a stamp of approval. This has always seemed to me strange, for tourists are on the increase in Louisiana, and I truly believe that anyone who would cater to their curiosity about Creole cookery at its best could make a fortune anywhere, any time—Emerson's man in the midst of a forest, manufacturing the best mousetrap, would not hold a candle to them as far as the beaten track is concerned! Then, if they could also be persuaded (1) that it is customary to supply a plate for the main course and not expect a guest to eat from the platter on which this is served; and (2) that elsewhere salad is eaten after and not before the main course and that the two merit equally careful preparation beforehand—why then I believe that these enterprising restaurateurs would not only have the world eating out of their hands, figuratively speaking, but off their tables, literally speaking!

But though there may be long hungry stretches outside of New Orleans, it is practically impossible to go more than a few blocks—often not more than a few steps—within its confines and still resist temptation to play havoc with both your waistline and your pocketbook. None of these restaurants—at least none with which I am familiar—is remarkable for its décor, for its table adornments or for the elegance of its service. Floors are usually tiled, walls bare or lined only with photographs, menus and inexpensive prints, an old-fashioned water carafe is a pivotal ornament and finger bowls apparently unknown. (At Brennan's the floors are carpeted and the tables lighted with candles; at Broussard's, the Patio Royale and the Court of Two Sisters the garden settings are delightful; and at Antoine's the 1840 Room and the Rex Room have unique character and decorations, but these are the exceptions that prove the rule.) Aside from the attractive Corinne Dunbar Dining Room on St. Charles Avenue, where the entire ground floor may be reserved for a private party, there are no *suites,* where the guests can meet their host and hostess in a drawing room for cocktails, go on into a dining room for the meal itself, and then return to the drawing room for coffee, liqueurs and conversation, as in a well-run residence or club; therefore, a general mingling is almost impossible;* you talk to the same persons from the beginning to the end of the party, for all amenities take place around the table itself, in one and the same place, though there is no lack of private dining rooms. But for the traveler or sojourner whose main interest is in what he eats, and not in stylish service, tasteful decorations or commodious surroundings, New Orleans is without a peer among American cities. Probably the most famous restaurants are Antoine's, Galatoire's, Arnaud's and La Louisianne, though I do not pretend to be enough of an authority to say in which order. "Diamond Jim" Moran has likewise built up a reputation for the somewhat spectacular combined with the substantial; and Tujague's, opposite the French Market supplies a moderate priced table d'hôte which is in a class by itself; but so much

* This omission will probably be rectified in the near future, as the Brennans are planning to provide such suites at the Patio Royale, which they will soon be taking over.

has already been written about these establishments that I should like to mention a few that are, apparently, not quite so well known but which, in my opinion, deserve to be, and in all of which I have greatly enjoyed myself.

One of these is Commander's Palace, on the edge of the so-called Garden District—that part of the city first made fashionable by the Anglo-Saxons who flocked there after the Louisiana Purchase and who, disdainfully designated as "Americans" by the Creoles of the French Quarter, located on the farther side of Canal Street and made their settlement one of great beauty. Many of the houses there are white-pillared and stately, and are set off to great advantage by their charming and spacious grounds. Commander's Palace, however, does not belong in this category; it is of the turreted, bay-windowed Victorian type, with no architectural merit whatsoever, and it stands flush to the street; within, one handsome crystal chandelier helps to illumine an otherwise nondescript room and seems somewhat out of place there. But the food! On a hot day, begin with Vichyssoise, which will be seasoned and chilled to perfection. Then accept the maître d'hôtel's suggestion that he be responsible for ordering the rest of the dinner. He will give you a Hearts of Palm Salad, mixing the dressing himself, and this time you will not mind having it before the main course, because the main course will have begun to seem unimportant already. Nevertheless, when this appears, and turns out to be Oysters Bienville, you will begin to regret your previous gourmandizing, for the sauce is superb. (Parenthetically, it is interesting to note that, in New Orleans, oysters are served the year round now—the old admonition, limiting their consumption to the months with an R in their names, has been dismissed as archaic!) And when the Stuffed Flounder, which is one of the *spécialités de la maison,* arrives you regret it still more, for it is impossible to do the noble fish justice, on top of everything else, and you resolve that the next time you will begin with that!

Another restaurant which I like immensely is Maylié's, on the corner of Poydras and Dryades streets—never a fashionable district. In fact, when the restaurant first opened, in 1876, the Poydras Street Market was directly opposite, and it was a simple matter for Madame Hypolite Esparbé, the wife of one of the co-founders—the other was Bernard Maylié—to shop there; and the establishment owed its foundation to the obvious necessity that someone should feed the butchers and fishmongers who came there before daybreak, and who, by 11:00 A.M., were famished. A breakfast hearty enough to serve as both the *petit déjeuner* and the *déjeuner à la fourchette* was the obvious answer—a forerunner of the currently popular brunch. This proved so popular—and so profitable!—that presently an extra building was erected on an adjoining lot, with a narrow passageway, pleasantly shaded by a wisteria vine, between the two sections of the restaurant; and soon thereafter dinner, as well as breakfast, was provided both for the original patrons and their rapidly increasing circle of friends. But there were three stipulations in regard to all these guests: they must buy the tickets for their dinners on the same day that they wished to be served, and before ten o'clock in the morning; only by the observance of this rule, Madame claimed, could she be sure there was plenty to eat, but no waste, and that the quality would be of the best, for she could then buy her supplies as soon as the tickets had been bought—no earlier, no later. Moreover, all ticket holders must be men!

In vain the fair residents of the city and the fair visitors to it pleaded and raged. Madame was adamant; no other woman, except her sister-in-law, would be admitted to the premises. And when Hypolite and Bernard were gathered to their fathers, the two widows managed the business by themselves, and eventually handed it down, in thriving condition, to the Maylié sons, who were, by then, "Willie" and "Johnnie" to the whole city. From then on, in unbroken succession from father to son, the line and the ownership have continued.

In some ways, the character of the place has changed though, fortunately, the aged bartender, Clement d'Azette, still presides at his old stand. For the past thirty years or so, women *have* been admitted—otherwise, I should not be able to describe the restaurant so feelingly! The one long table around which gentlemen formerly gathered at their ease has been supplanted by a number of small ones, and wine is secured by the bottle, instead of being supplied from casks and pitchers, in any desired quantity, with the price of the dinner. The passageway between the two buildings has been glassed over, to make communication easier in all weathers; but when this change took place, it was not permitted to make any difference in the important status of the wisteria vine, which by then had grown into a tree of considerable size. A hole was cut through the new glass roof, and the cascading purple blossoms continued to adorn the façade of the establishment and to provide colorful shade for passers-by; and to this day it continues to grow and to thrive, though it is no longer nourished with the dregs from the casks and pitchers. Like the customers, it has to get along with more moderate libations than those which the oldtime waiters proudly boasted they never left without offering it!

There is now some elasticity to the table d'hôte, though the guest is encouraged to stick to it rather closely, and Shrimps Remoulade and Sirloin Steak with Sauce Béarnaise are perennial standbys. The present Monsieur Maylié is a genial host, Gallic of manner and appearance, easy of conversation; and the present Madame Maylié is one of the most beautiful women I have ever seen in the Deep South. She is tall and slender, with classic features and a perfect carriage; and she wears her splendid black hair parted in the middle and smoothly drawn back over her ears into a great glossy bun at the nape of her neck. "Doesn't she look exactly like an Italian countess?" my host at dinner asked me recently. "Well," I answered cautiously, "she certainly looks the way an Italian countess is supposed to look and, unfortunately, seldom does!"

One of the questions I am most frequently asked about Creole cookery takes this form, "What in the world do you mean by *roux* when you talk about gumbos, soups and sauces?" This question is better and more clearly answered by the second

Madame Maylié, mother of the present proprietor, than by any-one else I know. "This is the foundation of all sauces. The Creole cook like the French holds that the success of sauces depends upon its brown or white *roux*. First of all it is well to remember that in making brown *roux*, it must never be burnt or over-browned. In making the *roux* melt the butter or lard slowly and gradually add the flour, stirring constantly till all is a deli-cate brown, remembering that as other ingredients are added the browning continues. The secret of good cooking lies in the gradual introduction of ingredients and it is a mistake to just throw in the last mentioned. A white *roux* is made like the brown except that flour and butter are blended together at the same time and not allowed to brown. This *roux* is used for sauce containing milk and cream. (Actual recipe: 1 or 2 tablespoons butter or good lard, 1 or more tablespoons of flour according to thickness desired.)"

The process of making Bouilli, the boiled beef which is an-other of the establishment's specialties, is also another which Madame Maylié describes with great clarity:

"When Bouilli is cooked at our restaurant, the meat is cut into large pieces of about 8 to 10 pounds, but for a small family, buy a piece of beef brisket about four pounds or more. Do not make the mistake of getting an inferior piece of soup meat, it must be brisket. To this amount of meat allow about 6 quarts or more water and boil for 4 hours slowly. This meat is not seasoned. It is suggested that a good sauce can be made by the guest of Creole mustard, horseradish, ketchup, and other season-ings. (In all our soups and gravies the stock from the boiled beef is added instead of water, thus making them richer and more palatable. There is, naturally, exception to this rule on Fridays.)"

As is natural, the French Quarter is more traditionally the home of Creole cookery than any other part of the city, and the coming restaurant there, in my opinion, is unquestionably Brennan's. It does not owe its existence to location or inheritance, like Commander's Palace and Maylié's, but to the sudden decision made by a denizen of the so-called "Irish Channel," whose occupation had hitherto been accounting, to become a restaurateur! Somewhat impetuously, he purchased a more or less moribund business on Bourbon Street, persuaded his sister, Ella—who, during her girlhood, had never evinced the slightest interest in cookery—to take over the supervision of the kitchen, and plunged in. The results have been electrifying. "Breakfast at Brennan's" has become a byword; but I think the delightfully unforced alliteration is partly responsible for that. As a matter of fact, luncheon and dinner are equally good, and the menu headed by the invitation, "Come as late as midnight for supper!" constitutes a welcome invitation to those who feel that the closing hour of most New Orleans restaurants is rather on the early side, and sorrowfully plagiarize Byron's comment on matrimony: "A holy estate, but what do you do with your evenings?"

Visitors to New Orleans will probably also find several of Owen Brennan's hard and fast rules extremely pleasing. He instructs his staff that everyone who comes to his restaurant is to be shown equal consideration and courtesy—a ruling in harmony with the inflexible statement made by Claude Terrail, proprietor of the famous Tour d'Argent in Paris, of which I shall have more to say later on—that all his guests are important to him. Unfortunately, there is more than one restaurant in New Orleans, however, where you get a superlative meal if you are considered important, but a very poor one if you get what is known as "typical tourist treatment." Brennan also instructs all members of his staff not to present a check until it is requested and then to do so promptly—a welcome change from getting the bill before you are halfway through your coffee, and an equally welcome one from searching vainly for a waiter when you are ready to leave and do not want to miss the first number of a symphony or the news reel at the movies, or even the train for California, or the plane to New York! He can be firm with his customers, too, though this firmness is mitigated by the most tactful means possible: no guest in a visible state of intoxication is permitted to annoy others or even to remain in the restaurant if he persists in immoderate drinking; and no male guest is seated unless and until he is wearing a coat. Before air conditioning relieved the atmosphere of New Orleans torrid summers, it was understandable, even excusable in many instances, that men should dress with great informality, to say the least, when dining out; now that a woman often finds it necessary to put on a light wrap over a low-cut dress, the short-sleeved, open-necked shirts, worn without a tie and often outside the trousers, affected by the escorts of such ladies, come as something of a shock to the "Easterners" who are always among the Crescent City's most profitable visitors. Owen Brennan has been quick to realize this.

Indubitably, all these factors have a bearing on Brennan's success, which is not so amazing, after all, if you stop to consider it. But, in the last analysis, a restaurant must stand or fall because of its food and, if Brennan's can be beaten any place in the United States, I do not know where this is. Until you have eaten Brennan's Jellied Consommé, topped with sour cream, you do not realize how a somewhat stereotyped dish can be transformed. The same gentleman who asked me the question about the Italian countess once went into ecstasies in my hearing about a certain soup that was formerly served at the Cabildo Restaurant, "As you tasted it, you began to see the heavens peopled with bands of cherubs," he said dreamily. The first vision he conjured up, as far as I was concerned, was of a Murillo painting. But now that I have eaten Jellied Consommé at Brennan's, I know exactly what he meant! Among other items equally worthy of mention are Buster Crabs Béarnaise, Chicken Pompadour, Cold Senegalese Soup, Eggs Hussarde, Tournedos LaBiche, Savarin or Rum Cakes, Jackson Salad, Petit Orange Brulôt, Ojen Cocktail, Absinthe Drip, Absinthe Frappé and Absinthe Suissesse, recipes for all of which the Brennans have been kind enough to give us.

Brennan's wine card offers as varied and as excellent a selection of beverages as are offered of food on the big red menus with New Orleans street scenes featured in the lower left-hand corner. My only criticism of it would be that none of the Spanish wines which I have found so surpassingly satisfactory, only one Portuguese wine, and very few Swiss and Italian wines, some of which are very good, too, appear on it. When it comes to American wines and French vintages, I venture to say that very few restaurants in this country can do better than the Brennan cellar. One of the reasons for this can doubtless be found in the fact that the representatives of the great companies dispensing these are received by Ella and Owen Brennan as friends and collaborators, that selections from their lists are made with the utmost care after thoughtful consideration of the products offered, and that replacements and additions to the stock on hand are never haphazardly undertaken.

Much of the social life in New Orleans centers in its restaurants. In this respect, it is more like New York than like Boston or Washington, where—though, of course, both possess excellent public eating places—the preference among the more conservative element seems still to be for home-cooked food and the more private reception of family and friends. But, with such an unlimited number of excellent places to choose among, it is not surprising that harassed or languid housekeepers in New Orleans frequently like to do much of their entertaining in restaurants. Since happily I do not belong to either of these groups—I knock on wood as I say it!—I still prefer to welcome my guests in my own home, or rather, in the private house that is serving as such, when I am absent from my own home. In New Orleans, this is Beauregard House and, to a large degree, the rear gallery, overlooking the flagstone patio with the fountain in the center, the box-bordered flower beds which surround it, and the crepe myrtle trees in the corners, has become the logical successor to my sycamore-shaded brick terrace in Alexandria. Beauregard House was built by a Spanish architect, Francisco Correjolles, one of the most outstanding of his day in New Orleans; and it has therefore seemed entirely fitting to equip this gallery in the Spanish style, with hempen rugs patterned in green and tan from Ubeda, rush-bottomed chairs with painted slats in ladder-back design and little tables painted to match the slats—that is to say, with plain green serving as a background for floral designs. (I found my furniture in Valencia, but it is in general use all over Andalucía for patios, galleries and country houses.) I invariably eat my evening meal on this gallery in the summertime, whether I have it alone or in company; not infrequently I can do so in the spring or the autumn; and I have occasionally been able to enjoy my supper there even in winter, for balmy weather may actually occur even in January. I have found that the Chicken Mousse and the Picket Fence Chocolate Pudding, which were so much appreciated in their original setting, taste just as good here; and I have actually overcome my aversion to "boughten" ice cream since it has been possible to send around the corner to my friend Mr. Brocato's shop and get Spumoni or Cassata at a moment's notice!

In the dining room, directly behind this gallery, the setting and the service are, naturally, both somewhat more formal. The large drawing room beyond—originally the ballroom—makes it possible to serve a seated supper for fifty guests quite easily, using the two rooms in conjunction with each other and putting the guests at small tables. For a formal dinner, using the dining room by itself, I must limit myself to eighteen and I prefer a limit of ten—from my viewpoint, the ideal number for a dinner in any case, as far as conversation is concerned. My grandmother's Fiddle Thread flat silver and tall silver epergne and my old Wedding Ring china and satin damask tablecloths seem especially suitable to use in this historic house, built in 1826; but so, perhaps incongruously, does the numerous treasure which I have gathered from various parts of the world: the amethyst crystal trees and jade grapes from Peking, as it was still called when I found them there; the Capo di Monte coffee set from Italy; the old lustreware and matching copper from Normandy. I try to vary my decorations, if not as frequently as my menus, at least often enough to give my guests occasional pleasant surprises. I recall that a company was equally enthusiastic about the soup plates of humble *terre à pipe* from Pont Audemer and the final offering at the same party: a sweet in which a decorated angel cake served as the skirt for a bisque doll, complete with crown, scepter and velvet train—the creation of that talented cateress, Mrs. Lucien Trosclair of Plaquemine, who therewith presented us with a Carnival Queen in miniature.

Like Tradition, Beauregard House has been the setting for the entertainment of certain celebrities. The Ambassador of France and Mme. Bonnet dined with me there, and one of the proudest moments in my life as a hostess came when Mme. Bonnet inquired what she was eating. (It was Caviar Soufflé!) Another proud moment came later that same evening when I found that a member of their staff, who had also been here to dinner, had written in my guest book, "*Combien suis-je loin de New York et près de mon pays! (How far I am from New York and how near to my own country!)*." The guests at a reception, given shortly thereafter in honor of M. Jacques de Lacretelle of the French Academy and his wife, were equally kind in the comments they left behind them—in fact, M. de Lacretelle himself wrote, "Why does not the French Academy stay at New Orleans? We should elect Mrs. Keyes '*à l'unanimité*.'" The Duke and Duchess of Windsor came there to a mint julep party, the most appropriate form of entertainment in their case—at least the Duchess and I both thought so—because, after all, it was her cousin, Lelia Barnett, who taught me how to make juleps in the first place. The Ambassador of Australia and Lady Spender spent ten days with me during the 1952 Carnival and though, of course, all major parties were held elsewhere, in connection with the balls, several minor ones, so to speak, took place at Beauregard House. Harold Lloyd and his wife and daughter; Carl Pforzheimer, the great bibliophile, and his wife; the Consul General of Italy and Signora Dalla Rosa; the late Roark Bradford, inimitable interpreter of Negro life through *The Green Pastures* and many other works; Frances Marion, Hedda Hopper and numerous famous publishers and authors are among the other celebrities whose names I find recorded in my guest book.

During the course of my first winter in New Orleans which, as I have already said, I spent so comfortably and agreeably with the Favrots, I had promised their little daughter, Claire, that when she came out, I would give her a party. Time crept up on us, as it has a way of doing, and her debut occurred in the Carnival Season of '51; the long-promised party, complete with supper in the ballroom and dancing in the patio, took place the same evening that my good friend, Captain the Hon. John Mitford, arrived in New Orleans from England, primed for Carnival pleasures by our mutual friend, Bussey Hewes—incidentally, the man who originally persuaded me I should make New Orleans the scene of a story. So the Captain's first party in the Crescent City was the one given in honor of Claire's debut; and, a week later, he was the guest at a dinner I gave in compliment to him and to the delightful French Consul General, Lionel Vasse, and his charming blonde wife, on the eve of their departure for Panama, where M. Vasse went to assume the post of French Ambassador.

I have mentioned these parties more or less at random, as typical of many others, and elsewhere I am giving recipes characteristic of such occasions. The entertainment of larger groups has been so extensive that I can hardly do more than hint at it and, indeed, a suggestion is probably all that is appropriate in a cookbook, for the menus on such occasions have not amounted to much. But I have been proud to welcome such organizations as the Garden Club of Virginia, the National Editorial Association and the National Catholic Education Association en masse, to open the patio to the public on the occasion of the annual Spring Fiestas and, in short, to share my sense of privilege in having Beauregard House as my winter residence with as many persons as I could. Since, like many another woman whose heritage is one of hospitality, I dislike to have even the most casual caller leave my rooftree without some form of entertainment, this has been offered whenever possible; but with groups of two or three hundred, these refreshments have generally been limited to coffee, punch, sandwiches and cake and with larger groups sometimes even limited to Coca-Cola, beer and sandwiches.

When I first came to live in Louisiana, I could not suppress some pangs of regret at seeing practically the entire male portion of my acquaintance disappear on the first day of the open season and reappear no more, or very little, until the season closed. These regrets soon evaporated, for I found that I was almost invariably the beneficiary of such absences. Wild ducks and wild geese began to find their way into my deep freeze with gratifying frequency; quail, partridge and pheasant made their appearance less often, but still they came. So did venison, though that gave me less of a thrill, as we had almost always been able to take "deer meat" for granted in New England during the hunters' moon. Since fisherman's luck may be tried at any time of the year in Louisiana, and since this luck is apt to be very good indeed, a day's catch is not infrequently stowed away beside a day's limit; and given any sort of game and any sort of fish as a basis, the hostess who cannot get up an acceptable dinner on short notice is not much of a housekeeper. I am glad to record here and now my unbounded gratitude to those sportsmen who have made many such dinners possible in my house.

My normal trek in Louisiana is between New Orleans and Crowley, which I can make either by the Airline to Baton Rouge and thence by way of Blanks, Lottie, Krotz Springs, Opelousas and Sunset to Lafayette; or over the Old Spanish Trail, which takes me through Raceland, Thibodaux, Morgan City, Franklin, Jeanerette and New Iberia to Lafayette. In the former case, I can feast at Roussel's, The Village or Didee's; in the latter case, Napoleonville is not too much of a detour to be practical, and White Castle and St. Martinville are quite feasible also; in both cases, Lafayette is on my direct route. This means that, besides having a good chance of eating at any one of three excellent restaurants, I may be privileged to dine with the Munsons, the Heberts, the Monteguts or the Nehrbasses in their homes—a most satisfactory variety. Every now and then, however, not because I am commuting from one of my obvious writing centers to another, but because I am especially fond of that part of the state and the people who live there, I head south instead of west, take the free ferry at Pointe a la Hache and pull up at Port Sulphur. I know I can count on a warm welcome there, under any circumstances; at the attractive guest house, a group of friends, headed by Mrs. Kenneth Price, the wife of the District Manager, will be on hand to meet me and Buster, its dusky presiding deity, will offer Creole Gumbo, Corn Soufflé Abbeville and Steak with "Rusty" Gravy for my delectation. If circumstances are favorable, I can ride along on top of the levee to Buras, where I can stop and get orange wine from my friends, the Lulichs; and when circumstances are most favorable of all, I can count on a boat trip to the mouth of the river, during the course of which Mrs. Pat Colligan—the charming wife of a self-styled "Irish Cajun"—will concoct her matchless Oyster Spaghetti as the *pièce de résistance* of a wonderful meal. With oyster "farms"—i.e., breeding grounds—and oyster "camps," where the men who operate the "farms" live, in the immediate vicinity, it is no wonder that the principal ingredient of this delicious dish is of superlative quality to begin with; but Mrs. Colligan has made the best possible use of a native product and that best is about the best ever!

I do not wish to give the impression that the wonderful food is the only, or even the greatest, attraction of such a trip, though I have culled—to use an oysterman's term—many wonderful recipes in the course of those I have made, which I am proud to pass on, with due credit to their originators. "I love its nearness to the levee, which is much lower than the levee farther north and, therefore, gives a greater sense of unity with the river," I wrote of the road to Pointe a la Hache some years ago. "I love the little beacons rising white above its verdure and, after nightfall, blinking cheerfully through the darkness. I love its abundant wild flowers, spider lilies and honeysuckle and iris. The thistles, which bloom at the same time, are beautiful, too, and the scent of orange blossoms is in the air, for we have begun to see scattered groves, though the road is not lined with them yet. But it is a lovely road all the way. . . . After we have crossed the river, we are about ten miles from Port Sulphur and our road is bordered on either side by citrus trees—not only the Louisiana 'Sweets' which, to my mind, are the best oranges in the world and the Louisiana navel oranges; but tangerines, kumquats, Satsumas and mandarins. As we approach Port Sulphur, we see the village on our right and, on our left, the huge crane and carrier by which sulphur is transferred from the barges which have brought it in from the mine to the freighters which take it to all the ports of the world. The heaped stockpiles, the laden barges and the burdened conveyor are all overflowing with beautiful yellow substance, some of it powdery and some of it lumpish, but all of it glistening. Whether our arrival takes place before or after dark, we see these docks fairly glowing with radiance. . . . Below Buras you may continue along the highway to Venice, where it ends, or you may go there on the levee road which follows the river. This is not a *river* road, in the same sense as the one I have talked about before; it is actually on top of the levee, which is wide enough for driving. On one side are pleasant little white houses, deep set in their luxuriant gardens; on the other, the great river, with ships riding proudly on its stream. On the piers are wooden benches where friends and neighbors go to chat at the end of the day's work. The pink clouds at sunset are reflected in the wide waters. And then the moon comes out and everything is bathed in silver. . . . It would be in the morning, however, that a pilot boat from Port Eads would be waiting to take us to the mouth of the river. . . . We are seeing fewer and fewer trees now and, at some distance from the river's mouth, we cease to see them at all; but indigo and Bermuda grass are abundant; horses and cattle feed on them with contentment and apparently with benefit. The presence of these creatures is another surprising feature of this Deep Delta Country, when there is no other sign of animal life except waterfowl. . . . This territory, where the land and water merge gradually into each other, has peculiar charm. The first time I saw it was under the light of a full moon, shining directly in front of the freighter on which I was traveling to South America. Under these circumstances, the scene has elements of magic in it; but it is beautiful at any time of day or night, and each time I go there, I find new glories in it. . . .

"However, the through traveler lacks one great opportunity offered to the privileged guest of a day: debarkation at Port Eads, and a hearty welcome from the bar pilots on duty and from such members of their families as may be vacationing there. In all, there are thirty-two bar pilots; they are a keen, hearty and courageous lot and I salute them.

"On the occasion of our [latest] visit to Port Eads, we were hospitably bidden to a bountiful dinner at Headquarters, and sat down in a company of ten or twelve; the group was congenial, the meal excellent."

So here I am back on the subject of food again—fried chicken, and I can taste and smell it still, in pleasant retrospect, though the meal about which I was writing, in the extract I have quoted,* was devoured several years ago. Farther than Port Eads, I cannot, as a southern writer, take you. For it is from here that vessels of all kinds go into the Gulf and the boundaries of Louisiana end. "Were you born south of the Deep Delta Country?" a certain Louisianian of my acquaintance was once asked. "If I had been, I wouldn't have been a man, I'd have been a soft-shelled crab," was the answer. This bit of repartee, I think, explains the reason why I can go no farther south myself.

* *All This Is Louisiana,* published by Harper & Brothers.

Breads

BUTTER CRUST ROLLS

(Creacy King)

½ cup butter
¼ cup vegetable shortening
1½ cups boiling water
1 tablespoon sugar

1 teaspoon salt
4 cups flour
½ yeast cake
¼ cup lukewarm water

Cream the butter and vegetable shortening together thoroughly. Combine the boiling water, sugar and salt, cool to lukewarm and stir in the flour. Soften the yeast cake in the lukewarm water and beat it into the dough. Beat in the creamed butter mixture and work into the dough enough additional flour to make a dough that is light but does not stick to the hands or bowl. Cover the bowl and set the dough in a warm place to rise for about 1 hour, or until the dough is double in bulk. Turn the dough out on a lightly floured board, knead it for a few minutes and return it to the bowl. Cover, and again put the dough in a warm place to double in bulk. Roll out the dough on a floured board and cut it into rolls of any desired shape. Place the rolls on an oiled baking sheet, cover, and let rise for 30 minutes. Bake the rolls in a moderate oven (350° F.) for about 20 minutes, or until golden.

PLAIN ROLLS

(Creacy King)

1¼ cups boiling water	4 cups flour
1 tablespoon sugar	½ yeast cake
1 teaspoon salt	¼ cup lukewarm water

Combine the boiling water, sugar and salt and cool to luke-warm. Stir in about 3 cups of the flour. Soften the yeast in the lukewarm water and stir it into the sponge. Beat in the additional cup of flour, cover and set the dough in a warm place to rise for about 1 hour, or until double in bulk. Turn the dough out onto a floured board and knead for a few minutes, adding more flour if necessary to make a dough that is light but does not stick to the hands. Return the dough to the mixing bowl, cover and again let rise to double in bulk.

Roll out the dough on a lightly floured board and shape it into rolls. Place the rolls on a lightly oiled baking sheet, cover and let rise in a warm spot for 30 minutes. Bake in a moderate oven (350° F.) for about 20 minutes, or until golden.

HUSH PUPPIES

(Mrs. T. P. Baker)

2 cups yellow corn meal	2 cups boiling water
1 teaspoon salt	1 tablespoon bacon drippings
1 tablespoon grated onion	¼ teaspoon Tabasco

Mix the meal, salt, baking powder and grated onion. Beat in the boiling water a little at a time. It may not be necessary to add all the water, so use just enough to make a thick dough. Stir in the bacon drippings and Tabasco and form the mixture into small thick cakes. Fry in hot deep fat (375° F.) until well browned and drain on absorbent paper.

FLANNEL CAKES

(Mrs. Allan F. Hebert)

1 *tablespoon butter*   1 *cup milk*
1 *tablespoon sugar*   2 *cups unsifted flour*
2 *eggs, separated*

Cream the butter and sugar together and beat in the egg yolks. Stir in the milk alternately with the flour and lastly fold in the egg whites, stiffly beaten. Bake in cakes on a hot greased griddle.

CINNAMON ROLLS

(Dorrie Blackstone)

¾ *cup milk*   1 *egg, beaten*
¼ *cup sugar*   3½ *cups flour*
3 *tablespoons butter*   *Soft butter*
1 *teaspoon salt*   ½ *cup brown sugar*
1 *cake yeast*   ½ *cup white sugar*
¼ *cup lukewarm water*   *Cinnamon*

Heat the milk to the scalding point, pour it over the sugar, butter and salt and cool to lukewarm. Soften the yeast in the lukewarm water and stir in the beaten egg. Combine the two mixtures, add half the flour and beat well. Add the remaining flour and mix well. Put the dough in the refrigerator for six hours, or overnight.

Roll the dough out on a floured board into a rectangle about ½ inch thick. Spread the dough with soft butter and sprinkle

with the sugars and cinnamon to taste. Roll the dough lengthwise like a jelly roll. Cut the roll crosswise into slices ½ inch
thick and place the slices on a buttered baking sheet. Let rise
until double in bulk, then bake in a moderate oven (375° F.)
for 20 to 25 minutes.

SALT RISING BREAD*

(Mrs. Edward Munson, Glenwood Plantation House)

1 cup milk	Sifted flour
1 cup white corn meal	1 tablespoon sugar
½ cup hot milk	1 teaspoon salt
½ cup cold water	

Heat the cup of milk to the boiling point, stir it into the corn
meal and mix well. Put the container holding the mush into a
pan of water just hot to the hand (120° F.), cover and let stand
in a warm place for 7 to 8 hours, or overnight to ferment. In the
morning combine the ½ cup of the hot milk and the water, add
it to the mush and beat well. Stir in enough flour to make a
stiff, thick batter, add the sugar and salt and beat well. Put the
batter, covered, in a warm place to rise for 3 or 4 hours. Then
stir in enough additional flour (you will need about 4½ cups in
all) to make a fairly stiff dough which does not stick to the
hands. Knead the dough for 10 minutes. Divide the dough in
half, shape into loaves, and put in generously buttered bread
pans. Brush the loaves with melted butter, cover with a light,
clean towel and put the pans in a warm place until the dough
is twice its original size. Bake in a hot oven (400° F.) for 10
minutes, reduce the oven temperature to 350° F. and bake for
30 minutes longer.

* This recipe was given to Mrs. Munson by her husband's old family
mammy.

SPOON BREAD

(Mrs. Richard Leche)

2 *cups milk*	1 *tablespoon sugar*
1 *cup white corn meal*	5 *eggs, separated*
2 *sticks soft butter (½ pound)*	1½ *tablespoons scotch or*
½ *teaspoon salt*	*bourbon*

Scald the milk and, while it is hot, stir in the corn meal and beat thoroughly. Add the butter, salt and sugar and beat vigorously until the butter is melted and well mixed with the meal. Set aside to cool. Beat the egg yolks and stir them into the mixture, then fold in the egg whites, stiffly beaten. Lastly add the whiskey. (The whiskey is supposed to help raise and hold the soufflé, but I have cooked it without the whiskey and it is equally as good.)

Turn the mixture into a buttered casserole and bake in a preheated moderate oven (350° F.) for about 40 minutes, or until a cake tester inserted in the center comes out clean. Serve immediately, as it tends to fall quickly. This does not affect the taste, however, but it doesn't look so wonderful as it does when it is high and handsome in its casserole.

SOUTHERN SPOON BREAD

(Mrs. Edward Munson, Glenwood Plantation House)

2 *cups white corn meal*	1½ *cups milk*
2 *cups boiling water*	3 *eggs, separated*
1 *teaspoon salt*	1 *teaspoon baking powder*
3 *tablespoons melted butter*	

Sift the corn meal three times and mix it into the boiling water, stirring until the mush is smooth and free of lumps. Add the salt, butter and milk and stir thoroughly. Add the beaten egg yolks. Add the baking powder to the egg whites and beat until they are stiff and fluffy. Fold the egg whites into the batter and turn the batter into a buttered baking dish. Bake in a moderate oven (350° F.) for about 45 minutes and serve immediately from the dish in which it is baked.

PAIN PERDU (LOST BREAD)

(Mrs. L. Perry Adams, née Helene Delery)

6 slices of stale bread, cut ¾ inch thick
1 cup milk
Sugar to taste
⅛ teaspoon salt

½ teaspoon vanilla or 1 tablespoon brandy
2 eggs
2 tablespoons butter or bacon drippings

Soak the bread in the milk, sweetened to taste, to which is added the salt and vanilla or brandy. Drain the slices of bread and dip them one at a time in the beaten eggs, turning each slice to coat it well on both sides. Sauté the bread slices in an iron or heavy aluminum skillet in the butter or bacon drippings until they are golden on both sides. Serve hot from the skillet with powdered sugar or sugar cane syrup.

HOG EARS*

(Mrs. Lester Montegut)

1 cup flour
¼ teaspoon salt

About ¼ cup water
¾ cup cane syrup

* When sons of French families returned to St. Martinville after spending two or three years in France on a grand tour, they were welcomed home by their colored nurses, who always served their breakfast in bed. Such delicacies as "hog ears" could always be found on the breakfast tray.

Sift the flour and salt into a small bowl and stir in the water, or enough to make a stiff dough. Divide the dough into 12 portions and roll out each portion as thinly as possible. Drop each portion into hot deep fat (370° F.), giving the dough a swift twist in the center with a long-handled fork. This forms the "ear." Fry the "ears" a few at a time until light brown in color.

Boil the cane syrup until a few drops form a soft ball when dropped into cold water. Dip each "ear" into the hot syrup and place them on a platter to cool.

Soups, Stews, Bisques, Jambalaya, Courtbouillon* and Gumbos

COLD SENEGALESE SOUP

(Brennan's Restaurant)

3½ cups chicken stock
1 cup finely chopped cooked
    chicken meat
½ teaspoon curry powder
4 egg yolks
2 cups warm cream

Bring the chicken stock to a boil and add the chicken meat and curry, more or less to taste. Beat the egg yolks with a little of the hot stock and blend them with the cream. Stir the cream and egg mixture gradually into the chicken stock, stirring constantly over low heat, until the soup is just thickened. Be careful not to let the soup boil or the eggs will curdle. Correct the seasoning, cool, then chill in the refrigerator.

CREME VICHYSSOISE

(Clara E. Wilson's recipe for this cold potato and leek soup)

4 to 6 leeks, white part only
1 medium onion, peeled
2 tablespoons butter
5 potatoes, peeled and finely
    diced
4 cups chicken stock
1 tablespoon salt
2 cups milk
2 cups light cream
1 cup heavy cream

* Pronouncd Cou'biyon.

Slice the leeks and onion thinly and sauté them in the butter until golden. Turn the vegetables into a soup kettle and add the potatoes, chicken stock and salt. Bring the stock to a boil and simmer for 35 to 40 minutes. Rub the soup through a fine sieve and return it to the heat. Add the milk and thin cream, bring again to a boil and again strain. Cool and stir in the heavy cream, slightly whipped. Chill thoroughly and serve in bouillon cups over ice. Sprinkle with chopped chives or parsley.

TURTLE SOUP

(Mrs. Edward Munson, Glenwood Plantation House)

½ cup cooking oil
½ cup flour
1 large onion, chopped
1 small slice raw ham, finely chopped
1 green pepper, seeded and chopped
1 No. 2 can of tomatoes
1 can tomato paste
2 pounds turtle meat, cut into pieces
4 quarts water
2 cloves garlic

1 sprig thyme
2 bay leaves
6 cloves
½ teaspoon ground allspice
1 tablespoon Worcestershire sauce
Salt, cayenne and pepper to taste
Juice of 1 lemon
1 cup sherry
Lemon slices
5 hard-cooked eggs, finely chopped

In a heavy kettle heat the oil, stir in the flour and cook, stirring, until the *roux* is golden. Add the onion and cook for 2 or 3 minutes. Add the ham, green pepper, tomatoes and tomato paste and simmer for 10 minutes. Add the turtle meat and simmer for 5 minutes, stirring frequently. Gradually stir in the water and add the garlic, thyme, bay leaves, cloves, allspice, Worcestershire sauce, salt, cayenne and pepper. Bring the water slowly to a boil and simmer the soup for 1 hour. Finally, add the lemon juice and cook 10 minutes longer. Remove the soup from the fire and add the sherry. Serve at once in plates garnished with slices of lemon and the chopped hard-cooked eggs.

CRAB SOUP

(E. A. Lafaye)

Clean 1 dozen very fat crabs and cut them in half lengthwise. Put the crabs in a heavy iron pot with 1 tablespoon lard, barely cover them with boiling water, cover the kettle and steam the crabs over a gentle flame for 20 minutes.

In another heavy pot melt 2 tablespoons oil or lard, stir in 4 tablespoons flour and cook, stirring, over a low flame until the *roux* begins to darken. Add 2 onions and 6 shallots, both finely chopped, 1 cup water, and ½ cup butter and cook, stirring constantly, for 10 to 12 minutes. Add the crabs and the contents of two No. 2 cans of tomatoes, strained to remove the seeds and pulp. Add 2 quarts water and cook vigorously for 40 minutes. Add several stalks of celery including the leaves, 1 sweet green pepper, seeded and halved, and 1 lemon, thinly sliced, and cook gently for 30 minutes longer. Discard the celery, green pepper and lemon and season the soup to taste with salt and white pepper.

Ladle the soup boiling hot into serving dishes, add 1 tablespoon dry sherry to each serving and sprinkle with a little finely chopped hard-cooked egg and parsley. Serves 6.

OYSTER STEW

(Mrs. L. Perry Adams, née Helene Delery)

2 dozen freshly shucked oysters

1 tablespoon butter
2 cups rich milk, scalded

Heat the oysters in the butter until the edges curl. Gradually stir in the hot milk and cook over a low flame for 5 minutes. Add the butter and salt if necessary and serve at once.

OYSTER SOUP

(Mrs. L. Perry Adams, née Helene Delery)

2 tablespoons butter
1½ tablespoons flour
1 small onion, finely chopped
1 clove garlic, minced
2 cups hot oyster liquor, strained
1 tablespoon finely chopped parsley
2 shallots, minced
2 dozen freshly shucked oysters

In a saucepan heat the butter and stir in the flour. Add the onion and garlic and cook, stirring, until the *roux* is golden brown. Gradually stir in the oyster liquor and cook, stirring, until the liquid is slightly thickened. Add the parsley and shallots and simmer over a low flame for 30 minutes. Add the oysters and cook for 5 minutes longer.

This soup does not have to be served immediately. In fact, it is better if it is allowed to get cold and is then reheated. Serve with buttered crackers crisped in a hot oven.

TURTLE STEW

(Invention of Pearl and Jesse of the Hoo-Shoo-Too Club)

5 pounds turtle meat
2 pounds onions, peeled and chopped
2 cloves garlic
Red and black pepper to taste
1 cup lard
3 lemons, sliced
9 bay leaves
Ground clove and allspice
2½ cups flour
2 green peppers, seeded and chopped
1 stalk celery, chopped
3 large cans of tomatoes
2 cans tomato paste
8 hard-cooked eggs
½ cup butter
Several sprays of parsley
8 scallions, chopped
Sherry

Cut the turtle meat, bones and all, into small cubes and scald the cubes several times with boiling water. Drain the meat in a strainer and turn it into a heavy iron pot or Dutch oven. Add ½ cup of the chopped onions, 1 clove of the garlic and a little red and black pepper and cook, stirring frequently, until most of the moisture in the turtle meat and the vegetables is evaporated. Add 2 to 3 tablespoons of the lard and sauté the meat and vegetables, stirring frequently, until they are browned. Add the lemons and bay leaves, a dash each of clove and allspice and about 3 cups hot water and stir well. Cover the kettle tightly and simmer on a low fire.

Into another pot heat the rest of the lard. Gradually stir in the flour and cook, stirring, until the *roux* is a golden brown. Add all but ¼ cup of the chopped onions and cook until the onions are lightly browned. Then add the other clove of garlic, minced, and cook for 3 to 4 minutes. Add the green peppers and celery, the tomatoes and tomato paste and stir in enough hot water to almost fill the pot. Bring to a boil and simmer for 5 minutes. Pour the contents into the turtle pot and stir in enough hot water to bring the stew to the desired consistency. Simmer the stew for 5 hours, skimming off the grease as it forms on the surface and adding additional hot water if necessary. Separate the egg yolks from the egg whites. Mash the yolks with a few drops of water to make them smooth and chop the whites finely. Add yolks and whites to the stew.

In a small frying pan melt the butter and in it sauté the remaining ¼ cup of onions and a bit of chopped garlic until browned. Turn this mixture into the stew pot a few minutes before serving. Finally add the parsley and green onions.

Put 1 tablespoon of sherry into each soup plate and serve with hot toast.

CRAYFISH STEW

(Mrs. Charles Landry)

6 *pounds crayfish*	5 *cloves garlic, chopped*
3 *tablespoons butter*	3 *scallions, chopped*
3 *tablespoons flour*	1 *tablespoon chopped parsley*
1 *large onion, peeled and*	*Juice of ½ lemon*
chopped	*Salt and pepper to taste*

Scald the crayfish with boiling water and clean them, reserving the fat from the heads and also the claws. Crush the claws, cover with about 2 quarts water, bring to a boil and simmer for 30 minutes.

In a soup kettle melt the butter, add the flour and cook, stirring, until the *roux* is browned. Add the onion and simmer over a low flame until the onion is transparent. Add the garlic and the fat from the crayfish heads and simmer for a few minutes. Gradually stir in the hot stock from the crayfish claws and simmer for 30 minutes. Then add the crayfish tails, scallions, parsley, lemon and salt and pepper to taste and simmer for 30 minutes longer. Other spices may be added if desired. Serve with hot cooked rice.

BRUNSWICK STEW

("Sissy" Wilbert)

1 *plump chicken, cleaned*	½ *teaspoon sugar*
2 *tablespoons olive oil*	1 *tablespoon Lea & Perrins*
2 *tablespoons flour*	*sauce*
2 *medium onions, peeled and*	4 *bay leaves*
. *chopped*	3 *stalks celery, chopped*
2 *cloves garlic, chopped*	3 *teaspoons chili pepper*
2 *large cans tomatoes*	2 *tablespoons chopped parsley*
1 *can Italian gravy*	*Salt and pepper to taste*

¼ pound (½ cup) butter	1 can button mushrooms
1 can corn	1 tablespoon wine
1 can peas	6 hard-cooked eggs, chopped

Put the chicken in a kettle with water to cover, bring the water to a boil and simmer for about 2 hours, or until the chicken is very tender.

In another kettle heat the olive oil, add the flour and cook, stirring, until the *roux* is smooth. Add the onions and garlic and cook, stirring, until the mixture is a light brown. Add the tomatoes, gravy, sugar, Lea & Perrins sauce, bay leaves, celery, chili pepper, parsley and salt and pepper to taste and cook for about 20 minutes, stirring often. Add the butter and the liquid in which the chicken was poached, the corn and peas and cook for 15 minutes longer. Cut the chicken into serving pieces and add the pieces to the stew with the mushrooms and wine. Then add the eggs and simmer until ready to serve.

CRAYFISH BISQUE

(Mrs. Edward Munson, Glenwood Plantation House)

4 gallons crayfish	3 tablespoons lard
3 onions, chopped	One-half as much stale bread
1 clove garlic, chopped	crumbs as crayfish meat
2 tablespoons chopped onion	1 tablespoon chopped parsley
tops or chives	Salt, pepper and cayenne to
2 sprigs thyme	taste
2 bay leaves	1 egg, beaten
4 cloves	2 tablespoons butter
3 stalks celery, chopped	2 tablespoons flour
2 blades mace	

Soak the crayfish in a strong solution of salt water for 1 hour. Drain, plunge the crayfish into boiling water, and simmer for about 5 minutes, or until they turn red. Remove the crayfish, reserving the liquid, clean the heads, reserving the fat, and pick the meat from the tails. Save the largest heads to stuff.

To the reserved liquid add one third of the onions, half the garlic and onion tops, the thyme, bay leaves, cloves, celery and mace. Also add the shells and claws of the crayfish and the heads that are not going to be used for stuffing. Bring the liquid to a boil, simmer for 10 minutes and set aside while you stuff the heads.

In a skillet melt the lard and in it cook the remaining chopped onion until the onion is tender. Add the crayfish tails, chopped, the fat from the heads, and the bread crumbs, soaked in water and squeezed dry. Season the mixture with salt, pepper and cayenne, and add the parsley and the remaining onion tops and garlic. Cook slowly until the stuffing is well blended and stir in the beaten egg. Stuff the heads with this dressing, roll each head in flour and sauté in hot butter until brown on all sides.

In a large kettle melt the butter and stir in the flour. Cook, stirring, until the *roux* is smooth and then gradually stir in the hot liquid from the kettle in which the shells and vegetables were cooked. Add the stuffed heads and simmer slowly for 30 minutes. Serve with hot French twist bread.

CRAYFISH BISQUE

(Mrs. Charles Landry)

12 pounds crayfish
2 tablespoons butter
2 tablespoons flour
1 onion, peeled and finely chopped
3 cloves garlic, minced

3 green onions, or scallions, finely chopped
1 tablespoon minced parsley
1 tablespoon minced green pepper
Salt and pepper to taste
Juice of ½ lemon

Scald the crayfish with boiling water and clean them, reserving the fat from the heads and the claws. Save also about 3 dozen of the large head shells for stuffing. Crush the claws, cover generously with water, bring the water to a boil and simmer for 30 minutes.

In a soup kettle melt the butter, add the flour and stir until the *roux* is lightly browned. Add the onion and cook until the onion is transparent. Add half the crayfish fat, one quarter of the tails, the garlic, scallions, parsley and green pepper and gradually stir in the hot liquid from the crushed claws. Season with salt and pepper to taste, add the lemon juice and simmer for 1 hour. Add the stuffed crayfish heads (see below) and cook slowly for a few minutes longer.

STUFFED CRAYFISH HEADS

The remaining crayfish tails from the above ingredients
¼ pound (½ cup) butter
1 onion, minced
The remaining crayfish fat from the above ingredients
1 tablespoon minced green pepper
1 tablespoon minced parsley
1 tablespoon minced celery
1 tablespoon minced green onion tops or chives
2 cups bread crumbs
Salt and pepper to taste
2 eggs, beaten
Flour
Butter

Chop the crayfish tails. Melt the butter and in it cook the onion until the onion is tender. Add the crayfish fat and the minced vegetables and about 2 cups water and simmer for 15 minutes. Stir in the bread crumbs and salt and pepper to taste.

Stuff the reserved crayfish heads with this stuffing. Dip the heads in the beaten egg, roll in flour and brown on all sides in hot butter.

JAMBALAYA

(Mrs. L. Perry Adams, née Helene Delery)

½ pound chorizos, cut into pieces
A 2-pound chicken, boned and the meat cut into pieces
½ pound ham, diced
2 medium onions, chopped
1 green pepper, chopped
1 clove garlic, minced
2 tablespoons tomato paste
3½ cups peeled and quartered tomatoes
1 tablespoon chopped parsley
1 bay leaf
1½ teaspoons salt
1½ cups washed rice

In an iron pot or heavy aluminum kettle cook the chorizos until they are brown on all sides. Set the chorizos aside and pour off all but 2 tablespoons of the sausage drippings. To the drippings add the chicken and ham and cook until the meat is browned. Set aside the chicken and ham and in the drippings remaining in the pot sauté the onions, green pepper and garlic until the onion is golden. Add the tomato paste, tomatoes, parsley, bay leaf and salt and return the chicken, ham and chorizos to the pot, bring to a boil and simmer until the chicken is tender. Add the rice and stir until the juice boils again. Cover the pot and cook over a very low flame for about 45 minutes, or until the rice is tender and dry, adding from time to time a little water if necessary. If the rice is too moist bake in a moderate oven (350° F.) uncovered until it is dry.

Jambalaya may also be made with shrimp and oysters.

RED FISH COURTBOUILLON

(Mrs. Edward Munson, Glenwood Plantation House)

3 tablespoons olive oil
2 tablespoons flour
1 large onion, sliced
6 tomatoes, peeled and
   chopped
1 clove garlic, chopped
2 bay leaves

Several sprays of parsley
Thyme and sweet basil
4 cups water
Salt and pepper
6 slices, or 3 to 4 pounds red
   fish (red snapper)
1 cup white wine

In a saucepan heat the olive oil, stir in the flour, and cook, stirring, until the *roux* is lightly browned. Add the onion and cook until the onion is tender. Add the tomatoes, garlic, bay leaves, parsley, and a good pinch each of thyme and sweet basil and cook until the tomatoes are tender. Add the water and bring the liquid to a boil. Salt and pepper the fish slices, add them to the saucepan, and simmer for 15 minutes. Add the white wine and simmer for 15 minutes longer.

FISH COURTBOUILLON

(Mrs. Frederick Nehrbass)

1 cup olive oil
4 cups flour
6 large onions, finely chopped
1 large sweet pepper, finely
   chopped
1 bunch celery, finely
   chopped
1 head garlic, peeled and
   finely chopped
1 can Italian tomato paste

1 tablespoon Worcestershire
   sauce
1 dash Louisiana Hot Sauce
4 large fresh tomatoes, peeled
   and chopped
2 quarts hot water
½ cup butter
1 bunch parsley, chopped
1 bunch green onion tops,
   chopped

2 bay leaves   Salt and red pepper to taste
24 large slices of red snapper,   1 bottle dry red wine or claret
  or poisson rouge*   1 lemon, sliced

In a large kettle heat the olive oil, gradually stir in the flour, and cook, stirring constantly with a wooden spoon, until the *roux* is smooth and a delicate brown. Add the onions, sweet pepper, celery and garlic and cook over a gentle fire, stirring, until the vegetables are cooked. Be careful not to let the mixture burn. Add the tomato paste, Worcestershire sauce, hot sauce and the tomatoes and continue to cook until the mixture is well browned, but not burnt. Add the water and simmer for 30 minutes. Add the butter, parsley, green onion tops and bay leaves and simmer for 30 minutes longer. Add the fish and salt and pepper to taste and simmer for 10 minutes. Add the wine and lemon slices and cook for 20 minutes more. Before serving correct the seasoning with salt and pepper. Serves 12.

Serve with garlic bread and chilled white wine.

GARLIC BREAD

Cream together ¼ pound butter and 1 or 2 cloves garlic, finely chopped. Split loaf of French bread lengthwise, then cut it cross-wise in quarters. Spread the garlic butter on the bread and toast.

TROUT COURTBOUILLON

(Mrs. B. A. Landry)

4 to 6 pounds trout   1 celery heart, chopped
2 tablespoons lard   2 cans Italian tomato paste
1 bunch green onion tops,   2 cans tomato sauce
  chopped   2 quarts hot water
2 cloves garlic, chopped   Salt and pepper to taste

* Mrs. Nehrbass says if red snapper is not available gaspergou will serve as well. (It takes a firm-fleshed fish to keep from disintegrating.) She uses the less attractive parts of the fish to make a fish stock which she uses in place of the hot water specified, thus adding to the richness and succulence of the stew.

Poach the trout in boiling lightly salted water for about 15 minutes, or until the flesh flakes from the bones. Remove the fish from the water and, when cool enough to handle, lift the flesh from the bones, keeping it in as large pieces as possible. Set aside.

Heat the lard and in it sauté the green onion tops, garlic, and celery until the vegetables are tender. Stir in the tomato paste, tomato sauce and the water and bring to a boil. Add the fish and simmer for about 40 minutes. Before serving season with salt and plenty of freshly ground black pepper.

GENERAL COMMENT ON GUMBOS

Filé (pronounced fee-lay) is a powder made from young sassafras leaves that have been dried and pounded into a powder. It was originally made by the Choctaw Indians of Louisiana, and sold only by them. It can now be purchased from grocery stores, put up in sifter top cans or bottles.

Filé may be used with a lighter *roux** for gumbo, but filé should not be added until the end of the cooking period. When okra is used, no filé is necessary in a gumbo.

CHICKEN GUMBO FILÉ
(Mrs. L. Perry Adams, née Helene Delery)

1 pound chorizos (hot Mexican sausages)
1 pound ham, cubed
A 3-pound chicken, cut into serving pieces
Salt and pepper
3 tablespoons flour
2 large onions, minced
3 cloves garlic, minced
2 tablespoons tomato paste
1 green pepper, minced

3 quarts oyster liquor and water
2 tablespoons chopped parsley
2 sprigs thyme
5 scallions, or green onions, minced
1 bay leaf
Salt and pepper to taste
3 dozen oysters
2 tablespoons filé

* A *roux* is flour browned in shortening.

In a heavy skillet sauté the chorizos until they are well browned on all sides. Cut them into pieces and transfer to a deep kettle. Pour off and reserve all but 2 tablespoons of the drippings in the skillet and in it sauté the ham until it is browned. Transfer the ham to the kettle. Sprinkle the chicken with salt and pepper, sauté it in the same drippings until golden and transfer the chicken to the kettle. Add more chorizo drippings to the skillet to make 2 tablespoons and stir in the flour. Add the onions and garlic and cook until the mixture is browned. Add the tomato paste and cook for a few minutes, then stir in gradually 2 cups of the water and oyster liquid and cook, stirring, until the sauce is thickened. Add the sauce to the kettle with the green pepper, parsley, thyme, scallions and bay leaf and stir in oyster liquor or water 1 cup at a time until 3 quarts liquid in all have been added. Add salt and pepper to taste, remembering that the chorizos are hot, and cook over a low flame for 3 hours. Add the oysters and simmer for 15 minutes longer. Remove the gumbo from the fire and stir in gradually the filé. The gumbo must not cook after filé is added. Serve with rice cooked dry so that each grain is separate. This will serve 8 people—2 plates each.

GUMBO Z'HERBES

(Mrs. L. Perry Adams, née Helene Delery)

1 *pound chorizos** cut into pieces	8 *outside leaves green Creole cabbage*
1 *pound pickled pork, cubed*	12 *sprays parsley*
1 *ham bone*	6 *scallions, or green onions*
2 *bunches spinach*	4 *sprigs thyme*
1 *bunch turnip tops*	2 *tablespoons flour*
1 *bunch beet tops*	2 *large onions, chopped*
1 *bunch mustard greens*	2 *cloves garlic, minced*
1 *head lettuce*	*Salt and pepper to taste*

* Hot sausages.

Sauté the chorizos until they are well browned and cooked through. Drain, reserving the drippings. Put the pickled pork and ham bone in a kettle with water to cover, bring the water to a boil and simmer for about 1 hour, or until the meat is tender. Set aside. Wash all the greens carefully, including the scallions, and cook them until tender with as little water as possible to prevent them from burning. Drain, saving the liquor, and chop the greens finely.

Heat 2 tablespoons of the chorizo drippings, stir in the flour and add the onions and garlic. Cook, stirring, until the *roux* is golden brown. Add the chorizos, pork, ham bone, and minced greens and enough of the liquid from the vegetables and meat to make a thick purée, about 1 quart. Add salt and pepper to taste and simmer for 30 minutes. Serve with cooked rice.

SEAFOOD OKRA GUMBO

(Mrs. L. Perry Adams, née Helene Delery)

12 *small hard-shell crabs or*	2½ *quarts shrimp stock and*
2 *pounds crab meat*	*oyster liquor combined*
2 *pounds shrimp*	3 *sprays parsley*
2½ *pounds small tender okra*	3 *sprigs thyme*
3 *tablespoons shortening*	1 *bay leaf*
1 *large onion, sliced*	*Salt and pepper to taste*
1 *sweet pepper, minced*	3 *dozen freshly shucked*
3 *cloves garlic, minced*	*oysters*
3 *cups cooked tomatoes*	

Scald the crabs in boiling water and clean, removing the "dead man's fingers," the spongy substance and the sand bag. Remove the claws and crack them and cut the bodies in quarters. Wash the shrimp thoroughly, remove the heads and shells and discard the black vein that runs along the backs. Cook the shrimp heads for 30 minutes in 2½ quarts salted water and strain, reserving the liquid. Slice the okra ⅛ inch thick.

In a soup kettle melt the shortening and in it sauté the okra, onion, sweet pepper and garlic over a low flame for about 1 hour, or until the okra ceases to "rope," stirring frequently. Gradually stir in the tomatoes and the combined shrimp stock and oyster liquid. Add the parsley, thyme, bay leaf, crabs and shrimp and simmer over a low flame for 45 minutes. Add the oysters and simmer for 15 minutes longer. Serve with rice cooked so dry that every grain is separate.

CREOLE GUMBO

(Mrs. Allan F. Hebert)

2 tablespoons fat	2 quarts water
1½ tablespoons flour	3 dozen oysters
1 large fowl, cut into serving pieces	7 tablespoons minced parsley
2 teaspoons salt	Red and black pepper to taste
1 large onion, diced	1½ tablespoons filé powder
	¾ cup cooked rice

In a heavy pot melt the fat, stir in the flour, and cook until the *roux* is brown. Sprinkle the chicken pieces with the salt and cook them in the *roux* until the pieces are brown. Add the onion and sauté until the onion is transparent. Add the water, cover the pot and cook over a slow fire for 2 to 3 hours, or until the chicken is tender. Add the oysters, parsley and pepper to taste and cook until the oysters curl at the edges. Remove the gumbo from the fire and stir in the filé. Do not reheat the gumbo after the filé powder is added. Add 2 tablespoons cooked rice to each portion and serve with more cooked rice. Serves 6.

CREOLE GUMBO

(Nelson "Buster" Williams)

A 2½ pound chicken, cut
  into serving pieces
½ cup cooking oil
2½ tablespoons flour
1 onion, finely chopped
1 sweet green pepper, seeded
  and minced

½ cup minced celery
2 cloves garlic, minced
1 pint freshly shucked
  oysters
2 sprays parsley, chopped
4 green onion tops, chopped

Put the chicken in a kettle with water to cover generously, bring the water to a boil and simmer the chicken for 15 minutes.

In a heavy skillet heat the oil, stir in the flour and cook, stirring, until the *roux* is lightly browned. Add the finely chopped onion and cook for 3 minutes. Stir this *roux* gradually into the chicken stock. Add the green pepper, celery and garlic and simmer for 15 minutes longer.

About 5 minutes before serving the gumbo, add the oysters, parsley and chopped green onions. Serve with cooked rice, crackers or toast. Serves 6.

GUMBO

(Creacy King)

2 tablespoons shortening
2 pounds okra, sliced
½ cup finely chopped celery
2 cloves garlic, chopped
1 onion, finely chopped
½ sweet green pepper, finely
  chopped

1 can Italian tomato paste
1 tablespoon flour
1½ bay leaves
2 tablespoons salt
2 quarts water
3 pounds shrimp, shelled and
  deveined

In a heavy kettle heat the shortening and in it sauté the okra until it ceases to "rope." Add the celery, garlic, onion, pepper, tomato paste, flour, bay leaves, salt and water and cook over a gentle fire for at least 2½ hours. Add the shrimp and when they are cooked, the gumbo is ready to serve with boiled rice.

WILD GOOSE GUMBO

(Creacy King)

2 tablespoons shortening
2 pounds okra, sliced
1 tablespoon flour
½ cup chopped celery
2 cloves garlic, minced
1 onion, chopped

½ green pepper, finely chopped
1 can Italian tomato paste
1½ bay leaves
2 tablespoons salt
2 quarts water
1 goose

In a soup kettle heat the shortening and in it sauté the okra until it ceases to "rope." Stir in the flour, add the celery, garlic, onion and green pepper and cook until the onion is transparent. Add the tomato paste, bay leaves and salt and stir in the water. Bring to a boil and simmer for at least 2½ hours.

Meanwhile simmer the goose in salted water to cover until it is tender. Remove the meat from the bones and cut it in small pieces. Add the meat to the gumbo and keep hot until ready to serve.

POULE D'EAU GUMBO*

(Mrs. John Supple)

The breasts and gizzards of
4 moor hens†
Salt and pepper
5 tablespoons shortening
3 tablespoons flour
½ cup finely chopped onions
½ cup finely chopped celery

½ cup finely chopped sweet green pepper
½ cup finely chopped green onions
6 cups water
1 to 2 teaspoons filé to taste

* This delicacy is good only when made from *poule d'eau* secured during the early part of the season. Later the meat of the moor hen is so fishy it is unpalatable.   † *Poules d'eau.*

Wash the breasts and gizzards well, drain and sprinkle them with salt and pepper. Sauté the breasts and gizzards in 2 tablespoons of the shortening in a heavy skillet until browned on all sides.

In another skillet melt the remaining shortening, stir in the flour and cook, stirring, until the *roux* becomes dark tan in color. Add the onions and cook until the onions are golden. Add the celery, pepper and green onions and cook for a few minutes longer. Gradually stir in 1 cup of the water and bring to a boil. Transfer this thick sauce to a gumbo pot and add the browned breasts and gizzards. Add another cup of the water to the skillet in which the breasts were browned and bring to a boil, stirring in all the brown bits from the bottom and sides of the skillet. Add the liquid to the gumbo pot. Add the remaining water, bring to a boil and simmer for about 45 minutes, or until the meat is tender. Just before serving stir in the filé.

Main Dishes

1. EGGS AND FISH

CAVIAR SOUFFLÉ

(Frances Parkinson Keyes' own invention carried out by
Clara E. Wilson)

4 tablespoons butter	2 cups milk
4 tablespoons flour	2 4-ounce jars of whitefish
1 tablespoon tapioca	caviar
6 eggs, separated	

In the top of a double boiler melt the butter and stir in the flour and tapioca. Beat the egg yolks lightly, combine them with the milk and gradually stir the liquid into the butter-flour mixture. Cook over low heat, stirring constantly, until the sauce thickens, being careful not to let it boil. Stir in the caviar and cook over boiling water, stirring continuously, for 3 to 4 minutes longer. Set aside to cool.

When ready to bake, beat the egg whites until stiff and fold them into the caviar mixture. Pour the batter into a buttered quart casserole, set the casserole in a shallow pan containing about 1 inch of warm water, and bake in a moderate oven (350° F.) for 30 minutes. Increase the oven temperature to 450° F. and continue to bake for 10 to 15 minutes longer. Serve immediately and do not open the oven during the first 30 minutes of cooking.

CHEESE SOUFFLÉ

(Mrs. Edward Munson, Glenwood Plantation House)

4 *tablespoons butter*	1 *cup grated cheese*
4 *tablespoons flour*	1½ *cups cooked rice*
1½ *cups milk*	*Salt and cayenne pepper*
8 *eggs, separated*	

In a saucepan melt the butter, stir in the flour and gradually stir in the milk. Cook, stirring, until the sauce is smooth and thickened. Remove the sauce from the fire and stir in the egg yolks, lightly beaten. Stir in the cheese, rice, a little salt and a dash of cayenne pepper. Beat the egg whites until stiff and fold them into the egg yolk mixture. Turn the batter into a buttered 1½ quart casserole or soufflé dish and bake in a moderate oven (350° F.) for 45 minutes. Serve immediately.

MACARONI AND CHEESE

(Creacy King)

1 *pound elbow macroni*	1 *cup milk*
1½ *cups grated cheese*	2 *tablespoons melted butter*
2 *eggs, beaten*	1 *teaspoon salt*

Cook the macaroni in a large quantity of rapidly boiling salted water until tender. Drain in a collander and rinse in cold water. Put the macaroni in a baking dish or casserole. Combine 1¼ cups of the grated cheese, the eggs, milk, butter and salt and mix well with the macaroni. Sprinkle the remaining cheese on top and bake in a moderate oven (350° F.) for about 30 minutes.

EGGS HUSSARDE

(Brennan's Restaurant)

On a base of 2 rounds of Holland rusks, arrange several slices of grilled ham and 2 slices of ripe tomato. Cover with Marchand de Vin sauce (see below). Put a poached egg on each slice of tomato and cover with Hollandaise sauce (see below).

MARCHAND DE VIN SAUCE

*1 bunch finely chopped shal-
  lots or green onions
1 pound chopped mushrooms
½ pound finely chopped
  cooked ham
1 teaspoon minced garlic*

*2 tablespoons butter
2 tablespoons flour
4 cups hot beef stock
1 cup red wine
1 bunch finely chopped
  parsley*

Sauté the onion, mushrooms, ham and garlic in the butter until the onion is tender. Stir in the flour and blend well. Gradually stir in the hot beef stock and cook, stirring constantly, until the sauce is slightly thickened. Stir in the wine and parsley and bring again to a boil.

HOLLANDAISE SAUCE

*4 egg yolks
Juice of 1 lemon*

1 pound butter, melted

Beat the egg yolks lightly and stir in the lemon juice. Cook over simmering water, adding the melted butter little by little and whisking constantly with a wire whip until the sauce is thick. Add salt to taste.

BUSTER CRABS BÉARNAISE

(Brennan's Restaurant)

8 soft-shell crabs (two per person)

Remove the claws and legs and clean the crabs thoroughly. Season them with salt and pepper and cook them under a moderate broiler flame for about 5 minutes on each side. Serve on thin slices of toast and cover each crab with Béarnaise sauce.

BÉARNAISE SAUCE

4 egg yolks	1 teaspoon Lea & Perrins
Juice of 1 lemon	sauce
1 pound butter, melted	Pinch of cayenne
4 tablespoons chopped capers	Salt to taste
¼ cup chopped parsley	

In the top of a double boiler beat the egg yolks lightly and stir in the lemon juice. Cook over simmering water, whisking constantly with a wire whisk until the sauce begins to thicken. Whisk in the butter a little at a time. Remove the sauce from the fire and stir in the capers, parsley, Lea & Perrins sauce, cayenne and salt to taste.

BOILED RED FISH WITH SAUCE DE LERY

(Mrs. L. Perry Adams, née Helene Delery)

In a large kettle put 2 quarts water, 2 onions, sliced, 1 bay leaf, 12 sprays parsley, 2 sprigs thyme, 2 stalks celery with the leaves, 3 cloves garlic, 3 birdeye peppers, 1 lemon, quartered, 2 tablespoons wine vinegar and 4 teaspoons salt. Bring the water to a boil and simmer for 30 minutes. Add ½ cup olive oil.

Slash the sides of a 4 to 5 pound red snapper on both sides and cook the fish in the seasoned water for about 12 minutes, or until the flesh flakes from the bones. When done, remove the fish from the water, cool and discard the skin and bones. Arrange the pieces of fish on a platter, cover with Sauce de Lery and garnish with slices of hard-cooked eggs, thinly sliced cooked beets and sprays of parsley.

SAUCE DE LERY

6 hard-cooked eggs
1½ teaspoons dry mustard
1½ cups homemade mayon-
   naise

6 shallots, finely chopped
1½ teaspoons garlic oil
7 drops Tabasco
A few capers

Mash the egg yolks with the mustard and stir in the mayonnaise. Add the shallots, garlic oil and Tabasco. Chop the egg
whites finely and stir them into the sauce. Add capers and mix
well.

CREOLE OYSTERS

(Mrs. L. Perry Adams, née Helene Delery)

3 dozen large fresh oysters
3 tablespoons oyster liquor
3 tablespoons olive oil
2 tablespoons vinegar
2 cloves garlic, minced

1 tablespoon minced parsley
1 sprig thyme
3 shallots, minced
2 tablespoons minced onion
A few drops Tabasco

Shuck the oysters and drain them, reserving the liquor. Put
the oysters in a large-mouth jar, add the other ingredients and
chill in the refrigerator for 24 hours. Serve with large pieces of
buttered crisp crust from French bread.

OYSTER PIE

(Mrs. Edward Munson, Glenwood Plantation House)

Rich pie dough
1 tablespoon butter
1 tablespoon flour
1 onion, finely chopped
8 dozen oysters and their
   liquor
A pinch of thyme

1 bay leaf
Chopped parsley
Cayenne pepper and salt to
   taste
1 slice bread, grated
Butter
½ cup milk

Line a 2-quart glass baking dish with the pie dough and bake in a hot oven (450° F.) for about 5 minutes, or until the dough is set. Melt the butter and stir in the flour. Add the onion and cook until the onion is transparent. Stir in the liquor from the oysters and add the thyme, bay leaf, parsley, cayenne pepper and salt, and the bread crumbs and cook, stirring, until the sauce is slightly thickened.

Put the oysters into the baking dish, pour over them half the sauce and dot with butter. Cover with a thin layer of pie dough and cut an X-shaped hole in the center. Bake the pie in a hot oven (425° F.) for about 30 minutes, or until the crust is well browned. Add the milk to the remaining sauce and when the pie is almost done, put a funnel into the opening in the center of the pie and pour in as much of the sauce as the pie will hold. Reduce the oven temperature to 350° F. and cook for 10 minutes longer. If there is any sauce left over, serve it with the pie.

OYSTERS ROCKEFELLER

(Mrs. Mortimer Favrot and Roberta Chester Brown)

2 *dozen oysters*
2 *tablespoons finely chopped*
 green onion tops
2 *tablespoons finely chopped*
 parsley
1 *cup butter*

Salt, pepper and cayenne to
 taste
1 *cup finely chopped cooked*
 spinach
¼ *cup minced bacon*
Bread crumbs browned in
 butter

Wash the oysters thoroughly. Open the oysters, detaching them from their shells and put each oyster in the deep half of its shell. Mix the green onion tops and parsley with the butter and season well with salt, pepper and cayenne. Stir in the chopped spinach. Cover each oyster with a layer of this mixture and sprinkle with the minced bacon. Sprinkle sparingly with bread crumbs and arrange from 6 to 9 oysters in a shallow pie pan filled with ice cream salt to hold the shells in place and to preserve the heat. Bake the oysters in a hot oven (450° F.) for about 5 minutes, or until they begin to swell, and serve with hot crusty French bread.

OYSTER SPAGHETTI

(Mrs. J. P. Colligan)

4 tablespoons good fat or drippings
4 tablespoons flour
1 medium onion, chopped
1 can tomato sauce
2 stalks celery and celery leaves, chopped
2 cloves garlic, minced
½ sweet pepper, seeded and chopped
1 bay leaf
4 dozen oysters and their liquor
2 tablespoons chopped parsley
1 pound spaghetti

Heat the fat, stir in the flour and cook, stirring constantly, until the *roux* is dark brown. Add the onion and cook slowly until the onion is soft. Add the tomato sauce, celery, garlic, sweet pepper and bay leaf and stir in the oyster liquor. Simmer over a very low flame for at least 2 hours, but 6 is not too long. About 20 minutes before serving, add the oysters and parsley and cook for 10 minutes longer.

Cook the spaghetti in a large quantity of boiling salted water for about 20 minutes, or until done. Drain well, mix with the oyster mixture and let stand for 5 to 10 minutes before serving.

SHRIMP SAUCE PIQUANTE

(Eloise Carte)

3 large onions, finely chopped
2 tablespoons olive oil
2 tablespoons butter
2 tablespoons flour
1 can tomato sauce
2 cups hot water
2 pounds shrimp, shelled and deveined
2 tablespoons chopped green pepper
¼ cup chopped celery
1 clove garlic, minced

Sauté the onions in the oil until they are very soft and lightly browned. In a saucepan melt the butter, stir in the flour and cook, stirring, until the *roux* is well blended. Add the tomato sauce and cook, stirring, for a few minutes. Then stir in the water, the cooked onions, shrimp, green pepper, celery and garlic and simmer for 45 minutes. If the sauce is too thick, thin it with a little more hot water. Serves 4.

SHRIMP F.P.K.

(Hermann B. Deutsch)

Select about a dozen medium-size shrimp per person; more if the shrimp are small, and fewer if jumbo shrimp are used.

In a kettle put 2 quarts water. Add celery stalks, bay leaf, a scraped carrot, a few sprays of parsley, a pinch of dried basil or half a dozen leaves of fresh basil, an onion stuck with a couple of cloves, a seeded sweet pepper and a pod of hot pepper. Bring the water to a boil and simmer for 20 minutes. Add a package of any commercial crab-boil mixture or about 3 tablespoons of commercial pickling spices tied in a bag and simmer for 10 minutes longer. Simmer the shrimp in this courtbouillon for about 30 minutes, let them cool in the liquid and then shell them and remove the sand veins. Cut jumbo shrimp, if they are used, into serving pieces.

While the shrimp are cooling, simmer in sweet butter for each person to be served 1 length of scallion, shredded (not minced) making sure to use a length in which both the green and white portions are present. Simmer and toss the scallions until soft, then add for each length of green onion used 2 ounces red wine, using one of the heavier Burgundy or Pinot grape wines, and simmer until well blended. Add for each portion a scant teaspoon of soy sauce, stir well and season to taste with salt and a drop or so of Tabasco if needed. Finally, add enough dark rum to achieve a desirable flavor. It is impossible to give the exact quantities at this stage.

When the sauce is ready, drop the peeled shrimp into it, heat thoroughly and serve hot in sherbet or other similar glasses with bread sticks fried until golden in butter and sprinkled with a few drops of lemon juice.

SALMON LOAF

(Dorrie Blackstone)

2 *tablespoons butter*	1 *egg, well beaten*
A 1-*pound can red salmon*	*Salt, pepper and lemon juice*
1 *slice bread* 1½ *inches thick*	*to taste*
soaked in as much milk as	
it will absorb	

Put the butter in a 1-quart casserole and place the casserole in the oven, which is heating to 350° F. Discard the skin and bones from the salmon and mash the salmon with a fork. When the butter in the casserole is melted, remove from the oven and swirl the casserole to coat the sides and bottom thoroughly with the butter. Pour the remaining butter into the mashed salmon. Add the rest of the ingredients and mix well. Turn the mixture into the casserole and bake in the preheated oven for about 1 hour, or until lightly browned.

SOLE WITH SHRIMP AND MUSHROOM SAUCE

(Clara E. Wilson)

Salt and pepper	*Bread crumbs*
6 *slices filet of sole*	½ *cup* (¼ *pound*) *butter*
Milk	½ *cup hot water*

Salt and pepper the filets, dip in milk and then in crumbs. Arrange the filets in a buttered baking dish and dot with the butter. Add the water and bake in a moderate oven (350° F.) for about 40 minutes, or until the flesh flakes easily, basting often. Arrange the filets on a hot serving platter and cover with shrimp and mushroom sauce. Garnish with lemon slices and sprays of parsley.

SHRIMP AND MUSHROOM SAUCE

1 *package frozen shrimp*
2 *tablespoons butter*
2 *tablespoons flour*
2 *cups milk*
1 *can button mushrooms*
½ *cup sherry*

Cook the shrimp in boiling salted water for 20 minutes. Drain, shell and remove the sand veins. In a double boiler melt the butter and stir in the flour. Gradually stir in the milk and the liquor from the mushrooms and cook, stirring, until the sauce is smooth and thickened. Add the shrimp and mushrooms and cook over boiling water until very hot. Just before removing from the fire, stir in the wine.

RED SNAPPER MARGUERY

(Mrs. Mortimer Favrot and Roberta Chester Brown)

2 *pounds red snapper*
1 *can mushrooms*
1 *tablespoon chopped truffles*
½ *pound American cheese, grated*
3 *hard-cooked eggs, chopped*
2 *pounds shrimp, cooked and cleaned*
1 *dozen freshly shucked oysters if desired*
2 *tablespoons butter*
1½ *tablespoons flour*
1 *cup hot cream*
Salt, *pepper and cayenne to taste*
1 *tablespoon minced onion*
1 *tablespoon chopped parsley*
1 *bay leaf*
2 *tablespoons finely chopped green pepper*

Simmer the red snapper (or his ilk) in salted water for about 15 minutes, or until the flesh flakes from the bones. Cool the fish on ice and break the flesh into pieces, discarding the skin and bones. Mix the red fish with the mushrooms, truffles, cheese, eggs, shrimp and oysters, if the latter are used, and turn the mixture into a buttered baking dish. In a saucepan heat the butter until it bubbles and stir in the flour. Stir in gradually the hot cream and cook, stirring, until the sauce thickens. Add salt, pepper and cayenne to taste, stir in the onion, parsley, bay leaf and green pepper and cook for 2 minutes longer. Pour the sauce into the baking dish and bake in a moderate oven (350° F.) for about 1 hour.

TROUT MEUNIÈRE

(Mrs. Edward Munson, Glenwood Plantation House)

Dip filet of trout in milk, seasoned with salt and pepper. Then dip the filet into flour so that both sides are well covered. Melt a generous quantity of butter in a frying pan and when it is hot sauté the filet in it until golden on both sides. Put the filet on a serving plate. Add a little lemon juice to the butter remaining in the frying pan and pour the juice over the trout.

Main Dishes

2. MEAT AND POULTRY

CHICKEN POMPADOUR (for 4)

(Brennan's Restaurant)

Put the breast meat of 2 tender chickens in a saucepan with 3 shallots, chopped, and 3 truffles, sliced. Sprinkle with salt and pepper and add 1 cup champagne and ½ cup chicken stock. Bring the liquid to a boil and simmer for about 30 minutes, or until the chicken meat is tender. Remove the breasts to a serving plate and stir into the sauce 3 egg yolks lightly beaten with ½ cup heavy cream and a little of the hot sauce. Cook the sauce for about 3 minutes, stirring constantly, and being careful that it does not boil. Add 1 tablespoon butter and when the butter is melted pour the sauce over the chicken and sprinkle with a few drops of lemon juice. Garnish with cooked vegetables.

CHICKEN AND OKRA

(Mrs. Kenneth T. Price)

2 *pounds okra*	*Salt and pepper*
10 *tablespoons shortening*	1 *onion, chopped*
A 2½ *pound tender chicken,*	½ *cup water*
disjointed	

Do not wash the okra. Wipe it with a clean cloth and slice it thinly. Cook the okra in 6 tablespoons of the shortening over a gentle flame until it stops stringing, stirring occasionally.

In another pot melt the remaining shortening. Sprinkle the

chicken with salt and pepper and sauté it slowly in the hot fat until golden brown on all sides and half cooked. Add the onion and continue to cook until the chicken and onion are tender. Add the chicken and onion to the okra. Rinse the chicken pot with the water and add it to the chicken and okra. If the mixture is too thick, a little more water may be added. Heat thoroughly and serve over fluffy cooked rice.

CHICKEN WITH TOMATOES

(Mrs. Lester Montegut)

1 large stewing hen, cut into serving pieces	1 onion, ground
Salt and pepper	6 cloves garlic, minced
½ cup oil	Liver and gizzard of the chicken, ground
2 tablespoons flour	1 No. 2 can tomatoes, strained to remove the seeds
1 green pepper, seeded and ground	

Sprinkle the hen with salt and pepper and sauté it in the oil until it is golden brown on all sides. Remove the chicken and stir the flour into the oil remaining in the pot. Cook the *roux* for about 5 minutes, or until it is browned. Add the pepper, onion and garlic and continue to cook for about 5 minutes longer. Add the liver and gizzard and the tomatoes and simmer for 30 minutes. Return the chicken to the pot, cover and cook until the chicken is tender. Serve with cooked rice, French bread and red wine.

CHICKEN RICE DINNER

(Mrs. V. R. Hoag)

A 3-pound chicken cut into serving pieces	1 onion, chopped
Salt and pepper	¼ cup chopped sweet green pepper
2 tablespoons good fat	1 cup sliced mushrooms
1 cup washed rice	

Sprinkle the chicken with salt and pepper and brown the pieces in a heavy skillet in the fat. Add enough boiling water to just cover the chicken, cover the skillet and simmer for 20 minutes, or until the chicken is almost tender. Add the rice, onion, pepper and mushrooms and correct the seasoning with salt. Bake in a moderate oven (350° F.) for about 1½ hours. Serves 8.

PARLOW*

(Mrs. Richard Leche)

Melt 2 tablespoons sweet butter or olive oil in a heavy iron kettle and add ⅓ cup each of chopped scallions, or green onions (white and green parts both), chopped celery (stalk and leaves), and minced sweet pepper and 3 tablespoons finely chopped parsley. Simmer the vegetables in the butter until they are soft, but not brown, and set aside. In a skillet brown a baking or stewing chicken, cut into serving pieces, in butter or olive oil. When well browned add the chicken to the vegetables in the kettle and cover chicken and vegetables with chicken stock or water. Cover the kettle tightly and simmer for 2 hours, or until the chicken is quite tender. Season the pot liquor with salt and pepper to taste. Now sprinkle into the liquor, from a spoon, corn meal (preferably the water-ground kind from which the germ is not removed) until the pot liquor is the consistency of thick mush. Serve. Quartered hard-cooked eggs may be added with the corn meal if desired.

* "Parlow" is a pronouncing corruption of "pilau"—just as "gringo" is a corruption of "green grow" stemming from a song popular among the American soldiers during the Mexican War, which began "Green grow the rashes-O!"

Pilau is a Turkish and/or Persian dish. The name is applied to any cut-up fowl that is cooked with cracked grain. In Turkey or Persia the grain is invariably rice or cracked wheat. Hereabouts it is corn meal.

TURKEY À LA ALFEREZ

(This recipe, though given me by Hermann B. Deutsch, is, generally speaking, that of Enrique Alferez, the noted sculptor, who prepared it for a gathering on a little farm in Jefferson Parish.)

The prerequisites for this recipe are a dishpan, a pit about 18 inches deep, 2 feet wide and 3 feet long, floored with loose bricks, plenty of firewood, a dozen large-sized boulders, a long-handled shovel, 3 large cabbages, a turkey trussed and stuffed for roasting, and at least 8 hours.

Begin about 2 A.M. by building a brisk wood fire in the brick-floored pit and when a good bed of coals has been achieved, put in the boulders and cover with more wood fuel, feeding the flames for approximately 4 hours.

While this is going on, separate the cabbage leaves from their central core, wash them and lay them in a bed of about 3 to 4 inches thick in the bottom and along the sides of the dishpan. Slice a lemon over the cabbage, sprinkle with salt and empty over the leaves ½ cup of Worcestershire sauce and a 6-ounce bottle of your favorite cola beverage or a cup of sweet cider. Tuck 2 or 3 red pepper pods among the cabbage leaves, then lay the turkey, breast up, upon the bedding and cover it with more layers of cabbage leaves to a depth of about 3 inches. Wring a clean burlap bag out in clear water and tie it over the top of the pan, fastening it well in place with wire, and leaving a length of wire extending from each handle of the dishpan.

Now take the long-handled shovel and shovel fire, embers, boulders and all out of the pit, making it reasonably clean, and giving voice to suitable secular comments when you realize how short the shovel handle really is.

Carefully lower the dishpan down upon the floor of hot bricks, and cover it well with green twigs, green weeds, or any other such insulating material. (In Louisiana, we use fresh Spanish moss for this.) On top, place the hot boulders, but none of the coals or embers, and then fill in the pit completely with earth, sealing it effectively and providing what is really a sort of fireless cooker.

Leave the turkey buried for 4 to 5 hours. It can't burn. The worst that can happen to it is that it can cook to pieces. Exhume it carefully in the presence of the guests, for the delectable aromas that accompany its resurrection serve as a magnificent appetizer. The cabbage leaves will have cooked down, and the dishpan will be half full of a delicious rich brown gravy; so serve with plenty of crusty French bread or "frog loaves" for sopping purposes.

BONED GOOSE

(Hermann B. Deutsch)

It is assumed that the reader can either bone a goose or have it boned. While not exactly a question of major surgical skills, it is not the sort of technique which can be picked up from one of of those insert-tab-B-in-slot-7 treatises.

To prepare the stuffing, run 2 pounds lean veal three times through the finest blade of the meat grinder; oftener if necessary to convert the meat into a smooth paste. Blend this meat paste with a cream sauce, thickened and enriched with egg yolks and well chilled. Add to the blend a sprinkling of whole-half pecan meats, canned button mushrooms, minced parsley, and salt and white pepper to taste.

Spread the boned goose skin-side down on a cloth and spread the surface with a thick layer of the meat mixture. Arrange on this several halved poultry livers and, using the cloth, bring the two edges of the boned goose's back together into a roll, wrapped in the cloth. Tie the ends securely and tie the goose at intervals along its length. Put the cloth-wrapped roll in a kettle and cover it with chicken stock, seasoned to taste. Bring the stock to a boil and simmer the goose roll for 1½ hours. Remove the roll from the broth and unwrap. Serve as desired, slicing it at the table, or placing the slices on a heated platter and covering them with *marchand de vin* (see Index) or any similar sauce. Garnish to suit individual taste.

GRILLADES

(Mrs. L. Perry Adams, née Helene Delery)

Round steak of beef or veal cut ½ inch thick

2 tablespoons bacon drippings or good fat

1 tablespoon flour

2 medium onions, finely chopped

1 clove garlic, minced

1 green pepper, seeded and chopped

2 cups peeled and chopped tomatoes

1 tablespoon chopped parsley

2 sprigs thyme

Salt and pepper to taste

Cut the meat into individual serving pieces. In a large skillet heat the fat and in it brown the pieces of meat on both sides and set aside. In the fat remaining in the skillet brown the flour, onions and garlic. When brown add the green pepper, tomatoes, parsley and thyme and stir until the mixture is well blended. Return the meat to the skillet, season with salt and pepper, cover, and cook over a low flame for 1½ to 2 hours. If the gravy becomes too thick, stir in a little hot water. Serve with rice or grits.

GRILLADES PANNES

(Mrs. Edward Munson, Glenwood Plantation House)

2 veal rounds

1 egg

1 tablespoon water

Salt and pepper

Toasted bread crumbs

Good fat

Cut the rounds into pieces about 4 inches square. Beat the egg lightly with the water and salt and pepper. Dip each piece of meat in the egg mixture, then in the toasted crumbs, making sure that both sides are well covered. Sauté each piece in hot fat until they are golden brown on both sides.

Arrange the meat on a warm serving platter and serve with creamed Irish potatoes. Be sure to select only *veal* rounds for this dish.

TOURNEDOS LABICHE

(Brennan's Restaurant)

Use the center cut of a filet of beef (two small uniform slices per person) and grill them to taste. Top each slice with a slice of grilled tomato and put into a moderate oven so that the juices of the tomato will flavor the meat. Serve with fresh mushroom sauce.

MUSHROOM SAUCE

1 bunch shallots or green onions, finely chopped
1 teaspoon finely chopped garlic
2 tablespoons butter
2 tablespoons flour
4 cups beef stock
1 pound mushrooms, quartered
1 cup red wine
1 tablespoon chopped parsley

Sauté the shallots and garlic in the butter until golden. Stir in the flour and gradually stir in the beef stock. Cook, stirring, until the sauce is slightly thickened. Add the mushrooms and red wine and simmer for 8 minutes. Stir in the parsley.

DAUBE GLACÉE

(Mrs. Mortimer Favrot and Roberta Chester Brown)

2 large knuckles or 2 or 3 calf's or pig's feet
Celery tops
Bay leaves
10 cloves
1 clove garlic

1 teaspoon whole black
  pepper
¾ tablespoon salt
3 pounds lean beef

2 large onions
2 carrots
2 tablespoons fat

Cover the bones with water, add the celery tops, bay leaves, cloves, garlic and whole black pepper, all tied in a bag, and simmer for about 3 hours. Brown the meat with the onions and carrots in the fat, add them to the bones and cook for 2 hours longer. Discard the spice bag, shred the meat and put it in a mold. Strain the stock and add more salt and pepper if necessary. Cover the meat with the stock, cool, then chill in the refrigerator for 24 hours. All the grease will rise to the top of the mold. Scrape it off when you are ready to serve your *daube*, and invert it on the serving platter.

DAUBE GLACÉE

(Mrs. L. Perry Adams, née Helene Delery)

DAUBE

3 pounds top round of beef
2 tablespoons wine vinegar
3 cloves garlic
1 tablespoon chopped parsley
2 medium onions, sliced
1 bay leaf
2 birdeye peppers
3 sprigs thyme
2 tablespoons shortening
1 tablespoon tomato paste
3 carrots, sliced
Salt to taste

JELLY

3 pig's feet
2 calf's feet
2 veal joints
3 birdeye peppers
2 carrots
2 medium onions
3 cloves garlic
1 bay leaf
3 sprigs thyme
12 sprays parsley
⅛ teaspoon allspice
2½ quarts water
Salt to taste

Put the beef in a bowl with the vinegar, garlic, parsley, onions, bay leaf, peppers and thyme. Cover the bowl and store in the refrigerator overnight.

In the morning sauté the beef in the shortening in a heavy kettle until it is a dark brown on all sides. Add the tomato paste, the carrots, 1 cup water and the seasonings in which the meat marinated overnight. Cover the kettle and cook the meat very slowly for 3 to 4 hours, adding a little water now and then when necessary. The meat must be tender enough to shred.

In another pot, put all the ingredients for the jelly. Bring the water to a boil and simmer for 3 to 4 hours, or until the meat falls from the bones. Strain, reserving the liquid, and remove the meat from the bones. Shred the beef, add the reserved liquid and the meat removed from the bones and simmer for 30 minutes longer. Cool and remove the fat from the surface. Turn into molds or dishes and put in the refrigerator to jell.

MEAT PORCUPINES

(Mrs. T. P. Baker)

1½ pounds ground beef
¾ cup raw rice
2 teaspoons salt
¾ teaspoon black pepper
½ nutmeg, grated
1 medium onion, chopped

½ sweet pepper, seeded and chopped
2 tablespoons bacon drippings
3 8-ounce cans tomato sauce
½ teaspoon celery seed

Mix together the beef, rice, salt, pepper and nutmeg and form the mixture into 14 or 15 small balls. Put the balls in a 2-quart casserole. Sauté the onion and bell pepper until tender in the bacon drippings and add the tomato sauce and celery seed. Bring the sauce to a boil, pour it over the meat balls and cover the casserole. Cook in a moderate oven (350° F.) for 1 hour.

STUFFED BELL PEPPERS

(Nelson "Buster" Williams)

½ *pound ground meat*	1 *clove garlic*
1 *cup minced celery*	*Salt and black and red pepper*
1 *small onion, minced*	1½ *cups soft bread crumbs*
6 *large sweet peppers, halved*	*Dry bread crumbs*
lengthwise and seeded	*Butter*

Put the meat, celery and onion into a saucepan and cook it over a gentle flame for 10 minutes, stirring frequently. Add 3 of the peppers, finely chopped, and the garlic, season to taste with salt and black and red pepper and cook for 8 to 10 minutes longer. Stir in the soft bread crumbs and stuff the other 3 peppers with this mixture. Sprinkle with dry bread crumbs, dot with butter and bake the peppers in a hot oven (425° F.) for 12 to 15 minutes. Serves 6.

STUFFED BELL PEPPERS

(Mrs. Lester Montegut)

2 *tablespoons olive oil*	8 *slices toasted bread*
2 *tablespoons flour*	*Milk*
1 *large onion, finely chopped*	*Salt and pepper*
6 *cloves garlic, chopped*	3 *sweet peppers*
1 *cup ground meat*	

In a saucepan heat the oil, stir in the flour and cook, stirring, for about 5 minutes, or until the *roux* is browned. Add the onion, garlic and ground meat and brown well. Moisten the toast with milk, squeeze out the excess moisture and add the toast to the meat mixture. Mix well and cook for 15 minutes longer.

Cut the peppers in half lengthwise and remove the seeds. Stuff the shells with the stuffing and put the peppers in a baking pan containing a small amount of water. Bake the peppers in a hot oven (425° F.) for 15 minutes.

HAM LOAF

(Dorrie Blackstone)

½ pound ground ham   1 egg, beaten
½ pound ground beef   ¾ cup milk
½ pound ground pork   ½ cup tomato soup
½ cup cracker crumbs   ½ teaspoon salt

Mix all the ingredients together well and pack the mixture lightly into a buttered loaf pan. Bake in a moderate oven (350° F.) for about 1½ hours, basting frequently with the following glaze.

GLAZE

Bring to a boil ⅓ cup each of vinegar and water and 1 cup brown sugar and simmer for 10 minutes.

MEAT LOAF

(Margaret Woodland)

2 pounds ground beef   1½ tablespoons horseradish
10 tablespoons tapioca   mustard
1 onion, finely chopped   1 tablespoon A-1 sauce
2 eggs, beaten   Salt and pepper
Juice of 1 lemon   1 cup hot water

Mix all the ingredients well, adding the water last. Turn into a buttered loaf pan and bake in a moderate oven (350° F.) for 45 minutes. Cool for about 15 minutes, then slice. Makes 8 to 10 large slices.

BOUDAN

(Mrs. Forestier Monceaux)

2 *pounds fat pork, ground*
1 *pound pork liver, ground*
1 *large onion, chopped*
½ *cup chopped celery*
1 *cup chopped green onion*
  tops

1 *cup chopped parsley*
6 *to 8 cups water*
2 *cups cooked rice*
Salt and pepper

Combine all the ingredients except the rice and salt and pepper in a heavy pot, bring the water to a boil and simmer for about 1 hour, adding a little water from time to time if necessary. Remove the mixture from the fire, stir in the cooked rice and season to taste with salt and pepper. Stuff the mixture into sausage casings, tie the casings in sausage lengths and cook in simmering water for 10 minutes. Serve the sausages hot or cold.

CALALOU*

(Mary Land)

3 *pounds minced cooked pork*
  (*or other meat, fish or*
  fowl)
3 *cloves garlic, minced*
4 *green peppers, seeded and*
  minced
1 *large eggplant, peeled and*
  minced
1 *pound young okra, minced*

2 *pounds fresh scraped or 2*
  cans corn kernels
6 *green onions, minced*
4 *cups minced pumpkin*
4 *quarts stock*
2 *cups minced parsley*
2 *cups minced celery*
4 *cucumbers, peeled and*
  minced

* *Calalou* was brought to Louisiana during the period of commerce between the territory of Louisiana and the French West Indies. The *calalou* of Martinique was identical with that of the Louisiana colonists with the exception of the addition of filé powder—a touch supplied by the Choctaw Indians of Louisiana.

Put all the ingredients, except the parsley, celery and cucumbers, in a heavy iron pot and bring the liquid to a boil. Cover the kettle and simmer for 2 to 3 hours. When ready to serve season to taste with salt and pepper and add the parsley, celery and cucumbers. Serve with cooked rice and sprinkle with filé powder.

GIBLET AND OYSTER DRESSING FOR CHICKEN OR DUCK

(Nelson "Buster" Williams)

½ cup Wesson oil
3 tablespoons flour
1 onion, minced
½ pound chicken giblets, chopped
½ cup chopped celery
1 sweet pepper, seeded and finely chopped
1 pint oysters

2 cups water
2 cloves garlic, minced
2 tablespoons Lea & Perrins sauce
Pepper
1 tablespoon minced green onion tops
2 tablespoons minced parsley
2 cups cooked rice

In a skillet heat the oil, stir in the flour and cook until the *roux* is browned. Add the onion and simmer over a low flame for 5 minutes.

Put the giblets in a saucepan with water to cover and simmer for 15 minutes. Add the celery and sweet pepper and cook for 5 minutes longer.

Combine the two mixtures, add the oysters and water and simmer for about 10 minutes. Add the garlic, Lea & Perrins sauce and a dash of black pepper and simmer for another 10 minutes. Add the onion tops, parsley and rice, mix well and simmer for 5 minutes longer.

MUSHROOM STEAK SAUCE (RUSTY GRAVY)

(Nelson "Buster" Williams)

⅓ cup butter
⅓ cup Lea & Perrins sauce
Juice of ½ lemon

1 teaspoon prepared mustard
⅓ cup A-1 sauce
2 cups sliced mushrooms

In a saucepan melt the butter and add the Lea & Perrins sauce and the lemon. Mix together the mustard and A-1 sauce until smooth and stir into the sauce. Cover and cook over a slow fire for 5 to 8 minutes. Add the mushrooms and simmer for 5 minutes longer. Serves 4 to 6.

CHICKEN BARBECUE BASTING SAUCE AND GIBLET SAUCE

(Claude "Parrain" Colomb)

2 cups olive oil
1 tablespoon prepared mustard
2 pounds onions, finely chopped

1 sweet pepper, finely chopped
1 celery heart, finely chopped
3 cloves garlic, minced
Salt, red and black pepper to taste

Combine the oil, mustard, onions, sweet pepper, celery and garlic. Heat to a simmer and cook until the mixture cooks down to a paste. Season the paste to taste with salt and pepper and use to baste chickens on the grill, swabbing the sauce on the chickens frequently with a small brush.

Chicken barbecue is, of course, not complete without the giblet sauce. This is made by using the livers and gizzards from the chickens and adding 2 pounds ground meat: Chop the gizzards, mix with the ground meat and sauté in 2 tablespoons olive oil until brown. Add enough water to cover and simmer until the gizzards are tender. Add what is left over from the basting sauce and correct the seasoning. Add the chopped chicken livers and simmer for 5 minutes longer. When ready to serve, add finely chopped celery, green onion tops and parsley. Serve on bread or buns which have been split and toasted.

BARBECUE GLAZING SAUCE

(Hermann B. Deutsch)

Heat ¼ cup olive oil with ¼ cup sweet butter and in it simmer ½ cup minced shallots and three medium cloves garlic, either finely minced or crushed through a garlic press. Use both green and white portions of the shallots in the proportion of one-third green to two-thirds white. Drain two No. 2 cans tomatoes, reserving only the pulp, and mince a dozen fresh leaves of sweet basil, adding this (or in default of it, a level teaspoon of dried basil) and ½ teaspoon marjoram to the simmering garlic and shallots. Purée the drained pulp of the canned tomatoes by rubbing it through a sieve, passing it through a food mill, or putting it through an electric blender, and add the purée to the butter-garlic-shallot-spice mixture, along with ½ cup dark corn syrup, cane syrup or honey, or one loosely packed cup of dark brown sugar. Add the juice and pulp of two limes (or one lemon if limes are unavailable). Add ¼ cup each of finely minced celery leaves and parsley, and season with salt and red pepper to taste (minced or crushed birdeye peppers picked at the bronze stage, before they become bright red, for preference). Stir in ¼ to ⅓ cup light or dark rum, and cook in top of a double boiler for half an hour or more. Before using, add a little more rum and correct the seasoning with salt and a few drops of Tabasco sauce, if needed.

To use:

Sear the meat to be barbecued slowly over the coals, and when a crust has been formed, swab the sauce generously over the turning meat every few minutes with a small sink mop. In practice, the best results are obtained by swabbing the top side of the meat first, then turning, and immediately swabbing the opposite side. Naturally, a very large barbecue will require more sauce, but the proportions here given can readily be multiplied to yield a sufficient quantity of the glazing sauce. What is left can later be served with the sliced meat in a sauce boat.

BEAN BARBECUE SAUCE

(B. A. Axelrad)

1 large onion, chopped
2 cloves garlic, minced
½ sweet pepper, seeded and chopped
4 tablespoons bacon drippings
2 cups melted beef fat or bacon drippings
4 tablespoons vinegar
2 cups beef stock or water
1 tablespoon salt
1 teaspoon black pepper
2 teaspoons Louisiana Red Hot Sauce

8 tablespoons Worcestershire sauce
½ cup tomato juice
1 small can Spanish-style tomato sauce
½ bottle (7 ounces) Chili Club Pepper Catsup
1 tablespoon mustard
1 tablespoon prepared horse-radish
1 bay leaf
Dash of allspice
2 hot green peppers

In a large pot put the onion, garlic, sweet pepper and the 4 tablespoons bacon drippings and cook slowly, stirring constantly, for 5 to 7 minutes. Add all the rest of the ingredients and cook slowly for 1 hour. One and one-half quarts of the sauce is sufficient for four pounds of beans. The sauce will keep if stored in a glass container, and the sauce may be used for beans or stew.

For beans, dried pinto beans are recommended. Add equal amounts of sauce and water sufficient to cover the beans by several inches. Cook in a covered pot on a slow fire for about 5 hours or overnight in a deep well. Do not pre-soak the beans. During the cooking, add more water-sauce mixture if necessary and, near the end of the cooking, remove the cover to attain the desired consistency of sauce and beans.

Vegetable Dishes

CARROTS AND ONIONS BROUSSARD

(Eve Broussard)

1 medium bunch of carrots, sliced
2 medium onions, chopped

2 tablespoons bacon drippings
Salt and pepper to taste

Barely cover the vegetables with water and add the bacon drippings and salt and pepper. Cover tightly and cook for at least 2 hours, or until most of the water is gone and the vegetables are *very* soft.

"Gromom" Gautreaux used to brown 4 pork chops per bunch of carrots and add them when the vegetables were about half cooked. She stirred them from time to time during the rest of the cooking.

CORN SOUFFLÉ ABBEVILLE

(Nelson "Buster" Williams)

2 tablespoons butter
1 can cream-style corn
1 onion, minced
1 teaspoon sugar
1 teaspoon salt

¼ cup finely chopped green pepper
⅔ cup water
½ cup milk
2 eggs, separated

In a saucepan melt the butter, add the corn, onion, sugar, salt, green pepper and water and simmer for 6 to 8 minutes. Stir in the milk and remove from the fire. Stir in the beaten egg yolks and fold in the egg whites, beaten until stiff. Turn the batter into a buttered soufflé dish and bake in a moderate oven (350° F.) for 8 to 10 minutes.

CORN CREOLE

(Mrs. Lester Montegut)

1 small sweet green pepper, seeded
1 large onion, sliced
5 cloves garlic
3 tablespoons olive oil
1 No. 2 can corn kernels
1 egg
2 cups milk
½ cup corn meal
Salt and pepper to taste

Put the green pepper, onion and garlic through a meat grinder and sauté the mixture in the oil until the onion is golden. Add the corn and stir in the egg beaten with the milk. Bring almost to a boil and stir in the corn meal and salt and pepper to taste. Cook, stirring, until the mixture thickens, turn it into a buttered casserole and bake in a slow oven (250° F.) for about 1 hour.

RED BEANS CREOLE

(Mrs. L. Perry Adams, née Helene Delery)

1 pound red beans
1 large ham bone
1 pound pickled pork
2 onions, finely chopped
1 tablespoon chopped parsley
⅓ teaspoon baking soda
⅓ teaspoon prepared mustard
Boiling water to cover

Wash and pick over the beans and soak them overnight in water to cover. In the morning drain the beans and put them in a bean pot with the rest of the ingredients. Simmer the beans slowly for 2 to 3 hours, or until the meat is tender and the beans are soft. Add more water if necessary during the cooking and stir frequently. Before serving mash some of the beans to make a creamy gravy and serve with cooked rice.

RICE

(Mrs. L. Perry Adams, née Helene Delery)

1 cup long-grained rice	1 teaspoon sugar
1½ cups water	1 teaspoon vinegar
1 teaspoon salt	1 teaspoon butter

Pick over the rice and wash it thoroughly in several changes of cold water. In a heavy saucepan combine the water, salt, sugar, vinegar and butter and bring the water to a boil. Gradually stir in the rice and continue to stir until the water boils again. Turn the heat very low, cover the saucepan tightly and cook for about 30 minutes, or until the rice is tender and the water is absorbed. This rice should be dry enough so that each grain stands apart.

SPINACH SOUFFLÉ

(Mrs. Edward Munson, Glenwood Plantation House)

2 tablespoons butter	¼ cup grated cheese
3 tablespoons flour	½ teaspoon salt
2 cups hot milk	A dash of pepper
6 eggs, separated	½ teaspoon cream of tartar
1 cup cooked, chopped spinach	

In a saucepan melt the butter and stir in the flour. Gradually stir in the milk and cook, stirring, until the sauce is smooth and thickened. Add the beaten egg yolks and stir over a low heat for 3 minutes, being careful not to let the sauce boil. Remove the sauce from the fire and stir in the spinach, cheese, salt and pepper. Set aside to cool. Beat the egg whites until they are foamy. Add the cream of tartar and continue to beat until the whites are stiff and dry. Fold the whites into the spinach mixture, turn into a buttered baking dish and bake in a moderate oven (350° F.) for 35 to 40 minutes. Serve immediately.

SWEET POTATO PONE*

(Mrs. Edward Munson, Glenwood Plantation House)

4 eggs, well beaten	1 cup milk
1 cup brown sugar	1 cup molasses
½ cup melted butter	½ teaspoon grated nutmeg
4 large sweet potatoes, peeled and grated	½ teaspoon ground cloves
	½ teaspoon ground cinnamon
Grated peel of 1 orange	Pinch of salt
Grated peel of 1 lemon	

Combine the eggs, sugar, melted butter, sweet potatoes and the fruit peels and mix well. Stir in the milk, molasses, spices and salt and beat thoroughly. Turn the mixture into a buttered baking dish and bake in a slow oven (325° F.) for 1 hour. Serve hot or cold, cut in slices.

CAULIFLOWER

(Mrs. Richard Leche)

Wash and trim a large white cauliflower, leaving a circle of the green outside leaves around it. Simmer the cauliflower in water to cover for about 20 minutes, or until tender. Drain the

* This is an old plantation recipe given me by my husband's mammy.

cauliflower, put it in the center of a heated platter, and sprinkle it with salt and pepper. Surround the cauliflower with freshly cooked artichoke hearts and hot sliced carrots and beets and pour over it the following sauce.

DRESSING FOR COOKED VEGETABLES

⅔ cup cracker crumbs
½ cup grated Parmesan
   cheese
½ cup finely chopped pecans

2 canned pimientos, finely
   chopped
¼ cup melted butter
1 can sliced mushrooms

In a small bowl mix the crumbs, cheese, pecans and pimientos. Stir in the melted butter and mix well. Heat the mushrooms in their own juice, add to the crumb mixture and mix lightly. Pour the sauce over the cauliflower.

Cooked broccoli is equally delicious served with this dressing.

BAKED CUSHAW

(Mrs. Richard Leche)

1 cushaw*
1 cup water
½ cup butter

Sugar to taste
Cinnamon
Rum or bourbon or brandy

Cut the cushaw into pieces, discard the seeds and peel the pieces. Put the cushaw in a kettle with the water, bring to a boil and simmer for 30 minutes, mashing occasionally with a potato masher. Stir in the butter, sugar and a sprinkling of cinnamon and continue to cook for about 30 minutes longer, or until the cushaw is free of excess moisture. Put the cushaw into individual

* In areas where cushaw cannot be obtained, pumpkin or squash can be fixed in this way, though it is not as good as cushaw, which has its own distinctive flavor.

ramekins and pour 1 teaspoon rum, bourbon or brandy over the top of each. Sprinkle each with 1 teaspoon sugar and place the ramekins in a shallow pan containing ½ inch of hot water. Bake the cushaw in a hot oven (450° F.) for 20 minutes, or until a crust is formed on top. Remove from the oven and keep the ramekins in the pan of water until ready to serve.

EGGPLANT RICE DRESSING

(Wilbert Miller)

1 large eggplant, peeled and chopped	6 cloves garlic, minced
1 cup chopped celery	1½ pounds ground lean pork
2 sweet peppers, seeded and chopped	Salt and pepper
1 large onion, chopped	3 cups cooked rice
	Bread crumbs
	Butter

Put the eggplant, celery, peppers, onion and garlic in a saucepan with water to cover, bring to a boil and simmer until the vegetables are tender. Sauté the meat in its own fat until it is brown and thoroughly cooked. Add the vegetables with their liquid, mix well and season to taste with salt and pepper. Stir in the rice and turn the mixture into a buttered casserole. Sprinkle with bread crumbs, dot with butter and bake in a moderate oven (350° F.) for about 10 minutes, or until the crumbs are browned.

Salads and Dressings

GREEN SALAD

(Mrs. L. Perry Adams, née Helene Delery)

Mixed greens, washed and
   dried—chicory, lettuce,
   watercress, parsley
1 celery heart, chopped
Cooked hearts of artichokes
Hearts of palm, sliced
1 avocado, peeled and sliced

2 egg yolks
9 tablespoons olive oil
Garlic salt
Pinch of sugar
Salt and pepper
1 tablespoon garlic wine
   vinegar

In a salad bowl combine the mixed greens, celery, artichoke hearts, hearts of palm, and the avocado. In a small bowl beat the egg yolks and gradually beat in the olive oil. Add the seasonings and beat in the vinegar a few drops at a time. Pour the dressing over the salad, toss lightly and serve with garlic bread Varursia.

JACKSON SALAD FOR 4

(Brennan's Restaurant)

8 strips crisply fried bacon,
   crumbled
4 hard-cooked eggs, minced
4 tablespoons wine vinegar
1 tablespoon Lea & Perrins
   sauce

5 tablespoons olive oil
Juice of 1 lemon
Salt, pepper, paprika
Crisp salad greens, washed,
   dried and chilled

Combine the bacon and eggs and add the vinegar, Lea & Perrins sauce, olive oil and lemon juice. Blend well and season to taste with salt, pepper and paprika. Mix the dressing and greens together lightly.

OKRA SALAD

(Mrs. Edward Munson, Glenwood Plantation House)

Select 4 dozen small tender pods of okra. Wash the okra well and trim the ends. Cook the okra slowly in 1 quart simmering water with 1 teaspoon salt for about 15 minutes, or until the okra is tender. Drain and cool. Pour French dressing over the okra and chill in the refrigerator. Serve on lettuce leaves.

TOMATO AND CREAM CHEESE SALAD

(Clara E. Wilson)

2 *large cans tomatoes*	*Cold water*
1 *bay leaf*	4 *3-ounce packages Phila-*
½ *onion, chopped*	*delphia cream cheese*
½ *teaspoon salt*	*Cream*
1 *teaspoon sugar*	*Lettuce*
Gelatin	*French dressing*

Cook the tomatoes, bay leaf, onion, salt and sugar until the onion is tender. Strain through a fine sieve and measure. To each pint of juice, add 1 tablespoon gelatin, softened in ½ cup cold water, and stir over a low flame until the gelatin is dissolved. Turn the juice into a mold rinsed in cold water and put in the refrigerator to set.

When the aspic is set, mash the cream cheese and beat in enough heavy cream to make a thick creamy sauce. Soften 1 tablespoon gelatin in 2 tablespoons cold water for 5 minutes and stir over simmering water until the gelatin is dissolved. Add the gelatin to the cream cheese and mix thoroughly. Spread the cheese mixture on top of the tomato aspic and return the aspic to the refrigerator until the cheese topping is set. To serve, turn the aspic out onto a chilled serving platter, surround with lettuce leaves, and pour a little French dressing on the greens.

PINEAPPLE ROQUEFORT CHEESE SALAD

(Mrs. Frederick J. Nehrbass)

1 package lime Jello	½ teaspoon salt
1 tablespoon gelatin softened in 2 tablespoons cold water	½ cup chopped celery
	½ cup chopped stuffed olives
½ cup hot water	1 cup drained, crushed
1 cup canned pineapple juice	pineapple
1 tablespoon vinegar or lemon juice	¼ to ½ pound crumbled Roquefort cheese, to taste

Dissolve the jello and gelatin in the hot water. Add the pineapple juice, vinegar or lemon juice, salt, celery, olives and crushed pineapple and chill until slightly thickened. Add the cheese, turn into individual molds and chill until firm. Unmold on crisp lettuce leaves and serve with homemade mayonnaise.

SHRIMP ASPIC

(As served at the Simon Wile home in Shreveport)

2 pounds raw shrimp, shelled and deveined	2 tablespoons chopped capers
4 tablespoons gelatin	1 tablespoon Lea & Perrins sauce
1 cup cold water	2 tablespoons tarragon vinegar
3 avocados, peeled and sliced or diced	2 tablespoons grated onion and juice
French dressing	Salt and pepper
6 hard-cooked eggs, chopped	
2 cups chopped celery	

Wash the shrimp and cook them for 15 minutes in 1 quart boiling water to which are added 2 cloves garlic, 1 small onion, 1 tablespoon red pepper, salt, ½ lemon, sliced, 2 bay leaves, 2 whole cloves and 12 peppercorns. Cool the shrimp in the liquid, then drain them, reserving the liquor. It should measure 1 quart. If not, add enough water to make a quart of liquid. Soak the gelatin in the cold water for 5 minutes, add the shrimp liquor and heat, stirring, until the gelatin is dissolved. Cool.

Cover the bottom of 12 individual molds with a little of the cool but still liquid shrimp aspic and chill until the aspic is firm. Garnish with whole shrimp and pieces of avocado which have been marinated in a little French dressing. Cover the garnish with another layer of the liquid aspic and chill until set.

Mix the hard-cooked eggs, celery and capers with the remaining shrimp. Add the Lea & Perrins sauce, vinegar and grated onion and juice and season to taste with salt and pepper. Fill the center of the molds with this mixture, keeping it away from the sides, fill the molds with the liquid aspic, and chill until set. Turn out on individual salad plates, garnished with crisp lettuce leaves.

AVOCADO SALAD DRESSING

(Mrs. Kenneth T. Price)

¾ cup mashed ripe avocado   1 teaspoon lemon juice
⅔ cup olive oil   ½ teaspoon sugar
3 tablespoons vinegar   ⅓ cup minced onion
½ teaspoon prepared horse-   Salt and pepper to taste
   radish

Mix the ingredients thoroughly in the order given.

Cakes, Pies, Icings, Desserts and Pecan Pralines

BANANES EN DAUBE

(Mrs. L. Perry Adams, née Helene Delery)

8 yellow firm bananas
3 tablespoons butter, melted
1 cup brown sugar
2 teaspoons lemon juice

Peel the bananas and arrange them side by side in a buttered baking dish. Sprinkle the bananas with the butter, sugar and lemon juice and bake in a moderate oven (350° F.) for about 1 hour. Serve hot with or without heavy cream. These bananas are delicious served on a slice of pound cake.

BANANAS GLACÉES

(Mrs. Edward Munson, Glenwood Plantation House)

Arrange 8 whole peeled bananas in an 8 x 12 buttered baking dish. Add 1 lemon, sliced, and sprinkle with ½ cup each of brown sugar and white sugar. Sprinkle with freshly grated nutmeg and ¼ cup each of melted butter and water and bake in a moderate oven (350° F.) for 30 minutes.

FRUIT SALAD

(Mrs. Kenneth T. Price)

2 tablespoons gelatin
½ cup cold water
1 cup canned fruit juice
⅓ cup orange juice
⅓ cup lemon juice
½ cup sugar
2 eggs, well beaten

½ teaspoon salt
⅓ cup ginger ale
1 cup cream, whipped
1 No. 2½ can of fruits for salad
2 medium bananas, peeled and cubed

Soak the gelatin in the cold water and set aside. Put the fruit juices and sugar in a saucepan and heat, stirring, until the sugar is melted. Stir the fruit juices gradually into the beaten eggs, return the mixture to the pan and cook over simmering water until the custard coats the spoon. Add the gelatin and salt, stir until the gelatin is thoroughly dissolved and cool. When cool stir in the ginger ale and fold in the cream. Combine the fruit and bananas in a 9-inch square pan, pour the cream over the fruit and chill in the refrigerator until set.

CHEESE TORTE

(Mrs. Edith Deutsch Lashman)

1 box zwieback, crumbed and sifted
2 cups sugar
½ cup melted butter
5 eggs, separated
3 8-ounce packages Philadelphia cream cheese

3 tablespoons cornstarch
Juice of 1 lemon
Pinch of salt
Pinch of nutmeg
½ teaspoon vanilla
2 cups cream, whipped

Combine the zwieback crumbs, 1 cup of the sugar and the

melted butter and line a well-buttered 10-inch spring-form pan with the mixture.

Beat the egg yolks with the remaining cup of sugar. Press the cream cheese through a potato ricer and stir it into the egg yolk mixture. Stir in the cornstarch, lemon juice, salt, nutmeg and vanilla. Fold in the cream and lastly fold in the stiffly beaten egg whites. Pour the filling into the crust-lined pan. Loosen the crust around the top of the pan to form an edge around the filling and bake in a slow oven (300° F.) for 1½ to 1¾ hours.

DATE TORTE

(Mrs. Mortimer Favrot and Roberta Chester Brown)

½ cup flour	2 eggs, beaten
⅛ teaspoon salt	½ teaspoon vanilla
1 teaspoon baking powder	1 cup chopped pecan meats
½ cup sugar	1 package dates, sliced

Sift the dry ingredients. Beat the sugar gradually into the eggs and stir in the vanilla, nuts and dates. Stir in the dry ingredients, turn the mixture into a casserole or shallow pan, lined with paper and oiled, and bake in a moderate oven (350° F.) for about 1 hour, or until a cake tester inserted in the center comes out clean. Cool and serve with whipped cream or ice cream.

DATE SOUFFLÉ CAKE

(Mrs. Edward Munson, Glenwood Plantation House)

2 eggs, beaten	1 cup chopped dates
½ cup sugar	½ cup chopped pecans
1 teaspoon baking powder	1 teaspoon vanilla
4 tablespoons flour	

Mix the eggs and sugar. Sprinkle the baking powder and flour over the dates and pecans, mix lightly and stir into the egg-sugar mixture. Stir in the vanilla and beat vigorously. Turn the batter into a shallow pan, lined with paper and oiled, and bake in a moderate oven (325° F.) for about 45 minutes.

PLUM PUDDING

(Mrs. L. Perry Adams, née Helene Delery)

2 cups self-rising flour
1 cup soft bread crumbs
½ cup white raisins
½ cup dark raisins
1 cup pecan meats
1 cup chopped figs
1 cup chopped prunes
½ cup currants
2 tablespoons each grated orange and lemon peel

⅓ cup shortening
1 cup thick cane syrup
1 cup milk
1 teaspoon salt
1 teaspoon each ground cloves, cinnamon and allspice
1 teaspoon soda dissolved in 1 tablespoon hot water

Mix together the flour, bread crumbs, fruit and fruit peel. Cut in the shortening and stir in the remaining ingredients. Divide the batter between 2 buttered pudding molds or empty coffee cans, filling the containers two-thirds full. Place the molds in a kettle containing enough boiling water to reach halfway to the top of the molds. Bring the water to a boil, cover the kettle and steam the puddings for 2½ hours. If the pudding is steamed in one large mold, 5 hours' steaming is required.

Garnish with brandied cherries and serve hot with hard sauce.

HARD SAUCE

1 cup butter
3 cups sifted confectioners' sugar

⅛ teaspoon salt
Brandy

Cream the butter thoroughly. Beat in the sugar a little at a time and add the salt. Beat in brandy, 1 teaspoon at a time, until the sauce is creamy and thick enough to stand in a peak.

PUFF PUDDING

(Mrs. Allan F. Hebert)

½ cup sugar
½ cup flour
2 cups hot milk

5 eggs, separated
1 teaspoon vanilla

In a heavy saucepan combine the sugar and flour. Stir in ½ cup milk to make a smooth paste. Stir in the remaining milk and cook over a low flame, stirring constantly, until the sauce is smooth and thickened. Simmer for 3 minutes, stirring constantly. Beat the egg yolks until they are thick and pale in color, stir in a little of the hot sauce, then stir the mixture into the sauce. Mix well, stir in the vanilla and set aside to cool.

Beat the egg whites until stiff, but not dry, and fold them into the cold sauce. Turn the batter into a buttered casserole, place the casserole in a shallow pan containing 1 inch of hot water and bake in a moderate oven (350° F.) for 40 to 50 minutes, or until a knife inserted in the center comes out clean.

Serve with fruit or with hard sauce. Serves 6.

IRISH POTATO PUDDING

(Mrs. Nathaniel Wells Pope)

1 pound potatoes, cooked
3 eggs, lightly beaten
1½ cups (¾ pound) butter
2 cups sugar

½ cup mixed spices
½ cup white wine
½ cup brandy
Pastry

Mash the hot potatoes until they are perfectly smooth and stir in the remaining ingredients. Turn the mixture into a pie plate lined with rich pie dough and bake in a hot oven (450° F.) for 10 minutes. Reduce the oven temperature to 350° F. and continue to bake for about 30 minutes longer, or until the filling is set and the crust is browned.

ORANGE DATE RICE PUDDING

(Mrs. Clark Hoffpauir)

3 eggs	¼ cup orange juice
2 cups milk	Grated rind of ½ orange
¾ cup sugar	2 cups cooked rice
2 tablespoons melted butter	1 cup chopped dates
¼ teaspoon nutmeg	½ cup chopped pecans

Combine the eggs and milk and beat well. Stir in the remaining ingredients and turn the mixture into a buttered casserole. Place the casserole in a baking pan containing about 1 inch of hot water and bake in a moderate oven (350° F.) for 1 hour. The pudding may be topped with meringue ten minutes before the baking is finished, or it may be served with whipped cream or any favorite dessert sauce.

SAVARIN OR RUM CAKES

(Brennan's Restaurant)

½ cup milk	½ inch vanilla bean
1 cake yeast	1¾ cups flour
2 egg yolks	¾ cup apricot juice
1 cup sugar	1 teaspoon lemon juice
1 egg	4 tablespoons dark rum
½ cup sweet butter, melted	

Scald the milk, cool to lukewarm and dissolve the yeast in it. Beat the egg yolks until thick and gradually beat in ½ cup of the sugar. Add the egg and beat vigorously. Stir the melted butter into the egg mixture while it is still slightly warm. Stir in the pulp from the piece of vanilla bean and stir in the milk and yeast mixture. Stir in the flour to make a medium thick batter and put the batter in a warm place for 3½ hours to rise. Stir down the batter and fill individual buttered baking molds half full. Let the batter rise again until it is double in bulk and bake in a hot oven (400° F.) for about 15 minutes, or until a cake tester comes out clean. Take the cakes from the molds and cool.

Combine the remaining sugar, apricot juice, lemon juice and rum. Bring to a boil and simmer for 10 minutes. Pour the syrup over the cakes and put the cakes back into their molds to marinate. Additional rum may be added before serving.

VANILLA CRESCENTS

(Mrs. Edith Deutsch Lashman)

4 cups (1 pound) flour	Pinch of salt
2 cups (1 pound) butter	1 pound sifted confectioners'
¾ cup sugar	sugar
1 cup ground almonds (not	1 vanilla bean
blanched)	

Sift the flour into a bowl, add the butter, sugar, almonds and salt and knead these ingredients into a solid mass of dough. If the dough gets too soft because of hot weather, put it in the refrigerator until it is hard enough to shape with the hands. Divide the dough into quarters and shape each part into a roll about 1 inch in diameter. Cut the rolls crosswise at 1-inch intervals and shape each piece into a ball. Form each ball into the shape of a tiny cigar and bend both ends of the little "cigars" into crescent shape. Place the crescents on a buttered baking sheet and bake in a moderate oven (350° F.) for 10 to 20 minutes, or until the crescents are only a very light brown.

Mix the sugar with the pulp from the vanilla bean. Dip the hot crescents into the sugar until each is thoroughly coated and place on a platter to cool.

DATE PECAN CAKE

(Mrs. E. W. Gravolet, Sr.)

1 pound pitted dates, chopped	1 cup sugar
4 cups pecan meats	1 cup flour
3 eggs, beaten	1 teaspoon vanilla

Combine the dates and nuts and stir in the eggs, sugar, flour and vanilla. Line a ring pan with buttered brown paper and turn the batter into it. Put the pan in another pan containing a little hot water and bake in a very slow oven (200° F.) for 2 to 2½ hours.

CHOCOLATE CAKE

(Dorrie Blackstone)

2 squares bitter chocolate	½ teaspoon salt
½ cup shortening	1 teaspoon soda
1¼ cups sugar	1 cup sour milk
2 eggs, beaten	1 teaspoon vanilla
2 cups sifted flour	

Put the chocolate over hot water to melt. Cream the shortening, add the sugar gradually and cream thoroughly. Stir in the eggs. Sift together the flour, salt and soda and stir the dry ingredients into the creamed mixture alternately with the milk. Stir in the chocolate and vanilla. Turn the batter into two buttered and floured 8-inch pans and bake in a moderate oven (350° F.) for 30 minutes, or until a cake tester comes out clean.

FOOL'S CAKE (ANY FOOL CAN MAKE IT)

(Mrs. L. Perry Adams, née Helene Delery)

3 eggs, beaten
2 cups (1 pound) light brown sugar
2 cups broken pecan meats
1 pound pitted dates, chopped
1 cup chopped figs
½ cup white raisins
½ cup dark raisins
⅓ cup candied citron, chopped

⅓ cup candied pineapple, chopped
½ cup candied cherries
½ teaspoon each of ground cloves, cinnamon and allspice
½ teaspoon salt
½ cup milk
2 cups self-rising flour sifted twice

Mix the eggs and sugar thoroughly. Add the fruit and mix well. Stir in the spices and salt, then the milk. Gradually stir in the flour a little at a time and divide the batter between two buttered angel food pans lined with paper. Decorate with pecan halves and candied cherries and bake the cakes in a slow oven (280° F.) for about 1 hour, or until a cake tester comes out clean.

FRENCH CREAM CAKE*

(Mrs. Edward Munson, Glenwood Plantation House)

3 eggs
1 cup sugar
1½ cups sifted flour

2 teaspoons baking powder
3 tablespoons water

* This is an old family recipe of Mr. Munson's great-grandmother, Mrs. Ebenezer Eaton Kittredge of Elm Hall Plantation, Assumption Parish.

Beat the eggs until light, add the sugar and mix well. Sift the flour and baking powder and stir the dry ingredients into the egg and sugar mixture. Stir in the water and turn the batter into two buttered 9-inch layer cake pans. Bake the layers in a moderate oven (350° F.) for about 25 minutes, or until the layers test done. Remove the cakes from the pans to cool. Meanwhile make the following filling.

FILLING

½ cup sugar
2 eggs, beaten
4 tablespoons flour

2 cups scalded milk
1 tablespoon butter
1 teaspoon vanilla

In a saucepan combine the sugar, eggs and flour. Gradually stir in the hot milk and cook, stirring constantly, until the filling is smooth and thickened. Put the saucepan over boiling water and cook the filling for 10 minutes to remove the taste of uncooked flour. Remove from the fire and stir in the butter and vanilla. Cool. Split the layers of cake and put the filling between. Dust the tops of the cakes with sifted confectioners' sugar.

FRUITCAKE

(Mrs. Nora Viallon)

2 cups brown sugar
1 cup butter
4 eggs, well beaten
2 cups flour
1 teaspoon each of ground
   cinnamon and nutmeg

2 tablespoons baking powder
2 cups pecan meats
2 cups raisins
1 tablespoon flour
1 cup candied cherries
1¾ cups preserved figs

Cream the sugar and butter until the mixture is light and fluffy. Stir in the eggs and mix well. Sift together the 2 cups of flour, spices and baking powder and stir the dry ingredients gradually into the egg mixture. Dust the pecans and raisins with the tablespoon of flour and stir them into the batter. Stir in the cherries and figs. Turn the batter into a deep pan, lined with wax paper, and bake in a slow oven (250° F.) for about 3 hours. A shallow pan of warm water should be placed in the oven under the cake pan while the cake is baking.

FRUITCAKE*

(Mrs. Lucien Trosclair)

1 *pound candied pineapple, chopped*
1 *pound candied cherries*
1 *pound pitted dates, chopped*
1 *pound figs, chopped*
½ *pound candied citron, sliced*
1 *pound raisins*
1 *pound currants*
2 *pounds pecan meats*
1 *teaspoon grated lemon peel*
1 *tablespoon grated orange peel*
8 *cups (2 pounds) flour*
1 *pound butter*
2 *pounds brown sugar*
14 *eggs*
2 *teaspoons baking powder*
1 *teaspoon each of ground allspice, cinnamon and cloves*
1 *cup sherry*
1 *cup corn syrup*

Combine the fruit, nuts and fruit peel and dredge them with 2 cups of the flour. Cream together the butter and sugar, then beat in the eggs one at a time. Sift the remaining flour, baking powder and spices three times and stir the dry ingredients into the batter alternately with the sherry and syrup. Stir in the dredged fruit. Line cake pans, 14 x 10 inches and 3 inches high, with heavy paper, well oiled. Fill the pans almost full and bake in a slow oven (250° F.) for 4 hours. Makes about 16 pounds of fruitcake.

* This recipe is over 100 years old.

PECAN PIE

(Mrs. J. P. Colligan)

3 eggs, lightly beaten
1 cup sugar
2 cups Karo
Pastry

⅛ teaspoon salt
1 teaspoon vanilla
1 cup pecan meats

Mix the eggs, sugar and Karo and stir in the salt and vanilla.
Lastly stir in the nuts. Turn the mixture into a 9-inch pie pan
lined with rich pie dough and bake in a hot oven (450° F.) for
10 minutes. Reduce the heat to 350° F., and continue to bake
for about 30 minutes longer, or until a silver knife inserted in the
center of the filling comes out clean.

CHOCOLATE PIE

(Mrs. Nathaniel Wells Pope)

2 cups milk
3 tablespoon grated chocolate
¾ cup sugar
2 eggs, separated

1 tablespoon cornstarch
1 tablespoon butter
1 teaspoon vanilla
1 baked pie shell

Scald the milk and stir in the grated chocolate. In a saucepan
combine the sugar, egg yolks, cornstarch and butter. Gradually
stir in the hot chocolate milk and cook over boiling water, stirring constantly, until the filling is smooth and thick. Stir in the
vanilla and cool. Turn the filling into the pie shell and top with
a meringue made by beating the egg whites until stiff and
beating in gradually ¼ cup sugar.

ICE CREAM MAGDERLIN

(Mrs. Kenneth T. Price)

1 quart vanilla ice cream   ¼ nutmeg, grated
½ cup sherry

Mix all the ingredients and freeze until firm.

FROZEN LEMON CREAM

(Mrs. Edward Munson, Glenwood Plantation House)

2 eggs, separated   ½ cup sugar
3 tablespoons lemon juice   ¾ large can evaporated milk
1 teaspoon grated lemon rind   1 cup crushed vanilla wafers

Beat the egg yolks until thick and pale in color. Add the lemon juice, rind and sugar and cook the mixture over simmering water, stirring constantly, until thick. Remove the custard from the fire and chill. Scald the evaporated milk, chill it thoroughly in a freezing tray of the refrigerator and then whip it until it is stiff. Fold in the stiffly beaten egg whites and combine this mixture with the custard. Pour the cream into refrigerator trays lined with wax paper and the crushed vanilla wafers and freeze until firm.

SPANISH CREAM

(Mrs. O. O. Ashworth)

1 tablespoon gelatin   Pinch of salt
¼ cup cold water   3 eggs, separated
2 cups rich milk, scalded   1 teaspoon vanilla
½ cup sugar   A few drops almond extract

Soften the gelatin in the cold water and add to the scalded milk. Add the sugar and salt and stir until the gelatin and sugar are dissolved. Beat the egg yolks with a little of the hot milk and stir gradually into the hot milk. Cook over hot, but not boiling, water, stirring constantly, for 4 to 5 minutes, or until the custard is slightly thickened. Stir in the vanilla and almond flavoring and fold in the egg whites, stiffly beaten. Turn into a mold and chill until firm.

If the egg whites are added as soon as the custard is removed from the stove, a clear jelly will form on top of the mold. This gives the appearance of two different jellies, one creamy and the other clear. When the egg whites are added after the custard is cool, the result is an even, creamy jelly. Serves 6.

Serve with sherry jelly made in individual molds, garnished with whipped cream and cherries, strawberries or other fruit.

SHERRY JELLY*

2 tablespoons gelatin   ¼ teaspoon salt
½ cup cold water   ½ cup orange juice
1 cup boiling water   2 tablespoons lemon juice
¾ cup sugar   1½ cups sherry

Soften the gelatin in the cold water, add the boiling water, sugar and salt and stir until the gelatin and sugar are dissolved. Cool and stir in the orange juice, lemon juice and sherry. Pour into individual molds and chill until firm.

* Mrs. Ashworth very kindly allowed me to attribute this dessert to the heroine of my novel, *Steamboat Gothic.*

FRUIT RICE BAVARIAN CREAM

(Miss Bess Milliken)

1 tablespoon gelatin	1 teaspoon vanilla
½ cup cold water	½ cup crushed pineapple
1 cup hot cooked rice	1 cup heavy cream, whipped
¼ cup sugar	Pecan halves and maraschino
¼ teaspoon salt	cherries

In a small bowl soak the gelatin in the cold water for 5 minutes. Place the bowl over hot water and stir until the gelatin is dissolved. Add the dissolved gelatin to the hot rice and mix well. Stir in the sugar, salt, vanilla and pineapple and beat until the mixture is cool and begins to thicken. Fold in the whipped cream.

Garnish a decorative mold with pecans and maraschino cherries. Fill the mold with the rice mixture and chill until firm.

CHOCOLATE ICING

(Dorrie Blackstone)

2 tablespoons butter	1 pound sifted confectioners'
2 squares bitter chocolate,	sugar
melted	Cream

Cream the butter thoroughly and stir in the melted chocolate. Gradually beat in the sugar a little at a time, thinning the icing with cream when it becomes too hard. Be careful not to add too much cream or the icing will be "runny."

SOUR CREAM CAKE FROSTING

(Mrs. Edward Munson, Glenwood Plantation House)

2 cups sour cream
2 cups brown sugar
½ cup chopped nuts

1 teaspoon vanilla
½ teaspoon salt

Combine the sour cream and brown sugar, bring to a boil and boil until the syrup reaches the soft ball stage (238° F.). Stir in the nuts, vanilla and salt and beat vigorously until the frosting is of a spreading consistency.

CREOLE PECAN PRALINES

(Mrs. Allan F. Hebert)

1½ cups sugar
⅓ cup cane syrup
⅔ cup water

⅛ teaspoon salt
2 cups pecan meats
1 tablespoon butter

In a saucepan combine the sugar, syrup, water and salt. Stir until the sugar is dissolved, then cook over a low fire until the syrup reaches the soft ball stage, or 238° F. on a candy thermometer. Add the pecans and butter and beat vigorously until the mixture begins to thicken. Drop by the tablespoon on a buttered baking sheet to cool.

Beverages, Canapés and Preserves

ABSINTHE DRIP

(Brennan's Restaurant)

1 cube sugar   1 ounce absinthe

Place the sugar in the bottom of a drip glass. Fill the drip saucer with cracked ice and pour the absinthe over the ice. Let drip for a few minutes, then pour water over the ice in the saucer to fill the glass.

ABSINTHE FRAPPÉ

(Brennan's Restaurant)

1 teaspoon simple syrup   2 tablespoons water
1½ ounces Herbsaint
  (absinthe substitute)

Pour into an 8-ounce glass filled with shaved ice and serve.

ABSINTHE SUISSESSE

(Brennan's Restaurant)

1½ ounces absinthe   1 tablespoon Orgeat
1 tablespoon cream   1 egg white

Blend the ingredients with crushed ice in an electric blender and serve in an old-fashioned glass.

CAFÉ BRULÔT

(Clara E. Wilson)

Into a brulôt bowl put 42 lumps of sugar, 40 whole cloves, the thinly sliced peel of 1 orange and 1 lemon and 2 sticks of cinnamon, broken into pieces. When ready to serve, heat 1 cup brandy and pour it into the bowl. Ignite the brandy, let it burn for a few minutes, then gradually pour into the flames 1 quart of hot strong coffee.

PETIT ORANGE BRULÔT

(Brennan's Restaurant)

Take an ordinary sized thick-skinned orange. Cut through the peel all around the orange like the line of the equator, then force off the peel by passing the handle of a spoon between it and the pulp. Into the cup thus formed, put 1 lump of sugar and, if desired, a pinch of cinnamon. Fill the cup with warm cognac and ignite. The brulôt will be found to have a pleasant flavor given to it by the orange.

OJEN COCKTAIL

(Brennan's Restaurant)

Add about 1 ounce of Ojen (Spanish absinthe) and 2 or 3 dashes of New Orleans (Peychaud) bitters to cracked ice in a cocktail shaker. Stir until the mixture is very cold and strain into a cocktail glass. A little seltzer can be added to reduce the strength of the drink if desired.

POUSSE CAFÉ*

(Mrs. Edward Munson, Glenwood Plantation House)

A pousse café is served in a very slender liqueur glass and it is necessary to pour the liqueurs in the order in which they are listed. The drink is served after dinner after demitasse.

Pour slowly into the liqueur glass, with a steady hand, the following—

1 tablespoon each:

Grenadine	Curaçao
Benedictine	Crème d'Yvette
Green Chartreuse	Cognac
Yellow Chartreuse	

None of these liqueurs should blend in the glass, but each one should remain a distinct band of color.

SAZERAC

Rinse an old-fashioned glass with absinthe and empty. Put a lump of sugar in the glass and add 3 drops Peychaud bitters, 1 dash Angostura bitters, 1 dash absinthe, 1 slice of lemon peel and 1 jigger of rye whiskey.

SAZERAC COCKTAIL

(Mrs. Edward Munson, Glenwood Plantation House)

In an old-fashioned glass moisten 1 lump of sugar. Stir and add 1½ jiggers of rye whiskey. Add a dash of Angostura bitters

* The above recipe was given to Mrs. Munson by a famous bartender—affectionately known as "Creole" to his many friends along Bayou Lafourche, but whose family name was De Laune—Leon de Laune.

and a dash of Peychaud bitters. Add a cube of ice and stir until the drink is chilled. In another chilled glass, put a dash of absinthe, twirl the glass, and drain. Pour the mixed drink into this glass and add a twist of lemon peel. Do not serve any ice in a Sazerac.

RAMOS GIN FIZZ*

Juice of ½ lemon or lime
2 ounces gin
1 teaspoon almond syrup

1 teaspoon orange-flower water
1 tablespoon heavy cream

Shake well with cracked ice and strain into a cocktail glass.

WHISKEY FLIP

("Sissy" Wilbert)

3 teaspoons sugar
1 ounce whiskey
1 egg yolk

3 tablespoons heavy cream
Dash of vanilla
Nutmeg

Combine all the ingredients except the nutmeg and shake well with cracked ice. Strain into a flip glass and sprinkle the top with nutmeg.

HOT TOM AND JERRY

("Sissy" Wilbert)

Separate the whites and yolks of 6 eggs. Beat the yolks until they are thick and pale in color and stir in enough confectioners'

* This recipe was given to Mr. Joseph Montgomery for a wedding present.

sugar to make a very thick batter. Beat the egg whites to a froth and fold them into the yolks. Place a spoonful of this mixture in each cup, add 1 jigger of whiskey to each cup and fill the cups with boiling water.

SOUR ORANGE WINE

(Ladies of the Sacred Heart, St. Michael's)

To 5 gallons of rain water, add 1 gallon of strained sour orange juice and 25 pounds of sugar. Add 2 egg whites, stiffly beaten, and bring the mixture to a boil, stirring constantly. Set aside for 5 minutes, skim well and stir in another quart of strained sour orange juice. Strain the liquid through a flannel cloth wrung out of cold water into glass demijohns and set in a cool place for 6 months, when fermentation will have ceased. Do not cork the jars, cover the jars with cloth to keep out the dust. Draw the wine off carefully from the sediment in the bottom of the jars, bottle and cork tightly. Set the bottles in a dry warm place for 4 to 6 months. The wine will be superb, and it will continue to improve with time.

QUEEN'S SAUCE

(Mrs. Lester Montegut)

Bring 4 cups milk to a boil. Stir in 4 eggs beaten with a little of the hot milk, add 1 cup sugar and cook, stirring over a low flame for 10 minutes, being careful not to let the custard boil. Stir in 1 cup whiskey and serve hot. This is a wonderful drink made over an open fireplace and served before retiring for the night.

COCKTAIL TIDBITS

(Mrs. L. Perry Adams, née Helene Delery)

1 pound butter
1 tablespoon cayenne pepper
3 tablespoons Worcestershire
    sauce
½ bottle garlic salt

1 box Cheerios
1 box pretzel sticks
1 box Ralstons
1 pound peanuts
2 pounds mixed nuts

Melt the butter and add the cayenne, Worcestershire and garlic salt. Put the Cheerios, pretzels, Ralstons and nuts in a large baking pan, pour the seasoned butter over them and bake in a slow oven (300° F.) for 1 hour, stirring every 10 minutes.

CHEESE BALLS

(Mrs. Allan F. Hebert)

½ pound grated American
    cheese
2 cups soft bread crumbs
1 teaspoon Worcestershire
    sauce

⅛ teaspoon salt
Pinch of cayenne
3 eggs, beaten
Tomato sauce

Combine the cheese with 1½ cups of the bread crumbs, the Worcestershire, salt and cayenne. Stir in enough of the beaten egg to make a firm dough. Shape the dough into balls. Add a little water to the remaining beaten egg, dip the balls into the egg and roll them in the remaining bread crumbs. Fry in hot deep fat (380° F.) until golden and drain on absorbent paper. Serve hot with tomato sauce.

HOT CHEESE SANDWICHES   - 311

(Mary Louise Bartlett)

Grate half a small onion and mix it into 2 cups grated sharp cheese. Add 1 teaspoon horseradish mustard, ½ teaspoon Louisiana Hot Sauce, ½ teaspoon Lea & Perrins sauce, ½ teaspoon caraway seeds, 1½ tablespoons minced green onion tops or chives and 1 tablespoon finely chopped parsley and mix well. Stir in enough warm milk to make a nice spreading consistency.

Make sandwiches with this filling and store until needed. When needed, put under the broiler flame and toast the sandwiches on both sides.

VEGETABLE SPREAD

(Creacy King)

2 or 3 carrots	1 avocado
1 medium onion	1 tablespoon sugar
½ head lettuce	2 tablespoons vinegar
½ green bell pepper	2 tablespoons olive oil
2 cups shredded cabbage	Mayonnaise
1 cucumber	Cayenne pepper
2 apples	

Prepare all the vegetables and the apples. Grind the carrots, onion, lettuce, green pepper, cabbage, cucumber and apples through a meat grinder. Mash the avocado with a fork and combine with the ground vegetables. Add the sugar, vinegar and oil and mix well. Stir in enough mayonnaise to bind the mixture and season to taste with cayenne. This spread is excellent for either canapés or sandwiches.

PUMPKIN PRESERVE

(Creacy King)

3 quarts peeled and cubed   3 cups sugar
    pumpkin   1 lemon, chopped

Put the pumpkin in a kettle, pour the sugar over it and let
stand overnight. In the morning add the lemon—more than one
may be used, according to the degree of tartness desired—bring
to a boil and cook until the syrup is thick. Turn into hot jars
and seal.

PUMPKIN MARMALADE

(Creacy King)

Follow the same procedure as for the preserve, but cut the
pumpkin into very thin slices.

FIG PRESERVES

(Mrs. Edward Munson, Glenwood Plantation House)

6 quarts Celeste figs   4 quarts water
6 pounds sugar   1 cup baking soda

Select only sound, firm Celeste figs. Discard any overripe or
broken figs. Put the figs in a large kettle, sprinkle them with
1 cup baking soda and cover with 6 quarts boiling water. Let
the figs stand for 15 minutes, drain and rinse in clear cold water.
Drain the figs thoroughly.

Combine the sugar and water, bring to a boil and simmer for 10 minutes, skimming when necessary. Add the figs and cook rapidly for about 2 hours, or until the figs are clear and tender. Lift out the figs and place them in shallow trays. Continue to cook the syrup until it is as thick as honey. Pour the syrup over the figs and let stand overnight. In the morning pack the figs cold in sterilized jars, fill each jar to overflowing with the syrup, and seal. Process the jars in simmering water for 25 minutes.

Part Four

THE WORLD TRAVELER

GOD HAS BEEN GOOD TO ME

God has been good to me, for I have sailed,
Into the Golden Horn—and through the Straits
Magellan glorified—and where the veiled
Harbor of Rio gleams and radiates.

God has been good to me, for I have stood
In the Red Square when it was white with snow—
And at the edge of a dark Chilean wood
When Aconcagua burned with Andean glow.

God has been good to me, for I have lingered
In the Alhambra when the moon was bright—
And in Damascus, dazzled, as I fingered
The brilliant wares spread out for my delight.

God has been good to me, for I have dwelt
Above the parapet at Carcasonne—
And on the pampas, where the shadows melt
Into mirage—and by the Rubicon.

God has been good to me, for I have tasted
Hymettus honey and Formosa tea—
Isfahan melons—and the rare, unwasted
Vintage of Jerez and of Hungary.

God has been good to me, for I have smelled
Night-blooming cereus on starlit hedges—
And waxen-white gardenias, which swelled
With fragrance, blossoming on window-ledges.

God has been good to me, for I have heard
The crush of Arctic ice around a boat
Jammed in the Neva River—and a bird
Piercing the Persian twilight with its note.

God has been good to me, for I have seen
The Wall of China, sprawling over space—
And Daibutsu, ageless and serene,
Looming at dusk above a holy place.

God has been good to me for I have felt
His glory all about me as I gazed
Upon Gethsemane—and as I knelt
In Chârtres Cathedral, overwhelmed and dazed.

God has been good to me, for I have known
All these His Wonders—and when He shall send
Me on the Last Great Enterprise, His own
Beatitude shall crown my journey's end.

The garden of the Marques of Santo Domingo
Avila, Spain

I DO NOT THINK that I consciously learned much of anything about Continental cuisine during the first year that I spent abroad, at the age of ten, except that there were many different ways of using rice which were new to me, though it had always appeared frequently on our table, both as a vegetable and a pudding. On the contrary, I spent most of that year in a state of active rebellion against the food that was put before me, clamoring for ice water, large glasses of rich cold milk and "Cousin Mary's bread," until my poor mother was nearly distracted. However, I did learn to drink *café au lait* since, as she could not provide the glasses of rich cold milk, my mother gradually persuaded me to drink large cups of thin boiled milk, to which a great deal of sugar and a small quantity of coffee had been added. Eventually, I came to tolerate it and, at the age of seventeen, when we next went abroad, and I was allowed more coffee in the mixture, I liked it very much indeed and the taste bcame a permanent one.

This taste has proved highly inconvenient as far as travel in the United States is concerned. The request for "coffee with hot milk" almost invariably meets with astonishment enhanced by incredulity. If such a strange beverage can be obtained at all, it is apt to appear under various peculiar and unappetizing guises —sometimes with the horrible weak coffee of the average hotel flanked by the usual pitcher of cream, with a pint bottle of milk, unsteadily wavering about in some sort of a container filled with hot water, elsewhere on the tray. But perhaps the most amusing

of all experiences in this connection was one I had in a mid-
western city which shall be nameless. As I was leaving the dining
room one evening in my hotel, I timidly told the head waitress
—a rather formidable personage, clad in black satin trimmed with
gold lace—that I would like to give an order then for toast and
coffee with hot milk, to be sent to my room at eight the following
morning; in the light of an early departure, I did not want to
risk a delay with room service. For the first time the imposing
functionary looked at me with something akin to pity instead of
the hauteur with which she had hitherto regarded me. "Well, I
won't put in the order right away," she said kindly, "you may
be feeling better after you've had a good night's sleep."

Outside of the United States, however, the taste for *café au
lait* has been a boon; unlike most Americans, I do not suffer
because of the so-called Continental breakfast, which, as a matter
of fact, is not only universal on the European Continent, but is
the accepted form of morning nourishment in all South and
Central American countries and also, in the Orient. On the
other hand, my early thirst for ice water, which has never abated,
has proved as inconvenient abroad as the taste for *café au lait*
in the United States. Nevertheless, in only one country—Persia,
as it was then still called—have I been absolutely defeated in
my efforts to secure it. In those days, there simply *wasn't* any
ice in Persia though, as far as I know, there may now be plenty
in Iran.

There was a lapse of nearly twenty years between my second
and third trips abroad, and the third time, I was accompanied
by my eldest son, Henry, who was just eighteen. I think it was
largely on his account that I began to interest myself seriously in
foreign dishes, for I had not forgotten my own childhood misery;
and when he set up a wail similar to mine, largely centering
around the absence of milk, I determined to find more nourishing and appetizing substitutes for him than *café au lait* with
which, in any case, he declined to be placated. At first, I had
some difficulty, for we were in Germany, where the normally
huge meals had been greatly reduced in both quantity and

quality, as this was in the inflation period, when conditions were very bad indeed. But after we reached Spain my troubles were practically at an end. A typical luncheon, in those days, consisted of hors d'oeuvres, an egg dish, red meat with vegetables, poultry with salad, a sweet, cheese and fruit; during the blissful coma into which he sank after doing full justice to every course, Henry forgot that his breakfast had been inadequate. Then came dinner, which began with soup instead of hors d'oeuvres and continued with fish instead of eggs, but which was otherwise the same as luncheon. Since no dining room opened before nine-thirty or ten, and we seldom finished our evening meal much earlier than midnight, Henry managed to get by until lunch time next day, despite *café au lait*.

Unquestionably, my interest in Spanish cooking dates from that time and I still think the cuisine of Spain, in the form this takes at private houses and in the best hotels, is one of the finest in the world. Unfortunately, in some provincial and second-class urban hotels, the oil used for cooking is not above reproach and, as it is the almost universal choice where we would use butter, cream or milk, it can at first be very upsetting to a digestive system unaccustomed to it, if it is rancid or unrefined. On the other hand, there is no more refreshing soup in the world than *gazpacho*, made of blended vegetables and served thoroughly chilled, and none more delicious than the hot cream soup flavored with the small artichokes typical of the South. There is no more delightful summer drink than *sangria*,* a glorified claret lemonade of a perfection we never seem to attain in this country. There is no more succulent a game than a Castilian pickled partridge; there is no more dainty a dish than *pollito tomatero*, a tiny plump chicken roasted whole and served crackling hot; and there is no more royal fare of any kind than a *paella*, also served so hot that the first mouthfuls must be taken with caution, and which is

* In some regions, notably in and around Granada, *sangria* is flavored with peach and plum juices, and a little brandy is mixed with the red wine; but wine, orange and lemon juice, and charged water, flavored to taste with sugar, are the usual ingredients.

preferably brought to the table in the heavy iron frying pot in which the rice, seafood and meat of which it is composed have all been blended together.

Though the *paella* may be found anywhere in Spain, it is a specialty of Valencia and, if I were pinned down and asked to state which Spanish city provides the finest food, I think I should have to name that one. I have made no secret of my predilection for any well-prepared dish which has rice as a base and Valencia offers the greatest variety of these that I have ever found. This is not surprising, considering its position in the center of a rice-growing community; and, in like measure, it is not surprising that its fresh orange juice is incomparable, since Valencia oranges are world famous. But fresh tomato juice, with enough of the strained pulp left in it so that it is best eaten with a spoon, is equally good in Seville; so are the numerous varieties of shrimp, both large and small, which are usually cooked, as they often are in Louisiana, in highly seasoned water and served with no other dressing. All over Spain the fresh fruits and vegetables seem to be equally plentiful and delicious; so does the white cheese made of goats' milk; so does veal, though it appears on menus somewhat too constantly for American tastes; while almost every locality has its own special sweets: *yemas de Santa Teresa* in Avila, *yemas de San Leandro* in Seville, *mazapán* in Toledo, *turrón* of Alicante (hard) and *jijona* (soft) and so on.

The wines of Spain are equally praiseworthy. With sherry, of course, most of us are familiar in the United States, though it is almost inevitably so "fortified" for export that the *finos* lose some of their flavor; while *manzanilla,* which is, so to speak, a half-sister of the *fino,* is almost unknown. So are the excellent red wines, such as the Marqués de Riscal, Marqués de Murrieta, Pomal and Valdepeñas, and the sparkling white wines which can bear comparison with all but the best vintage champagnes. We are so accustomed to thinking in terms of the superlative French wines, that we are apt to overlook the many excellent ones produced in other countries, Switzerland, Germany and Italy among them, Hungary—whose product is now unfortunately not obtainable—and, as I have just said, in Spain. Yet, as I have also said before, each of these wines complements the special dishes of the country from which it comes, in a way that no foreign product can ever do.

I did not mean to get sidetracked by Spain, though that is an easy thing for me to do, both literally and figuratively. Since that first visit with Henry, many years ago, I have now been there six times, each time with increasing pleasure. I have been almost as many times to Germany and Italy, four times to Denmark, oftener and for longer periods to France and at least once to nearly every country in Western Europe. I have been around the world, twice to both Japan and China, to every country in South America, several of them more than once, twice to Mexico, three times to Puerto Rico, and at least once to various other parts of the West Indies. To be sure, none of these trips has been undertaken primarily in the interests of the culinary art, but to keep abreast of international events, to authenticate hagiography, and to verify the local color which forms the *mise en scène* in current fiction—these being the fields which I have been called on to explore in connection with my writing. However, inevitably, during the course of my travels, my many visits to private homes, my occasional housekeeping and my frequent long sojourns in foreign lands, I have become interested in their cuisine. It would take too long to catalog all the dishes and drinks which have intrigued me to the point of experimenting with them myself if materials were available; but more or less at random, I have made a partial list of them and here it is:

West Indies

Guanabana Ice Cream, Fresh Coconut Ice Cream, Sole Amandine (I have eaten this many times elsewhere, but never as well prepared and seasoned as in Cuba), Frozen Daiquiris, Planter's Punch,* Green Devil Cocktails.

* So well described by Charles Poore of the New York *Times* as a "curative liquid."

Venezuela

Best Spanish type food outside of Spain itself, including *paella* as served at the Casa Maximo, The Bullfighters' Restaurant in Caracas; also *sancocho*—chicken and vegetable soup—and *salcocho*—beef and vegetable soup.

Peru

Pisco Sour.

Mexico

Baked Bananas as a dessert. (Usually I have found that no dish tastes quite as good as it does on its native heath. The exception which proves the rule is at La Fonda in San Antonio, also the city where the American food served at "Miss Alice's," as the old Argyle Hotel was almost universally called, used to reach a degree of perfection I have seldom seen attained.)

Brazil

Canja (Chicken Soup) and *Manjar de Coco* (Coconut Mold).

Hawaii

A chilled dessert made of chopped figs, chopped nuts and sweetened whipped cream mixed together and served in a large bowl. (The Chinese dishes in Hawaii are also excellent.)

Java

Rysttafel. (This may be had almost as good in certain restaurants in the Netherlands.)

Patagonia

Lamb in all forms.

Singapore and Ceylon

Curries.

Denmark

Pastries and *smörgåsbord.*

France

Moules Marinière; roast partridge with burgundy; Mère Chantal's veal and other special dishes at the Abbaye des Bénédictines; Mme. Nielsen's ham in pastry.

Italy

Pastas and zabaglione. (What I have said about Mexican food at La Fonda in San Antonio can be said with equal truth about Italian food at Giovanni's in New York.)

Canada

Pea soup (with peas unstrained); Habitant cocktails (a form of whiskey sour made with rye, instead of bourbon, and flavored with maple syrup instead of cane sugar—a substitution I was not surprised to find satisfactory after my experiments with mint juleps during World War II). I also greatly enjoyed the *Fricassée de Poulet à l'Angevine* as served at the Ritz Carlton Hotel in Montreal during the recent French Exposition, but this was rightly captioned as belonging to La France à Montreal and is French rather than Canadian.

England

Roast grouse in season; bread sauce with roast chicken; mint sauce with roast lamb; Yorkshire pudding with roast beef; vegetable marrow.

Like every traveler who takes a normal interest in food, I have sought out at least a few of the famous restaurants in every region I have visited; and like most travelers, I have discovered some that are less famous, but which have proved to have a special attraction for me, because of their cuisine, their setting, their atmosphere—or all three. My list is probably not as extensive or impressive as that of many other globe-trotters, however, partly because I have been fortunate in having invitations to private homes almost everywhere I have gone—a far greater privilege, in my opinion, than eating in the best restaurants in the world, even if the refreshment offered is very simple—which has reduced the number of meals I have eaten in restaurants; and partly because once I find a restaurant I enjoy, I go to it over and over again, instead of seeking out new ones.

A good example of this is the Gourmet sans Chiqué on the rue de l'Échelle in Paris. My secretary, Deanie Bullock, and I stumbled on this quite by chance, one Sunday after we had been to Mass at St. Roch's, which is near by. The Alsatian *cadre* was so pleasant, the service so prompt and attentive, the food and wine so excellent, and the *patron*, M. Louis Jouanneau, so cordial that, the following Sunday, we agreed we would like to return there. Since then, there has never been any question about it; we have automatically gone to the Gourmet sans Chiqué after church every Sunday that we have been in Paris, unless there was some special reason why we should go elsewhere. Now the waiters know our preferences, both as to tables and as to what should go on them, which almost invariably includes hors d'oeuvres *variés, coquilles* St. Jacques, lamb chops and *bananes flambées*. M. Louis has become our firm friend. It may be a poor season for melons, but he always finds us some luscious ones. Once, when we were giving a dinner party—not at his restaurant, either!—and no one else could get caviar for us, he provided it in abundance and at a wholly reasonable price. After I had ransacked Paris for a doll dressed in Alsatian costume, he assured me that nothing could be simpler than to procure one —and after that, it was! He even helped me match up a set of china in a pattern which I wanted because of its connection with the plot of a story and I felt sure it would make good source material. If M. Louis is now one of my most faithful fans in France—as I believe he is!—I am certainly one of his most appreciative clients, nor do I believe that my enthusiasm is biased; all the friends I have taken to the Gourmet sans Chiqué have been equally delighted with it. Douglas Jerrold, the director of the ancient and honorable firm of Eyre & Spottiswoode, which publishes my books in England, once went there with Deanie and me to our customary Sunday lunch after Mass at St. Roch's. That was three or four years ago. Yet almost every time that I have dined at a restaurant with Douglas Jerrold since then, as he samples his wine, he has said, "Yes, very good, very good indeed. But do you remember the burgundy we had at that little restaurant on the rue de l'Échelle?"

In common with countless other travelers, I would also put the Tour d'Argent high on the list of Paris restaurants which I have greatly enjoyed. However, candor compels me to state that this is not because of its pressed duck, whose unquestionable excellence does not surpass that of the same delicacy as prepared in at least one restaurant and several private houses in Louisiana; or even because of its equally famous wine cellar, entrancing though this is to visit and intriguing to order from. But if any restaurant in the world has a view which can surpass the one from the great plate-glass windows on the top floor of the Tour d'Argent, I do not know what this is—or could be. The illuminated miracle of Notre Dame rises in all its Gothic splendor in the immediate foreground; and beyond are the lights, transfigured into jeweled chains, which outline the bridges of the Seine, and those which dot the small craft scurrying up and down the river and sparkle from the buildings on the bank beyond. If M. Claude Terrail, the *patron,* should place before me nothing but a glass of *vin ordinaire*—not that he could find any in his wonderful *cave!*—a crust of bread and a rind of hard cheese—which I am sure would be equally unobtainable in his restaurant!—I could still sit and look out at the matchless sight, unmindful of what I was eating until the *vin ordinaire* and the hard bread and stale cheese were snatched away from me.

And that, I am sure, is exactly what would happen. M. Terrail has an invaluable maître d'hôtel, a corps of excellent captains, and innumerable waiters and bus boys who not only know their jobs, but take pride in doing them which, unfortunately, is not always the same thing. And M. Terrail is here, there and everywhere himself. His father and his grandfather and I know not how many ancestors before that were all restaurateurs. (If I am not mistaken, the Tour d'Argent has been in the same family for several centuries.) It is a proud tradition.

Every year, in Washington—and probably in other cities as well—one special story enjoys extraordinary vogue. A few years ago, the favorite concerned a certain would-be social leader from the Capital who went to the Tour d'Argent without a reservation and who was dissatisfied with the table which was given her. She called for "the manager" and M. Terrail swiftly answered her summons. "I am a very important lady," she told him. "As you can see, my dress is one of Christian Dior's latest models. My jewels are all from Cartier. I insist upon having a better table." M. Terrail bowed. "Madame," he said quietly, "*all* my customers are important to me. I do not need to be told that one of them buys her dresses from Dior and her jewels from Cartier to recognize her as a lady—if she is one. I am sorry that, at the moment, I have no better table to offer you. But, of course, you are quite at liberty to leave my restaurant if this one does not please you."

I set this story down as legendary when I heard it in Washington; but the next time I went to Paris, I made some inquiries and found out that there was a considerable basis of truth in it. And at least one line in it is certainly true: whether he said it or not to a client of this type, everything about M. Terrail's attitude reveals the fact that all his customers are important to him. Moreover, he has succeeded in impressing his staff with the same feeling of responsibility for their tastes and needs. The first time I went to the Tour d'Argent, I was undergoing a peculiarly painful bout with the lameness which is always more or less of a handicap to me. Since no one had been apprized of this beforehand, no special preparations had been made for me; but a comfortable armchair was immediately brought forward and the straight-backed one at my place whisked away. It so happened that it was two years before I dined there again, and as I was then in exceptionally good health, once more nothing was said beforehand about my lameness; however, when I reached the restaurant, the armchair was already installed at my appointed place. It has been there every time since then, always without any reminder on my part or that of my host.

I have my favorites outside of Paris, also. Obviously, I cannot mention them all, but there are at least two more in France to which I must refer. One of these is the Auberge du Vieux Puits at Pont Audemer, a charming little Norman town most conveniently located—at least for my purposes—between Le Havre and Lisieux. The supplementary modern quarters which contained most of the bedrooms of this delightful inn were tragically destroyed during World War II; but fortunately the old, half-timbered building which houses the dining rooms and kitchen; a smaller one in similar style where a few overnight guests can be accommodated; and the old mill from which the establishment takes its name, and which was immortalized by Flaubert in *Madame Bovary*, all still survive. You will never know what cream soup and sole supreme and escalloped veal can taste like until you have eaten them as prepared under the watchful care of M. Albert Foltz, who, incidentally, is an artist with the palette as well as for the palate—since here again, the *patron* is even more important than the place over which he presides. And once you have met him and tasted his Cocktail Vieux Puits, and lunched or dined under the magic spell of his old mill and his old copper and his old pottery, either on the dishes I have mentioned as my favorites or on *truite Bovary*—you may choose your own trout from the pool in the garden—*poulet Vallée d'Auge* and *canard au cerises*, you will not care whether Pont Audemer lies conveniently on your route or not: you will find it "well worth a detour," as Michelin says in its invaluable handbook of the places it especially recommends.

My other favorite is at Gennes, near Saumur, and not too far from most of the famous cities along the Loire. Its official title is the Hôtel de la Loire, and its rear terrace "gives" directly on the river; the sunsets seen from there are among the most gorgeous I have ever beheld. But though it, too, can accommodate a certain number of guests who wish to stay overnight, or longer, its chief call to fame is in its restaurant, and it is better known by the name of the sisters who run it—Mesdames Barrau. *Brochet au beurre blanc, vol-au-vent* of mushrooms and *poulet gennois à l'angevine* are the *spécialités de la maison;* and you should wash these down with Brézé and Champigny and end up with Sparkling Saumur, while you sit and chat with the Barraux about this, that and the other thing. They know practically everyone worth knowing in France and many celebrities• far beyond its borders; and they are almost as well informed about European affairs generally as they are about what is happening in and around Gennes and in their own kitchen and dining room. They are shrewd, jovial, generous and witty, and it will be hard to tell which you will enjoy more—the intimate visits when you are gathered around a small table in the dining room and taking coffee afterward in their little bureau, or the great feasts like the one they gave when their goddaughter was married, for instance, which began with a luncheon that went on until five in the afternoon, and did not really end until the midnight supper which followed the dancing. And it will also be hard to tell under which conditions you will learn more about the art of cooking and the art of living.

A great deal of my time, while in France during recent years, has been spent among the Benedictines of Lisieux, first at their wonderful old *abbaye*—for which the land was given by William the Conqueror and of which his cousin was the first abbess— and later, when this *abbaye* was destroyed in World War II, at the Monteillerie, the pleasant manorial estate in the nearby village of Norolles, where the nuns took temporary refuge. (I am happy to say that they have now returned to newly built quarters on their original terrain, so that the next time I visit them, I can at least feel I am on long familiar ground, even though the stately structure which stood there for so many centuries is alas! no more.) The *Mère Cuisinière* at such an establishment, and sometimes the *Mère Hôtelière* as well, can be quite as much of a culinary artist as the *patron* or *patronne* of a famous restaurant; and the austere fare of the nuns themselves is no indication of the dishes they set before their guests. I am happy to present the recipes for one or two of these.

The food in the private houses belonging to my French friends, where I have been a fortunate guest, has been comparable, in both abundance and variety, to that in the best restaurants and, like that in every other country, gains in attractiveness because of its intimate and more personal setting. There is something about a hostess' own linen and silver and china, her own arrangement of flowers, even her own bearing when she entertains at home, with which entertainment in even the most luxurious restaurant cannot compete, because the atmosphere cannot be permeated with the same degree of individuality and privacy. I have been the recipient of so much hospitality in France that I cannot possibly give even passing mention to much of it. But I have singled out four homes, as examples of this, partly because I have had such unalloyed enjoyment in each and partly because each is so different from the other.

The first of these is an old Norman farmhouse at Vieux, a small village about twenty kilometres from Caen. Mme. Houlbey, my hostess here, is the mayor—one of the few women in France who have attained that position and one who richly deserves the general esteem in which she is held. Vieux was virtually demolished during the Invasion of 1944, and one of Mme. Houlbey's daughters was among the twenty-five in the village killed. After the burial service, hurried because bombs were falling all around the little cemetery, it was Mme. Houlbey who courageously led a small band of refugees to safety near Alençon; and when at last they returned to what had once been a rich, productive countryside, it was she who organized the reclamation of their ruined fields, and the reconstruction of their homes and church. The house in which she now lives was one of the few that escaped with only minor damages, and a huge table, covered with a cloth that is almost startlingly white in contrast to the dark wood of the beams and furniture and the plaster of the ancient walls, is lavishly spread in the great raftered kitchen where a fire burns brightly.

The dinner begins with hors d'oeuvres, melon, sardines and cold sliced ham among them, and newly baked bread and newly churned butter are already on the table; next comes soup from the iron *pot au feu,* transferred directly from this to a huge tureen and from the huge tureen to over-sized soup plates. This course is followed by a mammoth roast of beef, and the beef by a succulent roast goose, both withdrawn from the warm fire so close to the laden table and both accompanied by potatoes and green vegetables from the newly rescued fields and the nearby kitchen garden. Then comes a perfectly dressed green salad of crisp fresh lettuce—nothing else. (Why do we not take a lesson from the French and learn that no salad in the world is as good as this? Also, that it is much better made of so-called Boston lettuce or garden lettuce or Bibb lettuce than of iceberg lettuce, that it should be well marinated in a spacious bowl, at least a quarter of an hour before it is to be used, and that individual servings should not be dished out until after such marinating?) As a concession to my strange American tastes, the cheeses come with the salad, and a noble array they are: Camembert and Roquefort which have come from a distance, Pont l'Évêque and Livarot, which are products of nearby towns—the latter, especially, not nearly as well known as it ought to be—and the *petits Suisses*— individual cream cheeses, which have been made on the premises, and which everyone except Deanie and me eats with sugar instead of salt. After the salad and the cheese comes a *crème caramel* which, like the salad, always poses a question to me when I eat it in France: why is it so irresistibly delicious there, just as its correlative, *flan,* is so delicious in Spain, when caramel custard is so insipid, so suggestive of nursery suppers and invalid trays in the United States? I would give a good deal to find out.

A great epergne, not only filled but surmounted with multi-colored fruits, follows the *crème caramel;* but long before that comes on, I have had to "skip from there to there," as the Vermont farmer asked if he might do when confronted for the first time with an à la carte menu at a metropolitan hotel. Deanie has yielded to the temptation of the Livarot, which is one of her favorites, I have yielded to the temptation of the *crème caramel* and both of us have at least tasted each of the excellent wines which have accompanied every course. But now we have to say no to the glowing fruits and the Calvados—the strong apple brandy of the region—which takes the place of cognac with the coffee. It is a true saying that the Norman is a mighty trencher-man and few Americans can keep up with him at table, even when the so-called *trou Normand** divides a gargantuan meal in two. As a matter of fact, I do not personally care for fruit in its natural state after a sweet dessert, any more than I care for a sweet fruit cup, instead of soup or hors d'oeuvres, at the beginning of a meal; I like it *instead* of the sweet dessert, or by itself at bedtime, or in the form of well-chilled juice halfway through a long hard afternoon's work, or at the end of a long hot day of motoring, or in limitless supplies at all hours when I am sick in bed. But of course that is merely a matter of taste. And I have wandered far from the Norman scene, whereas I meant to go no further from Vieux than Caen.

At Caen, in the venerable house on the rue Vauquelin, which was the birthplace of the poet, Malherbe, live my friends, Marie and Marguerite LeBoeuf. Marguerite is a water-colorist of note, a member of several important societies whose importance in art is comparable to the Académie Française in literature and whose aquarelles have been used to illustrate many important regional books and have formed the backbone of many important expositions. Her sister shares her exquisite taste in furnishings and household decorations, and they are fortunate in the many inherited possessions which have been handed down

* Literally, a Norman hole; actually, an interval of conversation and wine sipping between the heartier courses.

from generation to generation in their family. Their dining room, as well as their two connecting salons, is a feast for the eyes. But on the table which forms its central ornament another feast is spread before us. Deanie says the LeBoeufs have the best meringues in the world and I am inclined to agree with her; however, you have eaten a good many other things before you get to these meringues which, incidentally, are always *meringues Chantilly*—i.e., served with whipped cream and not with ice cream. Because we simply could not do the meringues justice the first times we lunched or dined with the LeBoeufs, we have gradually persuaded them to reduce the number of the previous courses, since nothing could impair the irresistible attributes of each. But such dishes as *foie gras* in delicate rolls of pink ham, *poulet doré* and the superlative salads and cheeses are never displaced.

Chinon, in Indre et Loire, is, like Caen, another provincial city where I always find a warm welcome waiting for me. The home of my friend Mme. Delannoy is on one of those steep, slit-like streets, so secluded that there is almost a secret quality about it; and the house itself has a blank facade flush to the pavement and a high wall which conceals the side garden. But inside, it opens up harmoniously and spaciously. Next to the front door with its well-polished brass is the formal salon; and next to that is the much larger *pièce,* which serves as both dining room and living room, with the accent on the former, for here, too, a large central table, covered with a white cloth, is the predominant feature. An American family, occupying the same house, or one similarly arranged, would probably do away with the formal salon, convert that into a dining room, and use the larger room, with its side entrance to the pleasant garden, as a family living room, where afternoon tea, after dinner coffee and cocktails would be served, but never entire meals. However, the dining room table with its white cloth, its large monogrammed napkins—and may we admit in passing, its napkin rings!—its glass decanters and goblets, is not infrequently the focal point of a French provincial living room,* and logically so, because it is the consumption of well-prepared food, and not some other diversion, which is the main event of the day in many well-ordered French lives. The small table near an easy chair and a good reading lamp, the comfortable seats grouped around a radio, are relegated to second place if they have any at all; and the attention paid to television, outside of the main centers, is still negligible.

But I have digressed again. Let us return to Mme. Delannoy, who gives us an *apéritif* in the formal salon and then takes us straight to the well-spread table around which we sit until we leave, except for a brief visit to the outbuildings and a short stay in the garden where again, an American family would be apt to do more of its living than our present hostess. Even Mère Poulard's omelettes at Mont St. Michel cannot surpass Mme. Delannoy's *omelettes gargamelles*—a specialty of Chinon. Her mushroom dishes are the peer of the Barrau *croûte au champignons*, and her roast veal with its macedoine of vegetables can vie with M. Foltz's scallop. Then, when we get to the sweet, not one, but two open-faced fruit pies are offered for our delectation. My young grandson, Peter, who happened to have his first meal at a private house in France with Mme. Delannoy, made the great mistake of taking "seconds" for several of the earlier courses, including the mushrooms, which he said he had never before eaten with relish; when the first fruit pie, with its filling of luscious-looking gooseberries, began to circulate, he realized, too late, his error; when the second, a great raspberry tart, appeared, he groaned aloud. I knew exactly how he felt. Like the little boy in the well-known story, he could still chew, but he could no longer swallow. His disappointment was bitter.

I am glad that, unlike most Americans, I have not concentrated on Paris to the exclusion of the provinces when I have

* The beautifully paneled living room at Château Malou in Norolles is among the others so centered, where I have been invited to delicious and delightful meals; and so, incidentally, is the unchanged living room at Les Buissonets, the childhood home of the Little Ste. Thérèse.

been in France. But Paris is, of course, the *ville lumierè* for me
no less than for thousands of others, and never more so than
when I look out on the river, its banks and its bridges, from the
apartment of my friends, the Nielsens, on the quai Voltaire.
Sven Nielsen, the director of the Presses de la Cité, publishes
the French editions of my books; his lovely wife, Lolotte, herself
a writer of charming tales for teen-agers, edits them and advises
in the matter of their adaptation to Gallic tastes. Both Nielsens
are experts along these lines, and I respect their talent, judg-
ment and experience; but it is when they become my host and
hostess and my association with them is personal rather than
professional, that one of the greatest treats of my Paris sojourns
begins.

For the superb view from the long windows of their immense
salon is no more remarkable in its way than the *mise en scène*
of the interior is in another. The transformed *palais* where the
Nielsens live was built by Cardinal Mazarin and used by him
for the lodgment of his beautiful and disturbing nieces and—no
doubt!—of other beautiful and disturbing ladies, not to mention
handsome and beguiling gentlemen. Sometimes I am guilty of
remarking that the elevator, which runs by waterpower and is
large enough to accommodate only one person at a time—and
that at a tight squeeze!—probably also dates from the day of the
reign of the *Roi Soleil;* and I have been known to mutter that
the hallways and stairways are horribly cold and musty, after
the manner of nearly all European hallways and stairways with
which I am familiar. But the great salon of the Nielsens, where
styles of all periods, from the Renaissance to the present, are
skillfully, harmoniously and warmly blended; and the small
dining room which is more cool and classic in design, leave
nothing to be desired in elegance and refinement. Cocktails are
always served in full view of the river, as they should be; dinner
may be either at the rear of the salon—which must be at least
fifty feet long—or in the classic dining room. In either place, it
will be a triumph of culinary art. The hostess gives the cook,
Hélène, all the credit for this, but I think that is mistaken

modesty; Mme. Nielsen has written a cookbook herself, as well as those tales for teen-agers, and I do not believe for a moment that Hélène is wholly responsible for all the recipes. Certainly I do not believe she is wholly responsible for *jambon en croûte,* which Deanie and I are agreed is the masterpiece in this household, though there are many other dishes which are comparable to it in excellence, among them roast larks on toast.

I cannot truthfully say that I have greatly enjoyed most of the food that has been set before me in England. (The exceptions are the plain, hearty, well-cooked roasts—or, as they are called there, joints—and the fruit tarts served for the main meal of the day, in private houses; and the really wonderful teas, whether plain or elaborate, also as they are served in private houses, and which constitute something pretty close to a meal when they include sliced bread and butter, scones, crumpets, jam, fresh strawberries with cream, fruitcake and poundcake.) However, during my latest stay there, an American friend introduced me to the Elizabethan Room at the Gore Hotel in London, and I returned to it again and again, taking with me delighted guests, both English and American.

This room represents the inspiration of the hotel's owner, who conceived the idea of bringing there the old paneling, chimney-pieces and other accoutrements from his country place, which dates from the Elizabethan Era, and transforming the modern lounge of the hotel with these treasures of antiquity. Then he went a step further, procuring chairs, tables and tableware that were skillful copies of those used in the reign of Good Queen Bess; dug up recipes of the same period; and persuaded some personable and pleasant young women to dress in Elizabethan costume while serving, and some talented young musicians, both male and female, to play, at intervals, on virginals and the guitar. The result, far from seeming synthetic, has created an atmosphere of astonishing authenticity as well as great charm and originality; and though some of the great variety of dishes provided in the First and Second "Removes"—i.e., courses—like boar's head and roast peacock are rather on the fantastic side, the great majority lend themselves to practical adaptation. Again, I feel it is a privilege to present typical recipes.

As I have remarked before, usually no dish tastes quite as good elsewhere as it does on its native heath, and the only exception to that rule which I can call to mind lies in the excellence of the so-called "Mexican food" served in San Antonio. In connection with that remark, I stated that San Antonio is also the city where American food, as served by "Miss Alice" at the old Argyle Hotel, likewise used to reach a degree of perfection I have seldom seen attained; and I should like to enlarge on that before bringing to a close the comments connected with my experience as a world traveler. For these travels have included many parts of the United States, as well as many parts of the world beyond its borders; and certainly a special tribute should be paid to at least a few of them.

"Miss Alice makes magic," Mrs. Ralph Durkee, the kind friend who first took me to the Argyle told me; and everything that I saw and ate there strengthened my conviction that she did not exaggerate. I use the word "saw" advisedly, for Miss Alice maintained that "the eye must be pleased; otherwise food had better remain unseen." Golden oranges, nestling among their glossy leaves, formed the centerpiece which never lost natural color and contour; red roses, primly disposed on their natural foliage, glowed on either side of a great turkey platter; but it was in the decoration of her cakes that Miss Alice excelled. To the table each day would come one or more of these cakes on which the swirls of white frosting merely served as the background for pink roses and blue morning glories, made of spun sugar. Then, when it came to a wedding cake, Miss Alice really let herself go. One, which was four feet in diameter, had its central hollow surmounted by a miniature "bridge of dreams" leading, on either side, to a "garden of romance." Miss Alice would never ship one of these masterpieces. "A petal or a stem might get broken," she objected; and nothing could induce her to change her stand on this question. But a solution was found for the transportation of cakes ordered for distant weddings: a section in a Pullman was taken, and the cake was enthroned in state at the place reserved for it and the watchful attendant who cared for it.

It was as difficult to unravel the mystery surrounding the composition of these cakes as it was to arrange for their handling. Not that Miss Alice actually declined to give a recipe—nothing as harsh, nothing as final as that. She would call for George, and a neat, white-coated figure would appear from the screened section of the verandah, which was sweet with the scent of the honeysuckle clambering over it, and musical with the tinkle of the pans that formed the obbligato to George's voice as he sang, "There's a Glory in God's Mercy." George had been Miss Alice's cook for more than a quarter of a century already when I made his acquaintance; and by that time he was attending to all the mixing and baking of her cakes under her direction. He answered her summons respectfully, listened respectfully while instructed to give the ingredients for the cake under construction at the moment and, speaking respectfully, announced, "Well, ma'am, they is about 120 eggs in that cake and that much butter and sugar to match."

"Of course that will serve several hundred people," Miss Alice would inform you smilingly. "Thank you, George. That will be all." And it was.

Ah well, it is worth while to have eaten a few slices from some of Miss Alice's cakes, even though I could never have duplicated them; and the same is true of her cream sauce in which peanuts and mushrooms were skillfully blended, her Alamo bananas, her Argyle yams, her candied cushaw, her roast of venison rubbed with Wesson oil, garlic and currant jelly. "Why strive to understand or break the spell of pure enchantment?"

I feel much the same way about the roast duck at the Tavern in Painesville, Ohio; the soup garnished with marshmallows at Club Twenty-One and the zabaglione at Giovanni's in New York; the Indian pudding and apple pan dowdy at Durgin-Park, the broiled live lobster and clam chowder at the Ritz; and the scrod at the Parker House—all in Boston. (Why is it that no one ever sings the praises of scrod? There is no more delicious and delicate fish in the world, and nowhere does it come to the table so fresh from the sea and so beautifully cooked as at the Parker House—at least within my ken. And, as far as that goes, I do not think that anyone has ever sufficiently sung the praises of everything about the Parker House dining room: the mellowness of its paneled walls, the distinction of the portraits which adorn these, the lambency of the lighting, the shining order of the little white-covered tables, the lavishness of the menus, the calm courtesy and quiet efficiency of the colored waiters—they cannot be the same ones who were there when I was a girl, but they seem the same—indeed, everything seems the same!)

Once I am in Boston I am practically home again—much closer than halfway home, though sometimes I have called myself a semi-Bostonian, because I did spend most of my winters there, when I was growing up, and large parts of these during the early years of my married life. But it was never home to me in the same sense as the Oxbow and Pine Grove Farm. A great many intelligent observers have remarked that one of the surest signs of advancing age is the feeling of greater satisfaction in the return from a trip than in the trip itself. Well, I will freely admit to the advancing age. But it is nothing new for me to enjoy getting home. I have always done that. And home has always meant the Oxbow and Pine Grove Farm, more or less indivisibly, for, after all, they are only five miles apart, geographically, even though they are in different states; and they are still nearer together, through shared family traditions, which go back for generations, and personal associations, which go back a lifetime. (To a great degree, Boston, Washington and Virginia will always mean home too, for almost equally cogent reasons; but even so, they are not quite in the same category.)

I was amused, even more than annoyed, by the reasons given for the recent resignation from the University of Vermont by a young professor, a native of Iowa. He found Vermont "mentally snowed in"; he feels it needs to get over its "hick provincial attitude"; and he can't imagine a healthy future for a state "so bogged down in rural interests." He even feels its lack of crime is due to a corresponding lack of "effort and imagination."

Well, I would never attempt to argue with this gentleman, though I certainly was under the impression that Iowa also had some rural interests. Quite a famous song tells us that this is where the tall corn grows: two of the best Secretaries of Agriculture I have known—one a Democrat and one a Republican—hailed from there. No state is without a certain number of persons who are called "hicks" by those who in turn are called "city slickers" or—condescendingly if less scathingly—"summer people" by the "hicks"; and though as a hard-working novelist I would be the last to underestimate either effort or imagination, I can do without the kind that is conducive to crime. As for being "mentally snowed in" it has been my experience that the persons whose long, cold winter evenings give them time to read and reflect are the ones who are often far more mentally alert than those who dash madly about in pursuit of trivial amusement. Only in national capitals have I found men and women as much interested in world affairs and as well informed about them as I have the friends with whom I eagerly look forward to discussing these, when I myself am far from home. I have gone a long way, both literally and figuratively, since I wailed, in Geneva, for ice water, large glasses of rich cold milk and "Cousin Mary's bread." But I still look forward to ice water, to large glasses of rich cold milk and to the banana bread made by my Cousin Anna, who is Cousin Mary's daughter-in-law, and who cooks in the same house, in the same kitchen, and with the same skill as her predecessor. (Such egg fluff! Such salmon mousse! Such old-fashioned stew! Such popovers! Such squash pies! Such pineapple ice cream!)

I also look forward to the dishes which will be set before me in my own house by Frances Welch, a worthy successor, in every sense of the word, to Ina Danforth. Did you ever eat carrots fresh from your own garden, flavored and decorated with mint leaves? Or glazed beets? Or broccoli with cheese sauce, equally fresh, from the same place? Or ice cold applesauce with hot sponge cake? Well, come to my house and someone will see that you get them. If I am lucky, I shall be there to do it myself, with Frances' help; for I hope that all my wanderings will end, as they began, at the Oxbow.

Spain

GAZPACHO ANDALUZ

(Countess Yebes)

Crush 2 cloves of garlic with 3 kummel seeds and a little paprika. Stir in ⅓ cup olive oil and 3 tablespoons vinegar and mix thoroughly. Add 1 slice of bread moistened with a mixture of half vinegar and half water. Peel 12 large ripe tomatoes and press them through a fine sieve. Combine the tomato purée with 1 onion, grated, 1 cucumber, minced, and ½ cup minced green pepper. Combine the two mixtures, season to taste with salt and chill well. Serve *gazpacho* in individual bowls with an ice cube in each and serve with diced bread sautéed in butter or olive oil until crisp and golden, chopped cucumber, chopped green pepper and sieved hard-cooked eggs. Serves 6.

SOPA DE AJO

(Mrs. Luis Bolin)

4 cloves garlic, minced
2 tablespoons Spanish olive oil
1 small onion, finely chopped
2 large, ripe tomatoes, peeled and chopped

4 cups water
Salt and pepper to taste
6 slices toasted French bread
4 to 6 eggs

Sauté the garlic in the olive oil until it is golden. Add the onion and tomatoes and cook slowly until the onion is tender.

Press the vegetables through a fine sieve and add the water and salt and pepper to taste. Bring the liquid to a boil and simmer the soup for 2 minutes.

Line a casserole with the toast and pour the soup over it. Break the eggs into the broth (one for each person to be served) and bake in a moderate oven (350° F.) for about 8 minutes, or until the eggs are done.

PAELLA

(Mrs. Luis Bolin)

1 small chicken, cut into serving portions
½ pound pork or beef, cut into pieces
½ pound sausages, halved
6 tablespoons olive oil
1 large onion, chopped
2 cloves garlic
1 pound tomatoes, peeled, seeded and chopped
1 can pimiento, chopped
1 dozen small clams

½ pound large shrimp or prawns, shelled and cleaned
½ pound conger eel, cut into pieces
2 cups (1 pound) rice
4 cups water
½ pound cooked green peas
6 small cooked artichoke hearts
½ teaspoon saffron
1 tablespoon chopped parsley
Salt

In a large flameproof casserole sauté the chicken, meat and sausages in the olive oil until golden. Add the onion and 1 clove of garlic, minced, and cook until the onion is transparent. Add the tomatoes and pimiento.

Steam the clams until the shells open and discard half the shell from each clam. Add the shrimp and eel, bring to a boil and simmer for 3 minutes. Add the fish and juice to the casserole.

Wash the rice in several changes of cold water, cover it with the 4 cups water and bring to a rapid boil. Cover the pan tightly and cook the rice over a very low flame, without stirring, for about 5 minutes, or until just tender. Add the rice, green peas and artichoke hearts to the casserole.

Mash the other clove of garlic with the saffron, parsley and 1 tablespoon water and add to the *paella*. Correct the seasoning with salt and cook over a low flame for 20 minutes, stirring once. Then bake the casserole in a moderate oven (350° F.) for 10 minutes. Serve in the dish in which the *paella* was cooked, garnished with strips of pimiento.

ARROZ ABANDA

(Maria Luisa Caturla)

3 *pounds shrimp*
3 *pounds white fish*
2 *onions, finely chopped*
3 *tablespoons olive oil*

4 *tomatoes, peeled, seeded and chopped*
1 *pound rice, washed*
Salt and paprika

Wash and dry the shrimp and sauté them in the shells in a little olive oil, stirring constantly, until the shrimp turn pink. Peel the shrimp and discard the black vein that runs down the backs. Cover the shells with water, bring to a boil and simmer for 15 minutes. Cover the white fish with water, bring to a boil and simmer for 25 minutes, or until the flesh flakes easily.

In a heavy skillet sauté the onions in the olive oil until transparent. Add the tomatoes, rice and salt and paprika to taste. Combine the liquid from the shrimp shells and the white fish and measure 4 cups into the skillet. Bring the liquid to a boil, lower the flame and cook for about 30 minutes, or until the rice is tender and the broth is almost evaporated, shaking the skillet

almost constantly. Arrange the shrimp and the fish, cut into
small pieces, on top of the rice and put the *arroz abanda* in a
warm spot to "rest" until ready to serve. The longer it "rests,"
the better.

ARROZ CON POLLITOS MERCEDES

(Mrs. Luis Bolin)

½ pound ham
3 tablespoons lard
4 tablespoons olive oil
2 small chickens, each cut
 into 6 serving pieces
½ cup dry white wine
1 cup tomato sauce
4 cups broth

Salt and pepper
24 green, pitted olives
1 onion, finely chopped
2 cups washed rice
4 tablespoons grated Gruyère
 cheese
Butter and minced parsley

Cut 12 small squares from the ham and cut the rest of it into
long strips. In a heavy skillet heat 2 tablespoons each of the lard
and olive oil and in it sauté the chickens and the strips of ham
until golden. Add the wine, tomato sauce, a little of the broth
and salt and pepper, cover and cook slowly for 20 minutes.
Cover the olives with water and bring them to a boil. Drain, add
the olives to the skillet and cook for 10 minutes longer.

In a heavy saucepan heat the remaining lard and olive oil and
in it sauté the onion and the squares of ham until the onion
begins to brown. Add the rice and cook, stirring, for about 3
minutes, or until the rice is well coated with the olive oil. Add
the remaining broth and bring to a rapid boil. Stir in the grated
cheese, cover and cook in a moderate oven (375° F.) for about
16 minutes, or until the rice is thoroughly cooked.

Coat a crown-shaped mold generously with soft butter and
sprinkle it with minced parsley. Press the rice firmly into the
mold, then unmold on a warm serving platter. Place the chicken
in the center of the rice and cover with the sauce.

ARROZ CON POLLO DAMA-BLANCA

(Mrs. Luis Bolin)

½ cup butter
½ cup lard
1 chicken, cut into 10 serving
   pieces
Salt and pepper
3 medium onions, thinly
   sliced
1 carrot, thinly sliced
1 stalk celery
1 bay leaf
1 sprig tarragon
1 clove

2 cups white wine (sauterne)
Dash of nutmeg
3 egg yolks
1 cup warm milk
Lemon juice
2 cups washed rice
4 cups chicken broth or water
6 tablespoons grated cheese
10 tablespoons truffles,
   minced
Chopped, cooked mushrooms

In a saucepan heat half the butter and lard. Add the chicken, sprinkle with salt and pepper and cook over a slow fire for about 5 minutes, turning the pieces of chicken constantly. Before the chicken browns, add the onions, carrot, celery, bay leaf, tarragon and the clove. Cover the saucepan and cook slowly for 20 minutes. Add the wine, nutmeg and salt to taste and simmer until the chicken is tender. Strain the liquid from the chicken into a saucepan and cook it over simmering water for 5 minutes. Beat the egg yolks and milk and add to the sauce along with 1 tablespoon of the butter. Beat the sauce with a rotary beater until it thickens slightly, correct the seasoning with salt and lemon juice and pour the sauce over the chicken. Keep chicken and sauce hot over hot water.

In another saucepan heat the remaining lard, add the rice and stir until the rice is well coated with the lard. Add the broth or water and salt to taste and bring quickly to a boil. Stir in the grated cheese, cover and bake in a moderate oven (375° F.) for about 20 minutes, or until the rice is tender.

Butter 10 small molds with the remaining butter and sprinkle each mold with 1 tablespoon each of minced truffles and chopped, cooked mushrooms. Press the rice firmly into the molds.

When ready to serve, arrange the chicken in the center of a large round platter. Remove the rice from the molds and arrange around the chicken. Pour half the sauce over the chicken and serve the remainder in a sauceboat. Serves 4.

ARROZ ABANDA

(Mrs. Luis Bolin)

2 pounds fish (red mullet, hake, lobster)
8 cups water
2 onions
½ cup white wine
1 pound small potatoes, peeled
2 sprays parsley
¼ teaspoon saffron
Salt and cayenne pepper
5 tablespoons Spanish olive oil
2 large tomatoes, peeled and chopped
1 clove garlic, minced
1 pound washed rice

Wash the fish and cut it into pieces. In a kettle put the water, fish, one of the onions, sliced, wine, potatoes, parsley, saffron, and salt and cayenne to taste. Bring the water to a boil and simmer for 30 minutes, removing the foam that forms on the top.

In a saucepan heat the olive oil and in it sauté the tomatoes, the other onion, chopped, and the garlic until the onion begins to brown, stirring constantly. Add the rice and sauté, stirring, for a few minutes longer. Add 4 cups of the liquid in which the fish was cooked and a pinch of powdered saffron and boil rapidly for 2 minutes. Cover the saucepan and cook the rice in a moderate oven (375° F.) for about 15 minutes, or until the rice is tender.

Serve the rice in the dish in which it was cooked and the fish in a separate dish with mayonnaise.

FLAN

(Mrs. Luis Bolin)

2 eggs	2 cups milk
4 egg yolks	1 inch vanilla bean, split
11 tablespoons sugar	Burnt sugar

Beat the eggs, egg yolks and sugar until the mixture is thick and pale in color. Heat the milk with the vanilla bean, simmer for 2 minutes, and stir the hot milk very gradually into the egg mixture. Strain the custard through a fine sieve.

Coat a 7-inch mold with burnt sugar and fill the mold with the custard. Put the mold in a *baño maria** containing boiling water, being careful that no water can enter the mold, and cook for 2 minutes. Then bake in a moderate oven (350° F.) for 30 to 35 minutes, or until the custard is set. The custard must not boil, or it will curdle. Let the *flan* cool in the water and when ready to serve, turn it out of the mold onto a platter.

BURNT SUGAR

Put 4 tablespoons sugar and 1 teaspoon lemon juice in a heavy saucepan and cook over a moderate fire, stirring constantly, until the syrup turns caramel in color.

CREMA DE ARROZ FLOR DE VALENCIA

(Mrs. Luis Bolin)

6 cups milk	Peel of 1 orange
9 tablespoons powdered rice	2 tablespoons curaçao
14 tablespoons sugar	

* A *baño maria* is a saucepan, containing water, which is large enough to accommodate the mold.

Bring the milk to a boil and gradually stir in the rice mixed with the sugar. Add the orange peel and cook, stirring frequently with a wooden spoon, for about 15 minutes, or until the milk thickens to a smooth cream. Discard the orange peel and let the cream cool. When partially cool stir in the curaçao and pour the cream into individual glass cups. Serves 6.

ARROZ CON LECHE

(Mrs. Luis Bolin)

1 cup rice	1 teaspoon vanilla
2 cups milk	Grated rind of ½ lemon
¾ cup sugar	Cinnamon

In a saucepan combine the rice, milk and sugar and bring to a boil. Add the vanilla and lemon rind and cook over a gentle flame for about 30 minutes, stirring occasionally. If the rice becomes too thick, stir in a little more hot milk. Turn into a serving dish, sprinkle with sugar and cinnamon and cool.

YEMAS DE SANTA TERESA

(Mrs. Luis Bolin)

10 egg yolks	¾ cup sugar
2 eggs	1 teaspoon vanilla

Put the egg yolks in a saucepan. Beat the whole eggs, sugar and vanilla and combine with the egg yolks. Heat the mixture, stirring slowly, until it begins to thicken, then cook for 3 to 4 minutes, stirring rapidly, until the mixture begins to stiffen. Pour onto a marble slab to cool. Form into small balls and roll the balls in fine granulated sugar.

West Indies

GREEN DEVIL COCKTAIL

2 *parts gin*   *Juice of ½ lime*
1 *part green curaçao*

Shake the ingredients with cracked ice and strain into a cocktail glass.

South America

CANJA

(Chicken Soup)

1 stewing chicken, disjointed   1 onion, sliced
Salt and pepper   ½ cup washed rice
Fresh mint

Sprinkle the pieces of chicken with salt and pepper and put them in a kettle with enough water to cover them generously. Add the mint and onion, bring the liquid to a boil and simmer until the chicken is almost tender. Add the rice and continue to simmer until the chicken is tender and the broth is slightly thickened. Take out the pieces of chicken, remove the bones and cut the meat into small pieces. Return the meat to the broth and serve very hot.

SANCOCHO

(Chicken and Vegetable Soup)

2 chickens, cut into serving   1 teaspoon cumin seeds
  pieces   Salt to taste
1 leek, split and washed free   1 pound yucca, peeled and
  of sand   diced
2 tomatoes, peeled and   1 pound yams, peeled and
  quartered   diced
2 cloves garlic   1 pound cabbage, shredded

1 *pound ocumo, peeled and sliced*

1 *pound pumpkin, peeled and sliced*

1 *pound small potatoes, peeled*

1 *pound "mapuey" (cushcush or yampee)*

1 *pound yellow turnips*

4 *ears corn on the cob*

Parsley, celery stalks with the leaves, and mint, all tied together

1 *large onion, peeled*

1 *green pepper, seeded*

Chopped sour pickles

Capers

Put the pieces of chicken in a large soup kettle with water to cover them generously. Add the leek, tomatoes, garlic, cumin seeds and salt, bring to a boil and simmer until the chickens are almost tender. Add all the remaining ingredients except the pickles and capers and continue to cook until the chickens and vegetables are tender. Correct the seasoning with salt and serve with the pickles and capers, which are added to taste.

SALCOCHO

(Beef and Vegetable Soup)

2 *pounds top sirloin bones*

2 *pounds brisket*

Salt and pepper to taste

1 *pound ocumo*

1 *pound yams*

1 *pound yellow turnip*

1 *pound yucca*

1 *pound pumpkin*

1 *pound shredded cabbage*

1 *pound potatoes*

1 *leek, chopped*

2 *large onions*

1 *clove garlic, crushed*

Combine the bones and brisket in a large kettle and add about 3 quarts water. Bring the water to a boil and simmer the meat and bones for about 3 hours, or until tender. Strain off the broth, discard the bones and cut the meat into pieces. Add the meat to the broth and season the broth with salt and pepper. Prepare all the vegetables, peeling them and cutting them into suitable squares or slices. Add the vegetables to the broth, cover the kettle and simmer until the vegetables are cooked.

The consommé may be served with the vegetables or separately.

MANJAR DE COCO

(Coconut Cream)

Peel and grate the flesh of a large coconut. Put the coconut in a bowl and pour 4 cups boiling water over it. Cover the bowl and when the coconut is almost cool, squeeze it through a napkin to remove as much of the liquid as possible. Sweeten the liquid with sugar to taste and bring it to a boil. Dissolve 2 tablespoons cornstarch in a little milk and stir it gradually into the liquid. Cook, stirring, until the liquid is the consistency of a thick cream. Turn the cream into a mold rinsed in cold water, cool and chill in the refrigerator.

France

BOUGÈRE

(Abbaye des Bénédictines)

2 cups water	1¾ cups flour
¾ cup butter	6 eggs
¾ teaspoon salt	½ cup grated Gruyère cheese

In a saucepan heat the water, butter and salt. When the butter is melted and the liquid is boiling, remove the saucepan from the fire and stir in the flour. Return the mixture to the fire and cook for about 30 minutes, stirring vigorously. Remove from the fire again and add the eggs, two at a time, beating vigorously after each addition. Stir in the grated cheese. Spoon the paste onto a buttered baking sheet in the form of a large crown. Brush with a little beaten egg and bake in a moderate oven (350° F.) for 40 minutes, or until the *bougère* is browned and crusty.

CROUSTADE DE BARBUE LAGRENÉ (for 2)

(La Tour d'Argent, Paris)

Put 2 filets of brill in a buttered saucepan and add enough water to cover. Add a few fish bones, 1 small onion, minced, a few sprays of parsley, a bit of bay leaf, 3 or 4 peppercorns, ½ cup white Bordeaux wine and a pinch of salt. Bring the liquid to a boil and simmer the fish filets for about 8 minutes, or until the flesh flakes easily.

In a saucepan combine 2 tablespoons Béchamel sauce and 4

tablespoons grated Parmesan cheese. Heat, stirring, until the cheese is melted and the sauce is smooth. Remove the sauce from the fire and stir in 1 egg yolk and salt and cayenne pepper to taste. Fold in 2 egg whites, stiffly beaten.

On a silver platter make a bed of dry mashed potatoes. Arrange the filets on the potatoes and cover the fish with the sauce. Sprinkle the sauce with dry bread crumbs mixed with a little grated Parmesan cheese and dot with butter. Bake in a hot oven (425° F.) for about 8 minutes, or until puffed and browned.

Strain the liquid in which the filets were poached into a saucepan, bring it to a boil and boil until it is reduced to 1 cup. Stir in 1 egg yolk beaten with a little of the hot liquid and cook, stirring, for about 3 minutes, being careful that the sauce does not boil. Stir in 1 tablespoon butter and serve the sauce separately with the fish.

SAUCE BÉCHAMEL

In a saucepan melt 1 tablespoon butter and blend in 1 tablespoon flour. Add a pinch of salt and pepper and stir in gradually ½ cup hot milk and ½ cup hot cream. Add a slice of onion and cook, stirring, until the sauce is thickened. Cook over simmering water for 5 minutes and strain through a fine sieve.

SOLE NORMANDY

(Mlles. LeBoeuf)

1 dozen mussels	Salt and pepper
½ cup white wine	1 sole, cleaned but not
4 mushrooms, sliced	beheaded
1 tablespoon lemon juice	1 dozen freshly shucked
4 tablespoons butter	oysters and their liquor
1 tablespoon flour	2 egg yolks
2 tablespoons brandy	¼ cup heavy cream

Scrub the mussels and steam them with the white wine until the shells open. Remove the mussels from the shells and strain and reserve the liquid. Simmer the mushrooms in water to half cover with the lemon juice for 3 minutes and drain the liquid into the mussel liquid.

In a baking dish melt the butter and stir in the flour. Gradually stir in the combined liquids and bring to a boil. Add the brandy and salt and pepper to taste. Place the fish in this sauce and bake in a slow oven (325° F.) for about 20 minutes, or until the flesh flakes, basting frequently. Discard the skin and head of the sole and place the fish on a heated platter. Surround the fish with the mushrooms and mussels and the oysters which have been poached in their own liquor until the edges curl. Keep the dish warm.

Strain the liquid from the baking dish into a saucepan, add the oyster liquor and bring to a boil. Stir in the egg yolks beaten with the cream and a little of the hot sauce and cook, stirring, for about 3 minutes, or until the sauce thickens, being careful not to let it boil. Pour the sauce over the sole and place in a hot oven (450°F.) for about 2 minutes before serving.

PIKE WITH WHITE BUTTER*

(Mmes. Barrau)

In a fish kettle large enough to hold a 5 to 6 pound pike put 2 quarts water, 1 bottle dry white wine, 1 onion, sliced, ½ carrot, sliced, salt, 6 crushed peppercorns and a *bouquet garni* consisting of 1 bay leaf and 1 sprig each of thyme, parsley and celery. Bring the liquid to a boil and simmer for 20 minutes. Tie the pike in cheesecloth and lower it gently into the simmering liquid. Simmer for about 30 minutes, or until the fish is done. Remove

* "White Butter" is also excellent made with turbot, colin fish or other white fish.

the fish from the liquid, unwrap it and place it on a hot platter. Pour white butter sauce over the fish and serve immediately.

WHITE BUTTER SAUCE

Simmer 3 shallots, finely chopped, in 4 tablespoons white wine vinegar and 6 tablespoons of the liquid in which the fish was poached until the combined liquids are reduced to about ¼ cup. Strain the liquid into an enameled saucepan and add, bit by bit, ½ pound sweet butter, beating constantly with a sauce whisk until the butter is melted and the sauce is thick and creamy white.

BRAISED TURBOT VALLÉE D'AUGE

(Mlles. LeBoeuf)

Place a turbot in a buttered turbot kettle and sprinkle it with salt and pepper, the finely chopped white part of 1 leek and 2 apples, thinly sliced. Add 1 cup white wine, bring the liquid to a boil, then cover the kettle and braise the fish in a moderate oven (350° F.) until the fish is cooked, basting frequently.

Place the turbot on a hot serving platter and strain the liquid from the kettle into a saucepan. Bring the liquid to a boil and simmer until it is reduced to ½ cup. Stir in 2 tablespoons butter and 1 cup heavy cream and heat to the simmering point. Pour the hot sauce over the turbot and garnish with creamed mushrooms.

MACKEREL WITH FENNEL

(Mlles. LeBoeuf)

Clean fresh mackerel and insert in each a stalk of fresh fennel. Wrap each fish in stalks of fennel and arrange them in a buttered baking pan. Bake in a hot oven (400° F.) for about 40 minutes, or until the fish are cooked. Place the fish on a serving platter. To the juices in the pan add about 2 tablespoons dry white wine for each fish cooked. Bring to a boil and strain the juice over the fish.

EEL WITH WHITE SAUCE

(Mlles. LeBoeuf)

Clean and skin a 3-pound eel. Wash it well and cut it into 2-inch pieces. Cover the bottom of a buttered saucepan with sliced onions and sprinkle the onion with 3 shallots, chopped, and 1 clove of garlic, minced. Sprinkle with a little freshly ground pepper and add a *bouquet garni* consisting of ½ bay leaf, 3 sprays of parsley, 1 sprig of thyme and 1 stalk of celery with the leaves. Place the pieces of eel on the vegetables, sprinkle lightly with salt and cover with dry white wine. Bring the wine to a simmer and poach the eel for 20 minutes. Transfer the pieces of eel to another saucepan and continue to cook the liquid until it is reduced by about one third its original quantity. Strain and keep hot.

In a saucepan melt 2 tablespoons butter and stir in 1 tablespoon flour. Gradually stir in the strained liquid and cook, stirring, until the sauce is smooth and thickened. Cook over simmering water for 5 minutes, then stir in 2 egg yolks beaten with ¼ cup heavy cream and a little of the hot sauce. Cook for 3 minutes longer. Add 6 mushrooms sliced and simmered in a little water until tender, 1 dozen mussels steamed and taken from their shells and 12 oysters poached in their own liquor until their edges curl. Pour the sauce over the eel and garnish with triangles of bread sautéed in butter until golden.

CHICKEN ANGEVINE

(Mmes. Barrau)

1 frying chicken, cut into serving pieces
4 tablespoons butter
6 small white onions, peeled
¼ cup warm brandy
1 cup dry white wine (Anjou)
½ cup heavy cream
Salt and pepper

1 pound mushroom caps
A bit of garlic
6 small tomatoes
6 cooked artichoke bottoms
Freshly cooked green peas
Potatoes
Parsley

Sauté the chicken in 3 tablespoons of the butter until golden on all sides. Add the onions and continue to cook until the onions are brown. Pour the brandy over the chicken, ignite it and let the flame die out. Add the white wine and cream and salt and pepper to taste, cover and simmer the chicken for 20 minutes, or until tender.

Meanwhile prepare the vegetables for garnish. Sauté the mushroom caps in a little butter with a small fragment of garlic until tender. Broil the tomatoes and fill the artichoke hearts with green peas. Cut some potatoes into small balls the size of hazelnuts with a French ball scoop and sauté them in butter until golden brown and tender.

Arrange the chicken in the center of a large, long dish, place the vegetables around it and sprinkle with chopped parsley.

CHICKEN SUPREME, SAUCE TOURAINE

(Mme. Jean Delannoy)

Put a stewing chicken in a deep iron kettle with 1 cup water, ¼ pound mushrooms, sliced, 2 medium onions and 1 carrot, both sliced, salt, pepper and a *bouquet garni* consisting of several sprays of parsley, a stalk of celery with the leaves, 1 bay leaf and a sprig of thyme. Cover the kettle tightly and cook the chicken over a very low fire from 2 to 3 hours, or until the chicken is tender, turning the chicken once during the cooking period.

In a saucepan melt 2 tablespoons butter and stir in 1 tablespoon flour. Stir in gradually 1½ cups cream and cook, stirring, until the sauce is smooth and thickened. Stir in 3 tablespoons of the liquid in the kettle and cook for 5 minutes. Stir in 2 egg yolks beaten with a little of the hot sauce and cook for 3 minutes longer, being careful that the sauce does not boil or it will curdle. Season to taste with salt and pepper.

Carve the chicken and arrange the pieces on a hot serving dish. Strain the sauce into a sauceboat and serve it separately.

CHICKEN WITH WHITE SAUCE

(Mlles. LeBoeuf)

In a kettle melt ¼ pound butter and stir in 1 tablespoon flour. Stir in gradually 1½ cups warm water and cook, stirring, until the sauce bubbles. Place a plump chicken in the sauce and add 1 onion, salt and pepper, a few sprays of parsley, ½ bay leaf and a sprig of thyme. Cover and cook the chicken over a gentle fire for at least 1½ hours, or until tender. Remove the chicken to a serving dish and keep it hot. To the sauce remaining in the kettle stir in 2 egg yolks beaten with 3 tablespoons cream and a little of the hot sauce and cook, stirring, over a very low flame for 3 minutes, or until the sauce thickens, being very careful not to let it boil. Strain the sauce over the chicken and serve with cooked rice. The dish may be garnished with broiled mushrooms, triangles of toast or even with small poached lobsters.

SAUTÉED CHICKEN, NORMANDY

(Mlles. LeBoeuf)

Cut a tender chicken into serving pieces and sauté the pieces in 4 tablespoons hot butter in a skillet until golden on all sides and half cooked. Transfer the chicken to a casserole. To the juices remaining in the skillet add ¼ cup apple brandy and bring to a boil, stirring in all the brown bits from the bottom and sides of the skillet. Pour the juice over the chicken and add ¾ pound of apples, peeled, cored and thinly sliced. Cover the casserole and bake in a moderate oven (350° F.) for about 30 minutes, or until the chicken and apples are thoroughly tender. Serve from the casserole.

ROOSTER IN RED WINE

(Mlles. LeBoeuf)

Clean and cut a young rooster into serving pieces, reserving the blood. Add 1 teaspoon vinegar to the blood and set aside. In a heavy kettle brown the pieces of rooster in 4 tablespoons hot butter with 3 slices of bacon, diced, 12 small white onions, peeled, and 12 mushrooms or morels. Add 2 cloves of garlic, crushed, and pour over the rooster ¼ cup warm brandy. Ignite the brandy and let the flame burn out. Add 2 cups dry wine, salt and pepper to taste and a *bouquet garni* of several sprays of parsley, 1 bay leaf, 1 stalk of celery with the leaves, and a sprig of thyme. Cover and cook the rooster over a gentle flame for about 40 minutes, or until tender. Five minutes before serving thicken the sauce by stirring in the blood which has been mixed with a little of the hot sauce from the kettle. Pour the rooster and sauce into a deep dish and arrange triangles of buttered toast around it.

CANETON À LA PRESS

(Frederic's Duck, from La Tour d'Argent in Paris)

To make this dish a very young duck, fattened for the last 15 days of his 8 weeks of life, must be killed by strangulation in order to keep all the blood.

Clean the duck, reserving the liver, and roast the duck in a hot oven (450° F.) for 15 minutes; the duck must be very rare. Place the duck on a heated platter and bring it to the table. Cut off the legs and return them to the kitchen to be broiled. They are served separately as a second course.

Slice the breasts thinly and arrange the slices in a hot chafing dish with the blood drained from the duck during the carving. Cover the chafing dish and turn up the flame.

Put the duck carcass in the well of a duck press. Crush the liver of the duck with ½ cup port wine, ⅓ cup madeira and 2 tablespoons cognac. Pour this mixture into the press with the juice of 1 lemon and ½ cup duck consommé. Turn the pressure wheel to crush the bones and force the juice and blood through the press into a heated dish. Return the sauce to the press and force it through again. Pour the sauce over the breast meat in the chafing dish and cook for about 20 minutes, beating the sauce continuously, until it becomes thick and dark chocolate brown in color. Add salt and pepper to taste.

DUCKLING ROUENNAISE

(Mlles. LeBoeuf)

To prepare duck in the Rouen style, the duck is not bled like other poultry, but is smothered in order to keep all the blood.

Pluck, clean and singe the duck. Sprinkle the bird inside and out with a little salt, put the washed liver in the cavity and truss the legs and wings close to the body. Spit-roast the duck for 20 to 22 minutes.

Meanwhile stew 1 large onion, chopped, in 2 tablespoons hot butter until the onion is transparent, but not browned. Cover the onion with equal parts of port wine and burgundy wine and simmer over a very low flame until the onion is very tender. When the duck is roasted, untruss it and remove the liver. Crush the liver and mix it with the onion purée.

To serve: Remove the legs and broil them under a lively flame for about 10 minutes. Remove the breastbone of the duck and put it on a hot serving dish. Carve the breast meat in long thin slices and arrange the slices around the breastbone. Put the duck carcass in the well of a duck press and turn the pressure wheel to crush the bones and force out the juice and blood. Mix the liquid with the onion purée, heat to almost boiling and pour the sauce over the breast meat. Arrange the broiled duck legs at the end of the serving dish.

DUCK WITH CHERRIES

(Auberge du Vieux Puits)

One duck will serve four persons.

Clean the duck and cut it into serving pieces. In a heavy skillet melt 3 tablespoons butter and in it sauté the pieces of duck until they are brown on all sides. Put the duck in a heavy iron or earthenware casserole and to the juices remaining in the skillet add 1 pound pitted Montmorency cherries (so-called jam cherries). Simmer the cherries in their own juice for 3 or 4 minutes and add them to the casserole. Sprinkle the duck with salt and pepper and pour over it 2 cups red Cinzano wine. Cover the casserole, bring the liquid to a boil and simmer over a very slow fire for 30 to 45 minutes.

PAUPIETTES

(Abbaye des Bénédictines)

Cut very thin slices of veal cutlet into 6 pieces about 5 by 3 inches in size. Place the pieces between wax paper and flatten them gently with the flat side of a cleaver.

Combine ¼ pound each of ground uncooked ham and fresh pork, the finely chopped stems from 12 mushrooms, 2 tablespoons chopped parsley and 2 shallots, minced. Season the mixture with salt and pepper and cook it in 3 tablespoons melted butter for about 20 minutes, stirring frequently. Stir in 1 egg, beaten, and ½ cup soft bread crumbs soaked in a little milk. Spread a layer of this stuffing on each slice of veal, roll the slices and tie them at each end with string to form tiny barrels.

Put the *paupiettes* in a buttered casserole and sprinkle them with salt and pepper. Add ½ cup beef stock, ¼ cup madeira wine, 12 small white onions and the 12 mushroom caps. Cover the casserole and bake in a moderate oven (350° F.) for 45 minutes. To serve, remove the strings and place the paupiettes on a hot serving platter. Surround them by the mushrooms and onions and pour the sauce over all.

SMOKED HAM

(Mlles. LeBoeuf)

Cut slices of smoked ham not too thinly. Put a piece of butter in a frying pan and sauté the ham slices in it. Arrange nicely in a dish. Thicken the ham gravy with cream and pour it over the slices.

MERIDIONAL VEAL SAUTÉ

(Abbaye des Bénédictines)

2 pounds veal shoulder, cut
    into pieces
4 tablespoons olive oil
Salt and pepper
4 tablespoons flour
2 cups dry white wine
¾ cup tomato sauce
Stock or water

2 onions, sliced
3 red peppers, seeded and
    cut into strips
4 tomatoes, peeled and
    chopped
1 clove garlic, minced
1 tablespoon chopped parsley

Sauté the veal in 2 tablespoons of the olive oil until it is well browned on all sides. Sprinkle the meat with salt and pepper and stir in the flour. Gradually stir in the red wine and tomato sauce, bring to a boil and simmer for 1 hour, adding a little stock or water if the sauce becomes too thick.

Sauté the onions, red peppers and tomatoes in the remaining olive oil until the onions are lightly browned. Add the garlic and parsley and sauté for about 5 minutes longer. Add the vegetables to the meat, cover, and simmer for 30 minutes longer, or until the meat is thoroughly cooked.

SCALLOPS OF VEAL NORMANDY

(Auberge du Vieux Puits)

1½ pounds thinly sliced veal
3 tablespoons butter
½ teaspoon flour
¼ cup dry white wine
¾ cup heavy cream

Salt and pepper
2 tablespoons Calvados (apple
    brandy)
Grated Gruyère cheese

Flatten each slice of veal with a wooden mallet or the side of a heavy cleaver and trim the edges neatly. Melt the butter in a skillet and sauté the veal slices slowly for about 5 minutes on each side, or until they are browned. Remove the slices to an ovenproof serving dish.

To the juices remaining in the skillet stir in the flour, add the wine and bring to a boil, stirring. Stir in the cream very gradually and heat, but do not boil. Season the sauce with salt and pepper to taste and stir in the apple brandy. Pour the sauce over the meat, sprinkle with grated cheese and put under the broiler flame for a few minutes to brown.

CUTLETS WITH SAUCE ROYAL

(Abbaye des Bénédictines)

4 *veal cutlets, ½-inch thick*	1 *teaspoon dry mustard*
4 *tablespoons butter*	3 *tablespoons heavy cream*
2 *tablespoons vinegar or the*	2 *tablespoons olive oil*
juice of 1 lemon	*Salt and pepper to taste*

Sauté the cutlets slowly in 2 tablespoons of the butter for about 30 minutes, or until browned on both sides and tender.

Meanwhile combine the remaining ingredients in a small saucepan and heat, without letting the mixture boil. Place the cutlets on a warm serving dish, pour the sauce over them and garnish with parsley or water cress.

This sauce is also good on steak, scallops of veal or mutton chops.

TRIPE À LA MODE DE CAEN

(Mlles. LeBoeuf)

In order to make a really good dish of *tripe à la mode de Caen* a whole paunch of beef or at least half a paunch should be used.

Clean the paunch thoroughly by soaking it in running water for several hours, then put it into steaming water until it is very white. Cool the tripe and cut it into pieces.

Arrange half the tripe in an earthenware casserole and add 3 or 4 onions, sliced, 3 carrots, quartered, 2 leeks, chopped, a spice bag containing 6 peppercorns and 4 cloves, ½ pound beef kidney fat, chopped, 2 tablespoons butter, a beef foot, split in half, and a *bouquet garni* consisting of a few sprays of parsley, a blade of mace, 1 bay leaf, and a sprig of thyme. Place the rest of the tripe on top and sprinkle with salt. Add ¼ cup cognac and enough water to completely cover the meat. Do NOT use any wine or cider, as this would cause the sauce to darken. Cover the pot and seal the edge with a thick paste made of flour and water and bake in a slow oven (250° F.) for 12 to 18 hours. When ready to serve, remove the lid, skim the sauce free of fat and serve boiling hot.

MUSHROOM PIE

(Mmes. Barrau)

Roll out flaky pie dough and line a mold—the mold may be a high-sided Charlotte mold or the flatter Savarin-type mold. Fill the mold with dry rice or beans and bake in a hot oven (450° F.) for about 10 minutes to set the dough. Remove the mold from the oven, empty out the rice or beans and brush the dough with beaten egg. Return the mold to the oven and continue to bake for about 10 minutes longer, or until the crust is dry and browned.

Remove the stems from 1½ pounds fresh mushrooms and use them for another purpose. Quarter the mushrooms if they are large; halve them if they are small and wash them thoroughly in lemon-flavored water. Drain well.

In a saucepan melt 6 tablespoons butter and stir in 6 tablespoons flour. Stir in gradually 3 cups heavy cream and cook, stirring, until the sauce is smooth and very thick. The juice from the mushrooms will thin the sauce to the right consistency. Season the sauce with salt and pepper, add the mushrooms and cook for 30 minutes, stirring constantly with a wooden spoon.

Remove the crust from the mold, pour the creamed mushrooms into it and serve very hot.

AIOLI SAUCE

(Abbaye des Bénédictines)

Crush 5 or 6 cloves of garlic in a mortar with salt and pepper until the garlic is reduced to a smooth paste. Add 1 egg yolk and blend thoroughly. Add 1 cup olive oil, at first drop by drop, and then in small dashes, beating vigorously, and adding a few drops of water from time to time when the sauce becomes too thick. Finally stir in a dash of lemon juice. The sauce should have the consistency of mayonnaise.

WELLS OF LOVE

(Mme. Jean Delannoy)

For each person to be served beat 1 egg yolk and 1 tablespoon confectioners' sugar until the mixture is pale in color and as thick as mayonnaise. Beat the egg white until stiff and beat in 1 tablespoon sugar.

In a champagne glass put a generous spoonful of red currant jelly. Cover the jelly with the egg yolk mixture, add 1 teaspoon kirsch and fill the glass with the meringue. Just before serving, a few fragments of candied fruit soaked in kirsch may be sprinkled on top.

THE DREAM

(Mme. Jean Delannoy)

1 cup milk	8 ounces semi-sweet
A 1-inch piece of vanilla bean,	chocolate
split	3 tablespoons water
4 tablespoons sugar	½ cup butter
1 egg	Ladyfingers
1 egg yolk	Coffee custard sauce

Put the milk, vanilla bean and sugar in a saucepan, bring to a boil and simmer for 10 minutes. Cool slightly. Stir in the egg and egg yolk beaten with a little of the hot milk and cook, stirring constantly, until the custard coats the spoon.

Break the chocolate into small pieces and melt them in a saucepan with the water, stirring until the chocolate is smooth. Stir in the butter.

Carefully line a Charlotte mold with ladyfingers, so that no space is left between them. Combine the chocolate butter and the custard and pour the mixture into the lined mold. Chill in the refrigerator overnight.

Next day, turn the chocolate custard from the mold onto a serving platter and pour cooled coffee custard around it.

This dessert should be prepared the day before it is served and it serves 8 people.

COFFEE CUSTARD

Heat ½ cup each of milk and strong coffee with ¼ cup sugar. Stir in 2 egg yolks or 1 egg and 1 egg yolk beaten with a little of the hot coffee milk and cook, stirring, until the custard coats the spoon. Cool.

RICE PUDDING

(Mlles. LeBoeuf)

Combine 1 cup rice, 2 quarts milk, 1 teaspoon cinnamon and sugar to taste. Turn the mixture into a casserole and bake in a very slow oven (300° F.) for 3 hours.

MERINGUES WITH CREAM

(Mlles. LeBoeuf)

> 6 *egg whites*
> 12 *tablespoons fine granulated*
> *sugar*
> *Whipped cream*

Beat the egg whites until stiff and fold in 6 tablespoons of the sugar, a tablespoon at a time. Drop the meringue by the spoonful on wax paper, leaving space between the mounds for the meringues to double in volume. Sprinkle the mounds with fine granulated sugar and bake in a slow oven (250° F.) for about 1 hour, or until dry but not colored in the least. Remove the meringues from the oven, loosen them from the paper and scoop out a hollow on the flat side of each. When ready to serve, fill the hollows with whipped cream. Makes 24 meringues.

BRETON CUSTARD

(Abbaye des Bénédictines)

4 *cups milk*	6 *eggs, beaten*
2 *cups flour*	¼ *pound chopped prunes*
1 *cup fine granulated sugar*	¼ *pound raisins*

Stir the milk gradually into the flour. Add the sugar and eggs and mix well. Pour the batter into a buttered casserole and sprinkle with the prunes and raisins. Bake in a moderate oven (375° F.) for 2 hours and serve cold.

ROYAL MAISON RICE CAKE

(Mme. Jean Delannoy)

Wash 1 cup rice several times in cold water and drain. Add the rice to 4 cups boiling water and boil, uncovered, for 2 minutes. Pour the rice into a strainer and rinse with cold water. Combine 4 cups milk, ½ cup sugar and a 1-inch piece of vanilla bean and bring the milk to a boil. Add the rice and cook over a slow fire until the rice is tender and the mixture is quite thick. Cool.

Combine 1 cup each of milk and cream and ½ cup sugar and bring to a boil. Stir in 4 egg yolks, lightly beaten with a little of the hot milk and cream and cook, stirring, over a low flame until the custard coats a spoon. Be careful not to let it boil or it will curdle. Remove from the fire, stir in 2 tablespoons kirsch and cool.

Combine the rice and kirsch custard and stir in 1 tablespoon gelatin softened in ¼ cup cold water and dissolved over hot water. Fold in 2 egg whites, stiffly beaten, ¼ pound melted and cooled butter and ½ cup finely cut assorted candied fruit. Turn the pudding into a buttered mold which has been sprinkled with chopped candied fruits and chill in the refrigerator for 12 hours.

CHOCOLATE CAKE BLAISOIS

(Abbaye des Bénédictines)

Cream together 6 tablespoons each of soft butter and fine granulated sugar and stir in gradually ⅔ cup flour. Break 4

---

ounces of semi-sweet chocolate into small bits and stir them over a low flame with 2 tablespoons water until the chocolate is melted and smooth. Add the melted chocolate to the flour mixture, mix well and fold in 4 egg whites, stiffly beaten. Turn the batter into a buttered and floured cake pan and bake in a moderate oven (350° F.) for about 25 minutes. Turn the cake out onto a cake rack to cool. Put the cake on a serving dish and pour over it the following icing.

CHOCOLATE ICING

Cut 2 ounces bitter chocolate into small pieces and stir them over a low flame with 1 tablespoon water until the chocolate is melted and smooth. Stir in enough sifted confectioners' sugar to make an icing that is sweet but not too thick.

SANDY GRIDDLECAKE

(Mlles. LeBoeuf)

½ pound butter   4 cups flour
½ cup sugar

Soften the butter. Sift together the flour and sugar and stir it into the butter. Turn the dough out on a floured board and knead until the dough cracks. Form the dough into a round cake about 1 inch thick and bake it slowly on a griddle for about 15 minutes on each side. The cake must be baked slowly if it is going to be uniformly "blond" in color.

Canada

SOUPE AUX POIS CANADIENNE

(Canadian Pea Soup)

2 cups dried whole yellow peas
2 quarts cold water
1 onion, minced
¼ pound salt pork
1 tablespoon chopped parsley or ½ teaspoon sage or 1 teaspoon salted herbs

Pick over the peas and wash them in several changes of cold water. Cover them with the 2 quarts cold water and let them soak overnight. In the morning add the remaining ingredients, bring the water to a boil and simmer for 3 to 4 hours. Correct the seasoning with salt and pepper. Serves 8 to 10.

PERDRIX AU CHOUX

(Partridge with Cabbage)

2 or 3 partridges
3 slices fat salt pork, diced
2 or 3 small cabbages
1 carrot, sliced
1 onion stuck with 3 cloves
Salt and pepper

Prepare the partridges for cooking. In a heavy skillet sauté the salt pork until crisp, add the partridges and brown them well on all sides. Dip the cabbages in boiling water for 1 minute, then remove the core, separate the leaves and drain them well.

Arrange a thick layer of cabbage leaves in the bottom of a small roasting pan. Put the partridges and the crisped pork on the bed of cabbage leaves and add the carrot and onion. Sprinkle with salt and pepper and cover with another thick layer of cabbage leaves. Add enough boiling water to cover the cabbage by a good inch and cook, covered, in a moderate oven (350° F.) for 1 to 1½ hours.

England

ARTICHOKE PIE

(As served in the Elizabethan Room at the Gore Hotel,
London, England)

Boil your artichokes well, then take the bottoms from the
leaves, and season them with a little beaten mace, and put to
them a pretty quantity of butter, lay a layer in the bottom, then
lay in the artichokes, sprinkle them with a little salt, put some
sugar over them, put in grated pieces of vegetable marrow rolled
up in the yolks of eggs, then put in a few gooseberries or grapes,
and lay upon it large mace and dates stoned, some yolks of hard
eggs, suckets, lettuce stalks, and citron, cover it with butter, and
when it is baked, put in scalded white wine and shake it together
and serve it up.

LOBSTER PIE

(As served in the Elizabethan Room at the Gore Hotel,
London, England)

Poach 2 large live lobsters in simmering water for 15 minutes
and let them cool a little in the water. When cool enough to
handle, split them and discard the intestines and the sac behind the heads. Remove the tail meat and cut each strip into
4 pieces. Put the pieces in a small deep pie dish. Remove any
edible meat left in the bodies, crack the claws and remove the
meat. Chop the claw meat finely and mix it and any other scraps

of meat with the coral and liver (tomalley) of the lobsters.
Season the mixture with salt and pepper and 2 tablespoons
vinegar or lemon juice and stir in 1 cup melted butter and 1
cup fine soft bread crumbs. Spread this mixture over the tail
meat and cover the dish with a thin layer of flaky pie dough.
Cut a few slashes in the dough to let the steam escape and bake
the pie in a moderate oven (350° F.) for about 30 minutes, or
until the crust is golden.

SYLLABUB

(As served in the Elizabethan Room at the Gore Hotel, London, England)

To 2 cups dry white wine and 2 cups raspberry juice add a
sprig of rosemary, 1 nutmeg, quartered, the juice of 1 lemon, a
few strips of lemon peel and sugar to taste. Cover and let stand
overnight. In the morning remove the lemon peel, rosemary and
nutmeg. Mix together 3 cups each of cream and milk. Add the
milk mixture to the wine mixture very gradually, whisking constantly with a wire whisk. Serve in tall glasses.

New England

AMADAMA BREAD

(Mrs. Haines Johnson)

½ cup corn meal
2 cups boiling water
2 tablespoons butter
½ cup molasses

1 teaspoon salt
1 yeast cake
¼ cup lukewarm water
5 cups flour

Stir the corn meal very gradually into the boiling water. Add the butter, molasses and salt, mix well and cool to lukewarm. Dissolve the yeast in the lukewarm water and add it to the meal. Sift in the flour, adding a little more if needed to make a stiff dough. Turn the dough out on a lightly floured board and knead well. Put the dough in a warm spot to rise until double in bulk. Punch the dough down, shape it into two loaves and let the loaves rise until double in bulk. Bake the loaves in a hot oven (400° F.) for 1 hour.

BANANA BREAD

(Mrs. Haines Johnson)

2 eggs
1 cup sugar
¼ cup soft butter
3 large ripe bananas, mashed

2 cups flour
¾ teaspoon salt
1 teaspoon baking soda
1 cup chopped nut meats

Beat the eggs until light and beat in the sugar and butter. Stir in the bananas and sift in the flour sifted with the salt and soda. Mix well and stir in the nuts. Turn the batter into a buttered bread pan and bake in a moderate oven (350° F.) for 45 minutes.

BANANA BREAD

(Mrs. Harold Hale)

2 eggs	2 cups flour
¾ cup sugar	½ teaspoon salt
½ cup butter	1 teaspoon baking soda
3 mashed bananas	½ cup chopped nut meats

Beat the eggs until light and beat in the sugar and butter. Stir in the bananas and sift in the flour sifted with the salt and soda. Mix well and stir in the nuts. Turn the batter into a buttered bread pan and bake in a moderate oven (350° F.) for about 1 hour.

DATE NUT BREAD

(Mrs. Plin Welch)

1 cup chopped dates	1 tablespoon melted butter
1 teaspoon soda	2 cups flour
1 cup boiling water	2 teaspoons baking powder
1 egg	½ teaspoon salt
⅔ cup sugar	½ cup chopped nut meats

Sprinkle the dates with the soda, pour the boiling water over them and cool to lukewarm. Beat the egg until light and stir in the sugar and butter. Sift the flour, baking powder and salt and stir in the dry ingredients alternately with the water from the dates. Fold in the dates and nuts, turn the batter into a buttered loaf pan and bake in a moderate oven (350° F.) for 1 hour.

FISH BISQUE

(Mrs. R. F. Chandler, Jr.)

4 cups fish stock	1 tablespoon minced parsley
1 cup minced cold fish	1 cup hot rich milk
3 tablespoons butter	⅞ cup cracker crumbs
1 tablespoon flour .	⅛ teaspoon soda

Bring the fish stock to a boil, add the fish and simmer for 5 minutes. Mix the butter, flour and parsley to a smooth paste and stir it into the fish stock, bit by bit. Add the milk, crumbs and soda and simmer for 1 minute longer.

JELLIED SALMON MOUSSE

(Mrs. Haines Johnson)

2 teaspoons salt	2 tablespoons melted butter
2 tablespoons sugar	1 cup milk
1 teaspoon dry mustard	⅓ cup vinegar
1 tablespoon flour	1 tablespoon gelatin
⅛ teaspoon pepper	3 tablespoons cold water
3 egg yolks, beaten	2 cups cooked, flaked salmon

In a sauce pan combine the salt, sugar, mustard, flour and pepper. Stir in the egg yolks, butter, milk and vinegar. Cook, stirring constantly, over simmering water until the mixture coats the spoon. Add the gelatin softened in the cold water and cook, stirring, until the gelatin is thoroughly dissolved. Add the salmon, turn the mixture into a mold and chill until set. Serve with cucumber sauce.

HAM PINEAPPLE LOAF

(Mrs. Plin Welch)

1 *pound ground ham*	2 *eggs, beaten*
1 *pound ground pork*	*Brown sugar*
1 *cup dry bread crumbs*	1 *cup drained crushed*
1 *cup tomato juice*	*pineapple*
1 *tablespoon minced onion*	

Combine the ham, pork, crumbs, tomato juice, onion and eggs. Put a one-quarter inch layer of brown sugar in a buttered loaf pan and cover the sugar with the crushed pineapple. Pack the meat mixture into the pan and bake in a moderate oven (350° F.) for 1 hour.

BRIDE'S PIE

(Mrs. Haines Johnson)

1 *cup scalded milk*	¼ *cup cold water*
3 *egg yolks, beaten*	3 *egg whites, stiffly beaten*
½ *cup sugar*	*Chocolate wafers*
Pinch of salt	½ *cup melted butter*
1 *teaspoon vanilla*	1 *cup heavy cream, whipped*
1 *tablespoon gelatin*	

Stir the milk gradually into the beaten egg yolks and add the sugar, salt and vanilla. Cook, stirring, over simmering water until the mixture coats the spoon, add the gelatin softened in the cold water and stir until the gelatin is thoroughly dissolved. Cool and fold in the stiffly beaten egg whites and the cream.

Crush and sieve enough chocolate wafers to make 1¼ cups crumbs. Mix the crumbs with the butter and line a pie plate with the crumb mixture, reserving about ⅓ cup. Pour the custard into the pie plate, cover with the reserved crumbs and chill the pie thoroughly before serving.

CHERRY COOKIES

(Mrs. Plin Welch)

1 cup vegetable shortening
⅔ cup sugar
1 egg
1¾ cups flour
½ teaspoon salt
1 teaspoon vanilla
⅓ cup chopped maraschino
cherries

Cream together the vegetable shortening and sugar until the mixture is light and fluffy. Add the egg and beat well. Stir in the flour and salt and add the vanilla and cherries. Mix well and roll the dough into small balls. Place the balls on an ungreased baking sheet and flatten them with the bottom of a small glass. Bake in a hot oven (400° F.) for 10 minutes, or until the cookies are golden and cool on cake racks. Makes 6 dozen cookies.

UNCOOKED RELISH

(Mrs. Harold Hale)

1 quart chopped raw beets
1 quart shredded cabbage
1 cup grated horseradish
1 cup white sugar
1 teaspoon salt
1 teaspoon pepper
Vinegar

Put the beets and cabbage through the fine blade of a meat chopper and mix the vegetables with the remaining ingredients.

Add enough vinegar to just cover the ingredients. Pack into sterilized jars and seal.

CHEESE PASTE

(Mrs. Harold Hale)

p 241

1 cup diced cheese
½ cup milk
2 tablespoons butter
1 teaspoon salt

1 teaspoon dry mustard
3 pimientos, chopped
2 eggs, beaten

Stir the cheese and milk over boiling water until the cheese is melted and the mixture is smooth. Stir in the butter, salt, mustard and pimientos and, lastly, stir in the beaten eggs. Turn into small crocks and store in the refrigerator. This is a delicious paste to serve on crackers or in sandwiches.

BLACKBERRY WINE

(Mrs. Haines Johnson)

7 quarts blackberries
15 pounds sugar

5 gallons water

Combine the ingredients, put in the cellar until through working and then bottle.

INDEX

Hard Sauce, 222–23
Hog Ears, 160–61
Hollandaise Sauce, 183
Hominy, Baked, 45
Hot Cabinet Pudding, 109–10
    Cheese Sandwiches, 241
    Raspberry Sauce, 39
    Tom and Jerry, 238–39
Hush Puppies, 156–57

Ice Box Cookies, 113
Ice Cream Magderlin, 231
    Peppermint Refrigerator, 114
    Plum Pudding, 39
Icing, Chocolate, 233, 301
Indian Pudding, 41
Irish Potato Pudding, 223–24

Jackson Salad, 215–16
Jambalaya, 171
Jam Cake, 112
Jellied Apples, 96
    Salmon Mousse, 308–9

Lady Baltimore Frosting, 26–27
Lady Cake, 26
Lemon Butter for Tea Biscuits,
    74–75
    Jelly Cakes, 88
        Filling, 88
    Pie, 84–85
    Sponge Pudding, 40
Little Sour Cream Cakes, 36
Lobster Chowder, 102
    Pie, 304–5
Lost Bread (Pain Perdu), 160
Louisiana Baked Fish à la Creole,
    78

Macaroni and Cheese, 182
Macaroons, Cornflake, 94–95
    Oatmeal, 36–37
    Quick Coconut, 113
Mackerel with Fennel, 286–87
Manja de Coco (Coconut Cream),
    282
Maple Mousse, 37

Sugar Frosting, 34
Marchand de Vin Sauce, 183
Marmalade, Orange, 97–98
    Pumpkin, 242
    Pudding, 41–42
Marshmallow Frosting, 90
Mayonnaise Dressing, 46–47
Meat
    Beef Steak Spanish, 76
    Boudan, 203
    Bouilli, 144
    Calalou, 203–4
    Cutlets with Sauce Royal, 295
    Daube Glacée, 198–99, 199–
        200
    Grillades, 197
        Pannes, 197
    Ham à la Breck, 105–6
        Loaf, 202
        Pineapple Loaf, 309
        Smoked, 293–94
    Meat Loaf, 202
        Porcupines, 200
    Meridional Veal Sauté, 294
    Paupiettes, 293
    Scallops of Veal Normandy,
        294–95
    Stuffed Bell Peppers (2),
        201–2
    Tournedos Labiche, 198
    Tripe à la Mode de Caen, 295–
        96
    Veal Birds, 75
Meridional Veal Sauté, 294
Meringues, 37
    with Cream, 299
Mincemeat, 42
Mint Julep, 60–62, 119, 149
Molasses Candy, 50
    Crumb Pie, 110
Mousse, Chicken, 106
    Jellied Salmon, 308–9
    Maple, 37
    Plain, 37–38
Muffins, Flour, 73
    Plain, 24–25
Mush Rolls, 99–100

4⁰⁰
de

The kitchen in the home of Mme. Houlbey, a "petit manoir" near
—drawing by Marguerite LeBoeuf and Leonard Flettrich.